The Selected Teachings of James Allen Vol. II

Eight Pillars of Prosperity
Foundation Stones to Happiness and Success
The Shining Gateway
James Allen's Book of Meditations
for Every Day in the Year

The Selected Teachings of James Allen Vol. II

by James Allen

©2008 Wilder Publications

Wilder Publications, LLC.
PO Box 243
Blacksburg VA 24060

ISBN 10: 1-60459-599-X
ISBN 13: 978-1-60459-599-4

Eight Pillars of Prosperity

Table of Contents

Preface. 6

Eight Pillars. 7

First Pillar – Energy. 14

Second Pillar – Economy. 22

Third Pillar – Integrity. 32

Fourth Pillar – System. 39

Fifth Pillar – Sympathy. 47

Sixth Pillar – Sincerity. 55

Seventh Pillar – Impartiality. 62

Eighth Pillar – Self-Reliance. 70

The Temple of Prosperity. 77

Preface

It is popularly supposed that a greater prosperity for individuals or nations can only come through a political and social reconstruction. This cannot be true apart from the practice of the moral virtues in the individuals that comprise a nation. Better laws and social conditions will always follow a higher realisation of morality among the individuals of a community, but no legal enactment can give prosperity to, nay it cannot prevent the ruin of, a man or a nation that has become lax and decadent in the pursuit and practice of virtue.

The moral virtues are the foundation and support of prosperity as they are the soul of greatness. They endure for ever, and all the works of man which endure are built upon them. Without them there is neither strength, stability, nor substantial reality, but only ephemeral dreams. To find moral principles is to have found prosperity, greatness, truth, and is therefore to be strong, valiant, joyful and free.

James Allen

Eight Pillars

Prosperity rests upon a moral foundation. It is popularly supposed to rest upon an immoral foundation — that is, upon trickery, sharp practice, deception and greed. One commonly hears even an otherwise intelligent man declare that "No man can be successful in business unless he is dishonest," thus regarding business prosperity – a good thing – as the effect of dishonesty – a bad thing. Such a statement is superficial and thoughtless, and reveals a total lack of knowledge of moral causation, as well as a very limited grasp of the facts of life. It is as though one should sow henbane and reap spinach, or erect a brick house on a quagmire — things impossible in the natural order of causation, and therefore not to be attempted. The spiritual or moral order of causation is not different in principle, but only in nature. The same law obtains in things unseen – in thoughts and deeds — as in things seen – in natural phenomena. Man sees the processes in natural objects, and acts in accordance with them, but not seeing the spiritual processes, he imagines that they do not obtain, and so he does not act in harmony with them.

Yet these spiritual processes are just as simple and just as sure as the natural processes. They are indeed the same natural modes manifesting in the world of mind. All the parables and a large number of the sayings of the Great Teachers are designed to illustrate this fact. The natural world is the mental world made visible. The seen is the mirror of the unseen. The upper half of a circle is in no way different from the lower half, but its sphericity is reversed. The material and the mental are not two detached arcs in the universe, they are the two halves of a complete circle. The natural and the spiritual are not at eternal enmity, but in the true order of the universe are eternally at one. It is in the unnatural — in the abuse of function and faculty – where division arises, and where main is wrested back, with repeated sufferings, from the perfect circle from which he has tried to depart. Every process in matter is also a process in mind. Every natural law has its spiritual counterpart.

Take any natural object, and you will find its fundamental processes in the mental sphere if you rightly search. Consider, for instance, the germination of a seed and its growth into a plant with the final development of a flower, and back to seed again. This also is a mental process. Thoughts are seeds which, falling in the soil of the mind, germinate and develop until they reach the completed stage, blossoming into deeds good or bad, brilliant or stupid, according to their nature, and ending as seeds of thought to be again sown in other minds. A teacher is a sower of seed, a spiritual agriculturist, while he who teaches himself is the wise farmer of his own mental plot. The growth of a thought is as the growth of a plant. The seed must be sown seasonably, and time is required for its full development into the plant of knowledge and the flower of wisdom.

While writing this, I pause, and turn to look through my study window, and there, a hundred yards away, is a tall tree in the top of which some enterprising rook from a rookery hard by, has, for the first time, built its nest. A strong, north-east wind is blowing, so that the top of the tree is swayed violently to and fro by the onset of the blast; yet there is no danger to that frail thing of sticks and hair, and the mother bird, sitting upon her eggs, has no fear of the storm. Why is this? It is because the bird has instinctively built her nest in harmony with principles which ensure the maximum strength and security. First, a fork is chosen as the foundation for the nest, and not a space between two separate branches, so that, however great may be the swaying of the tree top, the position of the nest is not altered, nor its structure disturbed; then the nest is built on a circular plan so as to offer the greatest resistance to any external pressure, as well as to obtain more perfect compactness within, in accordance with its purpose; and so, however the tempest may rage, the birds rest in comfort and security. This is a very simple and familiar object, and yet, in the strict obedience of its structure to mathematical law, it becomes, to the wise, a parable of enlightenment, teaching them that only by ordering one's deeds in accordance with fixed principles is perfect surety, perfect security, and perfect peace obtained amid the uncertainty of events and the turbulent tempests of life.

A house or a temple built by man is a much more complicated structure than a bird's nest, yet it is erected in accordance with those mathematical principles which are everywhere evidenced in nature. And here is seen how man, in material things, obeys universal principles. He never attempts to put up a building in defiance of geometrical proportions, for he knows that such a building would be unsafe, and that the first storm would, in all probability, level it to the ground, if, indeed, it did not fall about his ears during the process of erection. Man in his material building scrupulously obeys the fixed principles of circle, square and angle, and, aided by rule, plumbline, and compasses, he raises a structure which will resist the fiercest storms, and afford him a secure shelter and safe protection.

All this is very simple, the reader may say. Yes, it is simple because it is true and perfect; so true that it cannot admit the smallest compromise, and so perfect that no man can improve upon it. Man, through long experience, has learned these principles of the material world, and sees the wisdom of obeying them, and I have thus referred to them in order to lead up to a consideration of those fixed principles in the mental or spiritual world which are just as simple, and just as eternally true and perfect, yet are at present so little understood by man that he daily violates them, because ignorant of their nature, and unconscious of the harm he is all the time inflicting upon himself.

In mind as in matter, in thoughts as in things, in deeds as in natural processes, there is a fixed foundation of law which, if consciously or ignorantly ignored leads to disaster, and defeat. It is, indeed, the ignorant violation of this law which is the cause of the world's pain and sorrow. In matter, this law is presented as mathematical; in mind, it is perceived as moral. But the mathematical and the moral are not separate and opposed; they are but two aspects of a united whole. The fixed principles of mathematics, to which all matter is subject, are the body of which the spirit is ethical; while the eternal principles of morality are mathematical truisms operating in the universe of mind. It is as impossible to live successfully apart from moral principles, as to build successfully while ignoring mathematical principles. Characters, like houses, only stand firmly when built on a foundation of moral law — and they are built up slowly and laboriously, deed by deed, for in the building of character, the bricks are deeds. Business and all human enterprises are not exempt from the eternal order, but can only stand securely by the observance of fixed laws. Prosperity, to be stable and enduring, must rest on a solid foundation of moral principle, and be supported by the adamantine pillars of sterling character and moral worth. In the attempt to run a business in defiance of moral principles, disaster, of one kind or another, is inevitable. The permanently prosperous men in any community are not its tricksters and deceivers, but its reliable and upright men. The Quakers are acknowledged to be the most upright men in the British community, and, although their numbers are small, they are the most prosperous. The Jains in India are similar both in numbers and sterling worth, and they are the most prosperous people in India.

Men speak of "building up a business," and, indeed, a business is as much a building as is a brick house or a stone church, albeit the process of building is a mental one. Prosperity, like a house, is a roof over a man's head, affording him protection and comfort. A roof presupposes a support, and a support necessitates a foundation. The roof of prosperity, then, is supported by the following eight pillars which are cemented in a foundation of moral consistency:—

1. Energy
2. Economy
3. Integrity
4. System
5. Sympathy
6. Sincerity
7. Impartiality
8. Self-reliance

A business built up on the faultless practice of all these principles would be so firm and enduring as to be invincible. Nothing could injure it; nothing could undermine its prosperity, nothing could interrupt its success, or bring it to the ground; but that success would be assured with incessant increase so long as the principles were adhered to. On the other hand, where these principles were all absent, there could be no success of any kind; there could not even be a business at all, for there would be nothing to produce the adherence of one part with another; but there would be that lack of life, that absence of fibre and consistency which animates and gives body and form to anything whatsoever. Picture a man with all these principles absent from his mind, his daily life, and even if your knowledge of these principles is but slight and imperfect, yet you could not think of such a man as doing any successful work. You could picture him as leading the confused life of a shiftless tramp but to imagine him at the head of a business, as the centre of an organisation, or as a responsible and controlling agent in any department of life – this you could not do, because you realise its impossibility. The fact that no one of moderate morality and intelligence can think of such a man as commanding any success, should, to all those who have not yet grasped the import of these principles, and therefore declare that morality is not a factor, but rather a hindrance, in prosperity, be a sound proof to them that their conclusion is totally wrong, for if it was right, then the greater the lack of these moral principles, the greater would be the success.

These eight principles, then, in greater or lesser degree, are the causative factors in all success of whatsoever kind. Underneath all prosperity they are the strong supports, and, howsoever appearances may be against such a conclusion, a measure of them informs and sustains every effort which is crowned with that excellence which men name success.

It is true that comparatively few successful men practice, in their entirety and perfection, all these eight principles, but there are those who do, and they are the leaders, teachers, and guides of men, the supports of human society, and the strong pioneers in the van of human evolution.

But while few achieve that moral perfection which ensures the acme of success, all lesser successes come from the partial observance of these principles which are so powerful in the production of good results that even perfection in any two or three of them alone is sufficient to ensure an ordinary degree of prosperity, and maintain a measure of local influence at least for a time, while the same perfection in two or three with partial excellence in all, or nearly all, the others, will render permanent that limited success and influence which will, necessarily, grow and extend in exact ratio with a more intimate knowledge and practice of those principles which, at present, are only partially incorporated in the character.

The boundary lines of a man's morality mark the limits of his success. So true is this that to know a man's moral status would be to know – to mathematically gauge – his ultimate success or failure. The temple of prosperity only stands in so far as it is supported by its moral pillars; as they are weakened, it becomes insecure; in so far as they are withdrawn, it crumbles away and totters to ruin.

Ultimate failure and defeat are inevitable where moral principles are ignored or defied – inevitable in the nature of things as cause and effect. As a stone thrown upward returns to the earth, so every deed, good or bad, returns upon him that sent it forth. Every unmoral or immoral act frustrates the end at which it aims, and every such succeeding act puts it further and further away as an achieved realisation. On the other hand, every moral act is another solid brick in the temple of prosperity, another round of strength and sculptured beauty in the pillars which support it.

Individuals, families, nations grow and prosper in harmony with their growth in moral strength and knowledge; they fall and fail in accordance with their moral decadence.

Mentally, as physically, only that which has form and solidity can stand and endure. The unmoral is nothingness, and from it nothing can be formed. It is the negation of substance. The immoral is destruction. It is the negation of form. It is a process of spiritual denudation. While it undermines and disintegrates, it leaves the scattered material ready for the wise builder to put it into form again; and the wise builder is Morality. The moral is substance, form, and building power in one. Morality always builds up and preserves, for that is its nature, being the opposite of immorality, which always breaks down and destroys. Morality is the master–builder everywhere, whether in individuals or nations.

Morality is invincible, and he who stands upon it to the end, stands upon an impregnable rock, so that his defeat is impossible, his triumph certain. He will be tried, and that to the uttermost, for without fighting there can be no victory, and so only can his moral powers be perfected, and it is in the nature of fixed principles, as of everything finely and perfectly wrought, to have their strength tested and proved. The steel bars which are to perform the strongest and best uses in the world must be subjected to a severe strain by the ironmaster, as a test of their texture and efficiency, before they are sent from his foundry. The brickmaker throws aside the bricks which have given way under the severe heat. So he who is to be greatly and permanently successful will pass through the strain of adverse circumstances and the fire of temptation with his moral nature not merely not undermined, but strengthened and beautified. He will be like a bar of well-wrought steel, fit for the highest use, and the universe will see, as the ironmaster his finely-wrought steel, that the use does not escape him.

Immorality is assailable at every point, and he who tries to stand upon it, sinks into the morass of desolation. Even while his efforts seem to stand, they are crumbling away. The climax of failure is inevitable. While the immoral man is chuckling over his ill-gotten gains, there is already a hole in his pocket through which his gold is falling. While he who begins with morality, yet deserts it for gain in the hour of trial, is like the brick which breaks on the first application of heat; he is not fit for use, and the universe casts him aside, yet not finally, for he is a being, and not a brick; and he can live and learn, can repent and be restored.

Moral force is the life of all success, and the sustaining element in all prosperity; but there are various kinds of success, and it is frequently necessary that a man should fail in one direction that he may reach up to a greater and more far-reaching success. If, for instance, a literary, artistic, or spiritual genius should begin by trying to make money, it may be, and often is, to his advantage and the betterment of his genius that he should fail therein, so that he may achieve that more sublime success wherein lies his real power. Many a millionaire would doubtless be willing to barter his millions for the literary success of a Shakespeare or the spiritual success of a Buddha, and would thereby consider that he had made a good bargain. Exceptional spiritual success is rarely accompanied with riches, yet financial success cannot in any way compare with it in greatness and grandeur. But I am not, in this book, dealing with the success of the saint or spiritual genius but with that success which concerns the welfare, well-being, and happiness of the broadly average man and woman, in a word, with the prosperity which, while being more or less connected with money – being present and temporal – yet is not confined thereto, but extends to and embraces all human activities, and which particularly relates to that harmony of the individual with his circumstances which produces that satisfaction called happiness and that comfort known as prosperity. To the achievement of this end, so desirable to the mass of mankind, let us now see how the eight principles operate, how the roof of prosperity is raised and made secure upon the pillars by which it is supported.

First Pillar – Energy

Energy is the working power in all achievement. Inert coal it converts into fire, and water it transmutes into steam; it vivifies and intensifies the commonest talent until it approaches to genius, and when it touches the mind of the dullard, it turns into a living fire that which before was sleeping in inertia.

Energy is a moral virtue, its opposing vice being laziness. As a virtue, it can be cultivated, and the lazy man can become energetic by forcibly arousing himself to exertion. Compared with the energetic man, the lazy man is not half alive. Even while the latter is talking about the difficult of doing a thing, the former is doing it. the active man has done a considerable amount of work before the lazy man has roused himself from sleep. While the lazy man is waiting for an opportunity, the active man has gone out, and met and utilized half a dozen opportunities. He does things while the other is rubbing his eyes.

Energy is one of the primary forces: without it nothing can be accomplished. It is the basic element in all forms of action. The entire universe is a manifestation of tireless, though inscrutable energy. Energy is, indeed, life, and without it there would be no universe, no life. When a man has ceased to act, when the body lies inert, and all the functions have ceased to act, then we say he is dead; and in so far as a man fails to act, he is so far dead. Man, mentally and physically, is framed for action, and not for swinish ease. Every muscle of the body (being a lever for exertion) is a rebuke to the lazy man. Every bone and nerve is fashioned for resistance; every function and faculty is there for a legitimate use. All things have their end in action; al things are perfected in use.

This being so, there is no prosperity for the lazy man, no happiness, no refuge and no rest; for him, there is not even the ease which he covets, for he at last becomes a homeless outcast, a troubled, harried, despised man, so that the proverb wisely puts it that "The lazy man does the hardest work," in that, avoiding the systematic labour of skill, he brings upon himself the hardest lot.

Yet energy misapplied is better than no energy at all. This is powerfully put by St. John in the words: "I would have you either hot or cold; if you are lukewarm I will spew you out of my mouth." The extremes of heat and cold here symbolize the transforming agency of energy, in its good and bad aspects.

The lukewarm stage is colourless, lifeless, useless; it can scarcely be said to have either virtue or vice, and is merely barren empty, fruitless. The man who applies his abounding energy to bad ends, has, at the very power with which the strives to acquire his selfish ends, will bring upon him such difficulties, pains, and sorrows, that will compel him to learn by experience, and so at last to re-fashion his base of action. At the right moment, when his mental eyes open to better purposes, he will turn round and cut new and proper channels for the outflow of his power, and will then be just as strong in good as he formerly was in evil. This truth is beautifully crystallized in the old proverb, "The greater the sinner, the great the saint."

Energy is power, and without it there will be no accomplishment; there will not even be virtue, for virtue does not only consist of not doing evil, but also, primarily, of doing good. There are those who try, yet fail through insufficient energy. Their efforts are too feeble to produce positive results. Such are not vicious, and because they never do any deliberate harm, are usually spoken of as good men that fail. But to lack the initiative to do harm is not to be good; it is only to be weak and powerless. He is the truly good man who, having the power to do evil, yet chooses to direct his energies in ways that are good. Without a considerable degree of energy, therefore, there will be no moral power. What good there is, will be latent and sleeping; there will be no going forth of good, just as there can be no mechanical motion without the motive power.

Energy is the informing power in all doing in every department of life, and whether it be along material or spiritual lines. The call to action, which comes not only from the soldier but from the lips or pen of every teacher in every grade of thought, is a call to men to rouse their sleeping energy, and to do vigorously the task in hand. Even the men of contemplation and mediation never cease to rouse their disciples to exertion in meditative thought, is a call to men to rouse their sleeping energy, and to do vigorously the task in hand. Even the men of contemplation and meditation never cease to rouse their disciples to exertion in meditative thought. Energy is alike needed in all spheres of life, and not only are the rules of the soldier, the engineer and the merchant rules of action, but nearly all the percepts of the saviors, sages, and saints are precepts of doing.

The advice of one of the Great Teachers to his disciples – "Keep wide awake," tersely expresses the necessity for tireless energy if one's purpose is to be accomplished, and is equally good advice to the salesman as to the saint. "Eternal vigilance is the price of liberty," and liberty is the reaching of one's fixed end. It was the same Teacher that said: "If anything is to be done, let a man do it at once; let him attack it vigorously!" The wisdom of this advice is seen when it is remembered that action is creative, that increase and development follow upon legitimate use. To get more energy we must use to the full that which we already possess. Only to him that that is given. Only to him that puts his hand vigorously to some task does power and freedom come.

But energy, to be productive, must not only be directed towards good ends, it must be carefully controlled and conserved. "The conservation of energy" is a modern term expressive of that principle in nature by which no energy is wasted or lost, and the man whose energies are to be fruitful in results must work intelligently upon this principle. Noise and hurry are so much energy running to waste. "More haste, less speed." The maximum of noise usually accompanies the minimum of accomplishment. With much talk there is little doing. Working steam is not heard. It is the escaping steam which makes a great noise. It is the concentrated powder which drives the bullet to its mark.

In so far as a man intensifies his energies by conserving them, and concentrating them upon the accomplishment of his purpose, just so far does he gain quietness and silence, in response and calmness. It is great delusion that noise means power. There is no great baby than the blustering boaster. Physically a man, he is but an infant mentally, and having no strength to anything, and no work to show, he tries to make up for it by loudly proclaiming what he has done, or could do.

"Still waters run deep," and the great universal forces are inaudible. Where calmness is, there is the greatest power. Calmness is the sure indication of a strong, welltrained, patiently disciplined mind. The calm man knows his business, be sure of it. His words are few, but they tell. His schemes are well planned, and they work true, like a well balanced machine. He sees a long way ahead, and makes straight for his object. The enemy, Difficulty, he converts into a friend, and makes profitable use of him, for he has studied well how to "agree with his adversary while he is in the way with him," Like a wise general, he has anticipated all emergencies. Indeed, he is the man who is prepared beforehand. In his meditations, in the counsels of his judgement, he has conferred with causes, and has caught the bent of all contingencies. He is never taken by surprise; is never in a hurry, is safe in the keeping of his own steadfastness, and is sure of his ground. You may think you have got him, only to find, the next moment, that you have tripped in your haste, and that he has got you, or rather that you, wanting calmness, have hurried yourself into the dilemma which you had prepared for him. Your impulse cannot do battle with his deliberation, but is foiled at the first attack; your uncurbed energy cannot turn aside the wisely directed steam of his concentrated power. He is "armed at all points." By a mental Ju-Jitsu acquired through self discipline, he meets opposition in such a way that it destroys itself. Upbraid him with angry words, and the reproof hidden in his gentle reply searches to the very heart of your folly, and the fire of your anger sinks into the ashes of remorse. Approach him with a vulgar familiarity, and his look at once fill you with shame, and brings you back to your senses. As he is prepared for all events, so he is ready for all men; though no men are ready for him. All weaknesses are betrayed in his presence, and he commands by an inherent force which calmness has rendered habitual and unconscious.

Calmness, as distinguished from the dead placidity of languor, is the acme of concentrated energy. There is a focused mentality behind it. in agitation and excitement the mentality is dispersed. It is irresponsible, and is without force or weight. The fussy, peevish, irritable man has no influence. He repels, and not attracts. He wonders why his "easy going" neighbour succeeds, and is sought after, while he, who is always hurrying, worrying and troubling the miscalls it striving, falls and is avoided. His neighbour, being a calmer man, not more easy going but more deliberate, gets through more work, does it more skillfully, and is more self possessed and manly. This is the reason of his success and influence. His energy is controlled and used, while the other man's energy is dispersed and abused.

Energy, then, is the first pillar in the temple of prosperity, and without it, as the first and most essential equipment, there can be no prosperity. No energy means no capacity; there is no manly self respect and independence. Amongst the unemployed will be found many who are unemployable through sheer lack of this first essential of work energy. The man that stands many hours a day at a street corner with his hands in his pockets and a pipe in his mouth, waiting for some one to treat him to a glass of beer, is little likely to find employment, or to accept it should it come to him. Physically flabby and mentally inert, he is every day becoming more some, is making himself more unfit to work, and therefore unfit to live. The energetic man may pass through temporary periods of unemployment and suffering, but it is impossible for him to become one of the permanently unemployed. He will either find work or make it, for inertia is painful to him, and work is a delight; and he who delights in work will not long remain unemployed.

The lazy man does not wish to be employed. He is in his element when doing nothing. His chief study is how to avoid exertion. To vegetate in semi torpor is his idea of happiness. He is unfit and unemployable. Even the extreme Socialist, who places all unemployment, at the door of the rich, would discharge a lazy, neglectful and unprofitable servant, and so add one more to the arm of the unemployed; for laziness is one of the lowest vices repulsive to all active, right minded men.

But energy is a composite power. It does not stand alone. Involved in it are qualities which go to the making of vigorous character and the production of prosperity. Mainly, these qualities are contained in the four following characteristics:—

1. Promptitude
2. Vigilance
3. Industry
4. Earnestness

The pillar of energy is therefore a concrete mass composed of these four tenacious elements. They are through, enduring, and are calculated to withstanding the wildest weather of adversity. They all make for life, power, capacity, and progress.

Promptitude is valuable possession. It begets reliability. People who are alert, prompt, and punctual are relied upon. They can be trusted to do their duty, and to do it vigorously and well. Masters who are prompt are a tonic to their employees, and a whip to those who are inclined to shirk. They are a means of wholesome discipline to those who would not otherwise discipline themselves. Thus while aiding their own usefulness and success, they contribute to the usefulness and success of others. The perfunctory worker, who is ever procrastinating, and is always behind time, becomes a nuisance, if not go himself, to others, and his services come to be regarded as of little economic value. Deliberation and dispatch, handmaids of promptitude, are valuable aids in the achievement of prosperity. In ordinary business channels, alacrity is a saving power, and promptness spells profit. It is doubtful whether a confirmed procrastinator ever succeeded in business. I have not yet met one such, though I have known many who have failed.

Vigilance is the guard of all the faculties and powers of the mind. It is the detective that prevents the entrance of any violent and destructive element. It is the close companion and protector of all success, liberty, and wisdom. Without this watchful attitude of mind, a man is a fool, and there is no prosperity for a fool. The fool allows his mind to be ransacked and robbed of its gravity, serenity, and judgement by mean thoughts and violent passions as they come along to molest him. He is never on his guard, but leaves open the doors of his mind to every nefarious intruder. He is so weak and unsteady as to be swept off his balance by every gust of impulse that overtakes him. He is an example to others of what they should not be. He is always a failure, for the fool is an offence to all men, and there is no society that can receive him with respect. As wisdom is the acme of strength, so folly is the other extreme of weakness.

The lack of vigilance is shown in thoughtlessness and in a general looseness in the common details of life. Thoughtlessness is built another name for folly. It lies at the root of a great deal of failure and misery. No one who aims at any kind of usefulness and prosperity (for usefulness in the body politic and prosperity to one's self cannot be served)' can afford to be asleep with regard to his actions and the effect of those actions on other and reactively on himself. He must, at the outset of his career, wake up to a sense of his personnel responsibility. He must know that wherever he is – in the home, the counting — house, the pulpit, the store, in the schoolroom or behind the counter, in company or alone, at work or at play — his conduct will materially affect his career for good or bad; for there is a subtle influence in behavior which leaves its impression every man, woman, and child that it touches, and that impress is the determining factor in the attitude of persons towards one another. It is for the reason that the cultivation of good manners plays such an important part in all coherent society. If you carry about with you a disturbing or disagreeable mental defect, it needs not to be named and known to work its poison upon your affairs. Its corrosive influence will eat into all your efforts, and disfigure your happiness and prosperity, as powerful acid eats into and disfigures the finest steel. On the other hand, if you carry about an assuring and harmonious mental excellence, it needs no that those about you understand it to be influenced by it. They will be drawn towards you in good –will, often without knowing why, and that good quality will be the most powerful sport in all your affairs, bringing you friends and opportunities, and greatly aiding in the success of all your enterprises. It will even right your minor incapacitaties; covering a multitude of faults.

Thus we receive at the hands of the world according to the measure of our giving. For bad, bad; for good, good. For defective conduct, indifferent influence and imperfect success; for superior conduct lasting power and consummate achievement. We act, and the world responds. When the foolish man fails, he blames other, and sees no error in himself; but the wise man watches and corrects himself, and so is assured of success.

The man whose mind is vigilant and alert, has thereby a valuable equipment in the achievement of his aims; and if he be fully alive and wide-awake on all occasions, to all opportunities, and against all marring defects of character, what event, what circumstance, what enemy shall overtake him and find him unprepared? What shall prevent him from achieving the legitimate and at which he aims?

Industry brings cheerfulness and plenty. Vigorously industrious people are the happiest members of the community. They are not always the richest, if by riches is meant a superfluity of money; but they are always the most lighthearted and joyful, and the most satisfied with what they do and have, and are therefore the richer, if by richer we mean more abundantly blessed. Active people have no time for moping and brooding, or for dwelling selfishly upon their ailments and troubles. Things most used are kept the brightest, and people most employed best retain their brightness and buoyancy of spirit. Things unused tarnish quickest; and the time killer is attacked with ennui and morbid fancies. To talk of having to "kill time" is almost like a confession of imbecility; for who, in the short life at his disposal, and in a world so flooded with resources of knowledge with sound heads and good hearts can fill up every moment of every day usefully and happily, and if they refer to time at all, it is to the effect that it is all too short to enable them to do all that they would like to do.

Industry, too, promoted health and well being. The active man goes to bed tired every night; his rest is sound and sweet, and he wakes up early in the morning, fresh and strong for another day's delightful toil. His appetite and digestion are good. He has an excellent sauce in recreation, and a good tonic in toil. What companionship can such a man have with moping and melancholy? Such morbid spirits hang around those who do little and dine excessively. People who make themselves useful to the community, receive back from the community their full share of health, happiness, and prosperity. They brighten the daily task, and keep the world moving. They are the gold of the nation and the salt of the earth.

"Earnestness," said a Great Teacher, "is the path of immortality. They who are in earnest do not die; they who are not in earnest are as if dead already." Earnestness is the dedication of the entire mind to its task. We live only in what we do. Earnest people are dissatisfied with anything short of the highest excellence in whatever they do, and they always reach that excellence. They are so many that are careless and half hearted, so satisfied with a poor performance, that the earnest ones shine apart as it were, in their excellence. They are always plenty of "vacancies" in the ranks of usefulness and service for earnest people. There never was, and never will be, a deeply earnest man or woman who did not fill successfully some suitable sphere. Such people are scrupulous, conscientious, and painstaking, and cannot rest in ease until the very best is done, and the whole world is always on the lookout to reward the best. It always stands ready to pay the full price, whether in money, fame, friends, influence, happiness, scope or life, for that which is of surpassing excellence, whether it be in things material, intellectual, or spiritual. What ever you are – whether shopkeeper or saintly teacher you can safely give the very best to the world without any doubt or misgiving. If the indelible impress of your earnestness be on your goods in the one case, or on your words in the other, your business will flourish, or your precepts will live.

Earnest people make rapid progress both in their work and their character. It is thus that they live, and "do not die," for stagnation only is death, and where there is incessant progress and ever ascending excellence, stagnation and health are swallowed up in activity and life.

Thus is the making and masonry of the First pillar explained. He who builds it well, and sets it firm and straight, will have a powerful and enduring support in the business of his life.

Second Pillar – Economy

It is said of Nature that she knows on vacuum. She also knows no waste. In the divine economy my Nature everything is conserved and turned to good account. Even excreta are chemically transmitted, and utilized in the building up of new forms. Nature destroys every foulness, not by annihilation, but by transmutation, by sweetening and purifying it, and making it serve the ends of things beautiful, useful and good.

That economy which, in nature is a universal principle, is in man a moral quality and it is that quality by which he preserves his energies, and sustains his place as a working unit in the scheme of things.

Financial economy is merely a fragment of this principle, or rather it is a material symbol of that economy which is purely mental, and its transmutations spiritual. The financial economist exchanges coppers for silver, silver for gold, gold for notes, and the notes he converts into the figures of a bank account. By these conversions of money into more readily transmissible forms he is the gainer in the financial management of his affairs. The spiritual economist transmutes passions into intelligence, intelligence into principles, principles into wisdom, and wisdom is manifested in actions which are few but of powerful effect. By all these transmutations he is the gainer in character and in the management of his life.

True economy is the middle way in all things, whether material or mental, between waste and undue retention. That which is wasted, whether money or mental energy, is rendered powerless; that which is selfishly retained and hoarded up, is equally powerless. To secure power, whether of capital or mentality, there must be concentration, but concentration must be followed by legitimate use. The gathering up of money or energy is only a means; the end is use; and it is use only that produces power.

An all round economy consists in finding the middle way in the following seven things:— Money, Food, Clothing, Recreation, Rest, Time and Energy.

Money is the symbol of exchange, and represents purchasing power. He who is anxious to acquire financial wealth as well as he who wishes to avoid debt – must study how to apportion, his expenditure in accordance with his income, so as to leave a margin of ever increasing working capital, or to have a little store ready in hand for any emergency. Money spent in thoughtless expenditure – in worthless pleasures or harmful luxuries – is money wasted and power destroyed; for, although a limited and subordinate power, the means and capacity for legitimate and virtuous purchase is, nevertheless, a power, and one that enters largely into the details of our everyday life. The spendthrift can never become rich, but if he begin with riches, must soon become poor. The miser, with all his stored-away gold, cannot be said to be rich, for he is in want, and his gold, lying idle, is deprived of its power of purchase. The thrifty and prudent are on the way to riches, for while they spend wisely they save carefully, and gradually enlarge their spheres as their growing means allow.

The poor man who is to become rich must begin at the bottom, and must not wish, nor try to appear affluent by attempting something far beyond his means. There is always plenty of room and scope at the bottom, and it is a safe place from which to begin, as there is nothing below, and everything above. Many a young business man comes at once to grief by swagger and display which he foolishly imagines are necessary to success, but which, deceiving no one but himself, lead quickly to ruin. A modest and true beginning, in any sphere, will better ensure success than an exaggerated advertisement of one's standing and importance. The smaller the capital, the smaller should be the sphere of operations. Capital and scope are hand and glove, and they should fit. Concentrate your capital within the circle of its working power, and however circumscribed that circle may be it will continue to widen and extend as the gathering momentum of power presses for expression.

Above all take care always to avoid the two extremes of parsimony and prodigality.

Food represents life, vitality, and both physical and mental strength. There is a middle way in eating and drinking, as in all else. The man who is to achieve prosperity must be well nourished, but not overfed. The man that starves his body, whether through miserliness or asceticism (both forms of false economy), diminishes his mental energy, and renders his body too enfeebled to be the instrument for any strong achievement. Such a man courts sickly mindedness, a condition conducive only to failure.

The glutton, however, destroys himself by excess. His bestialized body becomes a stored up reservoir of poisons, which attract disease and corruption, while his mind becomes more and more brutalized and confused, and therefore more incapable. Gluttony is one of the lowest and most animal vices, and is obnoxious to all who pursue a moderate course.

The best workers and most successful men are they who are most moderate in eating and drinking. By taking enough nourishment, but not too much, they attain the maximum physical and mental fitness. Beings thus well equipped by moderation, they are enabled to vigorously and joyfully fight the battle of life.

Clothing is covering and protection for the body, though it is frequently wrested from this economic purpose, and made a means of vain display. The two extremes to be avoided here are negligence and vanity. Custom cannot, and need not, be ignored; and cleanliness is all important. The ill-dressed, unkempt man or woman invites failure and loneliness. A man's dress should harmonize with his station in life, and it should be of good quality, and be well made and appropriate. Clothing should not be cast aside while comparatively new, but should be well worn. If a man be poor, he will not lose in either self respect or the respect of others by wearing threadbare clothing if it be clean and his whole body be clean and neat. But vanity, leading to excessive luxury in clothing, is a vice which should be studiously avoided by virtuous people. I know a lady who had forty dresses in her wardrobe; also a man who had twenty walking-sticks, about the same number of hats, and some dozen mackintoshes; while another had some twenty or thirty pairs of boots. Rich people who thus squander money on piles of superfluous clothing, are courting poverty, for it is waste, and waste leads to want. The money so heedlessly spent could be better used, for suffering abounds and charity is noble.

An obtrusive display in clothing and jewellery bespeaks a vulgar and empty mind. Modest and cultured people are modest and becoming in their dress, and their spare money is wisely used in further enhancing their culture and virtue. Education and progress are of more importance to them than vain and needless apparel; and literature, art, and science are encouraged thereby. A true refinement is in the mind and behaviour, and a mind adorend with virtue and intelligence cannot add to its attractiveness though it may detract from it) by an ostentatious display of the body. Time spent in uselessly adorning the body could be more fruitfully employed. Simplicity in dress, as in other things, is the best. It touches the point of excellence in usefulness, comfort, and bodily grace, and bespeaks true taste and cultivated refinement.

Recreation is one of the necessities of life. Every man and women should have some definitive work as the main object of life, and to which a considerable amount of time should be devoted, and he should only turn from it at given and limited periods for recreation and rest. The object of recreation is greater buoyancy of both body and mind, with an increase of power in one's serious work. It is, therefore, a means, not an end; and this should ever be born in mind, for, to many, some forms of recreation innocent and good in themselves – become so fascinating that they are in danger of making them the end of life, and of thus abandoning duty for pleasure. To make of life a ceaseless round of games and pleasures, with no other object in life, is to turn living upside down, as it were, and it produces monotony and enervation. People who do it are the most unhappy of mortals, and suffer from languor, ennui, and peevishness. As sauce is an aid to digestion, and can only lead to misery when made the work of life. When a man has done his day's duty he can turn to his recreation with a free mind and a light heart, and both his work and his pleasure will be to him a source of happiness.

It is a true economy in this particular neither to devote the whole of one's time to work nor to recreation, but to apportion to each its time and place; and so fill out life with those changes which are necessary to a long life and a fruitful existence.

All agreeable changes is recreation and the mental worker will gain both in the quality and, quantity of his work by laying it down at the time appointed for restful and refreshing recreation; while the physical worker will improve in every way by turning to some form of study as a hobby or means of education.

As we do not spend all our time in eating or sleeping or resting, neither should we spend it in exercise or pleasure, but should give recreation its proper place as a natural tonic in the economic scheme of our life.

Rest is for recuperation after toil. Every self respecting human being should do sufficient work every day to make his sleep restful and sweet, and his rising up fresh and bright.

Enough sleep should be taken, but not too much, over indulgence on the one hand, or deprivation on the other, are both harmful. It is an easy matter to find out how much sleep one requires. By going to bed early, and getting up early (rising a little earlier every morning if one has been in the habit of spending long hours in bed), one can very soon accurately gauge and adjust the number of hours he or she requires for complete recuperation. It will be found as the sleeping hours are shortened that the sleep becomes more and more sound and sweet, and the waking up more and more alert and bright. People who are to prosper in their work must not give way to ignoble ease and over indulgence in sleep. Fruitful labour, and not ease, is the true end of life, and ease is only good in so far as it sub-serves the ends of work. Sloth and prosperity can never be companions can never even approach each other. The sluggard will never overtake success, but failure will speedily catch up with him, and leave him defeated. Rest is to fit us for greater labour, and not to pamper us in indolence. When the bodily vigour is restored, the end of rest is accomplished. A perfect balance between labour and rest contributes considerably to health, happiness, and prosperity.

Time is that which we all possess in equal measure. The day is not lengthened for any man. We should therefore see to it that we do not squander its precious minutes in unprofitable waste. He who spends his time in self indulgence and the pursuit of pleasure, presently finds himself old, and nothing has been accomplished. He who fills full with useful pursuits the minutes as they come and go, grows old in honour and wisdom, and prosperity abides with him. Money wasted can be restored; health wasted can be restored; but time wasted can never be restored.

It is an old saying that "time is money." It is, in the same way, health, and strength, and talent, and genius, and wisdom, in accordance with the manner in which it is used; and to properly use it, the minutes must be seized upon as they come, for once they are past they can never be recalled. The day should be divided into portions, and everything – work, leisure, meals, recreation – should be attend to in its proper time; and the time of preparation should not be overlooked or ignored. Whatever a man does, he will do it better and more successfully by utilizing some small portion of the day in preparing his mind for his work. The man who gets up early in order to think and plan, that he may weigh and consider and forecast, will always manifest greater skill and success in his particular pursuit, than the man who lives in bed till the last moment, and only gets up just in time to begin breakfast. An hour spend in this way before breakfast will prove of the greatest value in making one's efforts fruitful. It is a means of calming and clarifying the mind, and of focussing one's energies so as to render them more powerful and effective. The best and most abiding success is that which is made before eight o'clock in the morning. He who is at his business at six o'clock, will always other conditions being equal be a long way ahead of the man who is in bed at eight. The lie a bed heavily handicaps himself in the race of life. He gives his early-rising competitor two or three hours start every day. How can he ever hope to win with such a self imposed tax upon his time? At the end of a year that two or three hours start every day is shown in a success which is the synthesis of accumulated results. What, then, must be the difference between the efforts of these two men at the end, say, of twenty years! The lie-a-bed, too, after he gets up is always in a hurry trying to regain lost time, which results in more loss of time, for hurry always defeats its own end. The early rise, who thus economies his time, has no need to hurry, for he is always ahead of the hour, is always well up with his work; he can well afford to be calm and deliberate, and to do carefully and well whatever is in hand, for his good habit shows itself at the end of the day in the form of a happy frame of mind, and in bigger results in the shape of work skillfully and successfully done.

In the economizing of time, too, there will be many things which a man will have to eliminate from his life; some of things and pursuits which he loves, and desires to retain, will have to be sacrifice to the main purpose of his life. The studied elimination of non-essentials from one's daily life is a vital factor in all great achievement. All great men are adepts in this branch of economy, and it plays an important part in the making of their greatness. It is a form of economy which also enters into the mind, the actions, and the speech, eliminating from them all that is superfluous, and that impedes, and does not sub-serve, the end aimed at. Foolish and unsuccessful people talk carelessly and aimlessly, act carelessly and aimlessly, and allow everything that comes along good, bad, and different to lodge in their mind.

The mind of the true economist is a sieve which lets everything fall through except that which is of use to him in the business of his life. He also employs only necessary words, and does only necessary actions, thus vastly minimizing friction and waste of power.

To go to bed betime and to get up betime, to fill in every working minute with purposeful thought and effective action, this is the true economy of time.

Energy is economized by the formation of good habits. All vices are a reckless expenditure of energy. Sufficient energy is thoughtlessly wasted in bad habits to enable men to accomplish the greatest success, if conserved and used in right directions. If economy be practiced in the six points already considered, much will be done in the conservation of one's energies, but a man must go still further, and carefully husband his vitality by the avoidance of all forms of physical self indulgences and impurities, but also all those mental vices such as hurry, worry, excitement, despondency, anger, complaining and envy – which deplete the mind and render it unfit for any important work or admirable achievement. They are common forms of mental dissipation which a man of character should study how to avoid and overcome. The energy wasted in frequent fits of bad temper would, if controlled and properly directed, give a man strength of mind, force of character, and much power to achieve. The angry man is a strong man made weak by the dissipation of his mental energy. He needs self control to

manifest his strength. The calm man is always his superior in any department
of life, and will always take precedence of him, both in his success, and in the
estimation of others. No man can afford to disperse his energies in fostering
bad habits and bad tendencies of mind. Every vice, however, apparently small
will tell against him in the battle of life. Every harmful self indulgence will
come back to him in the form of some trouble or weakness. Every moment of
riot or of pandering to his lower inclinations will make his progress more
laborious, and will hold him back from scaling the high heaven of his wishes
for achievement. On the other hand, he who economizes his energies, and
bends them towards the main task of his life, will make rapid progress, and
nothing will prevent him from reaching the golden city of success.

It will be seen that economy is something far more profound and far
reaching than the mere saving of money. It touches every part of our nature
and every phase of our life. The old saying, "Take care of the pence, and the
pounds will take care of themselves," may be regarded as a parable, for the
lower passions as native energy; it is the abuse of that energy that is bad, and
if this personal energy be taken care of and stored up and transmuted, it
reappears as force of character. To waste this valuable energy in the pursuit
of vice is like wasting the pence, and so losing the pounds, but to take care
of it for good uses is to store up the pence of passions, and so gain the golden
pounds of good. Take care, therefore, of the lower energies, and the higher
achievements will take care of themselves.

The Pillar of Economy, when soundly built, will be found to be composed
largely of these four qualities:—

1. Moderation
2. Efficiency
3. Resourcefulness
4. Originality

Moderation is the strong core of economy. It avoids extremes, finding the
middle way in all things. It also consists in abstaining from the unnecessary
and the harmful. There can be no such things as moderation in that which
is evil, for that would be excess. A true moderation abstains from evil. It is
not a moderate use of fire to put our hands into it, but to warm them by it at
a safe distance. Evil is a fire that will burn a man though he but touch it. a
harmful luxury is best left severely alone. Smoking, snuff taking, alcoholic
drinking, gambling, and other such common vices, although they have
dragged thousands down to ill health, misery, and failure, have never helped
one towards health, happiness and success. The man who eschews them will
always be head of the man that pursues them, their talents and opportunities

being equal. Healthy, happy, and long lived people are always moderate and abstemious in their habits. By moderation the life forces are preserved; by excess they are destroyed. Men, also, who carry moderation into their thoughts, allaying their passions and feelings, avoiding all unwholesome extremes and morbid sensations and sentiments, add knowledge and wisdom to happiness and health, and thereby attain to the highest felicity and power. The immoderate destroy themselves by their own folly. They weaken their energies and stultify their capabilities, and instead of achieving an abiding success, reach only, at best, a fitful and precarious prosperity.

Efficiency proceeds from the right conservation of one's forces and powers. All skill is the use of concentrated energy. Superior skill, as talent and genius, is a higher degree of concentrated force. Men are always skillful in that which they love, because the mind is almost ceaselessly centered upon it. Skill is the result of that mental economy which transmutes thought into invention and action. There will be no prosperity without skill, and one's prosperity will be in the measure of one's skill. By a process of natural selection, the inefficient fall in to their right places. Among the badly paid or unemployed; for who will employ a man who cannot, or will not, do his work properly? An employer may occasionally keep such a man out of charity; but this will be exceptional; as places of business, offices, households, and all centers of organized activity, are not charitable institutions, but industrial bodies which stand or fall but the fitness and efficiency of their individual members.

Skill is gained by thoughtfulness and attention. Aimless and inattentive people are usually out of employment – to wit, the lounger at the street corner. They cannot do the simplest thing properly, because they will not rouse up the mind to thought and attention. Recently an acquaintance of mine employed a tramp to clean his windows, but the man had refrained from work and systematic thought for so long that he had become incapable of both, and could not even clean a window. Even when shown how to do it, he could not follow the simple instructions given. This is an instance, too, of the fact that the simplest thing requires a measure of skill in the doing. Efficiency largely determines a man's place among his fellows, and leads one on by steps to higher and higher positions as greater powers are developed. The good workman is skillful, with his tools, while the good man is skillful with his thoughts. Wisdom is the highest form of skill. Aptitude in incipient wisdom. There is one right way of doing everything, even the smallest, and a thousand wrong ways. Skill consists in finding the one right way, and adhering to it. The inefficient bungle confusedly about among the thousand wrong ways, and do not adopt the right even when it is pointed out to them. They do this in some cases because they think, in their ignorance, that they know best, thereby placing themselves in a position where it becomes impossible to learn, even though it be only to learn how to clean a window or sweep a floor. Thoughtlessness and inefficiency are all too common. There is plenty of room in the world for common. There is plenty of room in the world for thoughtful and efficient people. Employers of labour know how difficult it is to get the best workmanship. The good workman, whether with tools or brain, whether with speech or thought, will always find a place for the exercise of his skill.

Resourcefulness is the outcome of efficiency. It is an important element in prosperity, for the resourceful man is never confounded. He may have many falls, but he will always be equal to the occasion, and will be on his feet again immediately. Resourcefulness has its fundamental cause in the conservation of energy. It is energy transmuted. When a man cuts off certain mental or bodily vices which have been depleting him of his energy, what becomes of the energy so conserved? It is not destroyed or lost, for energy can never be destroyed or lost. It becomes productive energy. It reappears in the form of fruitful thought. The virtuous man is always more successful than the vicious man because he is teeming with resources. His entire mentality is alive and vigorous, abounding with stored up energy. What the vicious man wastes in barren indulgence, the virtuous man uses in fruitful industry. A new life and a new world, abounding with all fascinating pursuits and pure delights, open up to the man who shuts himself off from the old world of animal vice, and his place will be assured by the resources which will well up within him. Barren seed perishes in the earth; there is no place for it in the fruitful economy of nature. Barren minds sink in the struggle of life. Human society makes for good, and there is no room in it for the emptiness engendered by vice. But the barren mind will not sink for ever. When it wills, it can become fruitful and regain itself. By the very nature of existence, by the eternal law of progress, the vicious man must fall; but having fallen, he can rise again. He can turn from vice to virtue, and stand, self respecting and secure, upon his own resources.

The resourceful men invent, discover, initiate. They cannot fail, for they are in the stream of progress. They are full of new schemes, new methods, new hopes, and their life is so much fuller and richer thereby. They are men of supple minds. When a man fails to improve his business, his work, his methods, he falls out of the line of progress, and has begun to fail. His mind has become stiff and inert like the body of an aged man, and so fails to keep pace with the rapidly moving ideas and plans of resourceful minds. A resourceful mind is like a river which never runs dry, and which affords refreshment, and supplies new vigour, in times of drought. Men of resources are men of new ideas, and men of new ideas flourish where others fade and decay.

Originality is resourcefulness ripened and perfected. Where there is originality there is genius, and men of genius are the lights of the world. Whatever work a man does, he should fall back upon his own resources in the doing it. While learning from others, he should not slavishly imitate them, but should put himself into his work, and so make it new and original. Original men get the ear of the world. They may be neglected at first, but they are always ultimately accepted, and become patterns for mankind. Once a man has acquired the knack of originality, he takes his place as a leader among men in his particular department of knowledge and skill. But originality cannot be forced; it can only be developed; and it is developed by proceeding from excellence to excellence, by ascending in the scale of skill by the full and right use of one's mental powers. Let a man consecrate himself to his work, let him, so consecrated, concentrate all his energies upon it, and the day will come when the world will hail him as one of its strong sons; and he, too, like Balzac who, after many years of strenuous toil, one day exclaimed, "I am about to become a genius!, "I am about to become a genius" will at least discover, to his joy, that he has joined the company of original minds, the gods who lead mankind into newer, higher, and more beneficent ways.

The composition of the Second Pillar is thus revealed. Its building awaits the ready work man who will skillfully apply his mental energies.

Third Pillar – Integrity

There is no striking a cheap bargain with prosperity. It must be purchased, not only with intelligent labor, but with moral force. as the bubble cannot endure, so the fraud cannot prosper. He makes a feverish spurt in the acquirement of money, and then collapses. Nothing is ever gained, ever can be gained, by fraud. It is but wrested for a time, to be again returned with heavy interest. But fraud is not confined to the unscrupulous swindler. All who are getting, or trying to get, money without giving an equivalent are practicing fraud, whether they know it or not. Men who are anxiously scheming how to get money without working for it, are frauds, and mentally they are closely allied to the thief and swindler under whose influence they come, sooner or later, and who deprives them of their capital. What is a thief but a man who carries to its logical or later, and who deprives them of their capital. What is a thief but a man who carries to its logical extreme the desire to possess without giving a just return – that is, unlawfully? The man that courts prosperity must, in all his transactions, whether material or mental, study how to give a just return for that which he receives. This is the great fundamental principle in all sound commerce, while in spiritual things it becomes the doing to others that which we would have them do to us, and applied to the forces of the universe, it is scientifically stated in the formula, "Action and Reaction are equal."

Human life is reciprocal, not rapacious, and the man who regards all others as his legitimate prey will soon find himself stranded in the desert of ruin, far away from the path of prosperity. He is too far behind in the process of evolution to cope successfully with honest man. The fittest, the best, always survive, and he being the worst, cannot therefore continue. His end, unless the change in time, is sure it is the goal, the filthy hovel, or the place of the deserted outcast. His efforts are destructive, and not constructive, and he thereby destroys himself.

It was Carlyle who, referring to Mohammed being then universally regarded by Christians as an impostor, exclaimed, "An impostor found a religion! An impostor couldn't built a brick house" an impostor, a liar a cheat the man of dishonesty cannot build as he has neither tools or material with which to build. He can no more build up a business, a character, a career, a success, than he can found a religion or build a brick house. He not only does not build, but all his energies are bent on undermining what others have built, but his being impossible, he undermines himself.

Without integrity, energy and economy will at last fail, but aided by integrity, their strength will be greatly augmented. There is not an occasion in life in which the moral factor does not play an important part. Sterling integrity tell wherever it is, and stamps it hall mark on all transactions; and it does this because of its wonderful coherence and consistency, and its invincible strength. For the man of integrity is in line with the fixed laws of things – not only with the fundamental principles on which human society rests, but with the laws which hold the vast universe together. Who shall set these at naught? Who, then, shall undermine the man of unblemished integrity? He is like a strong tree whose roots are fed by perennial springs, and which no tempest can law low.

To be complete and strong, integrity must embrace the whole man, and extend to all the details of his life; and it must be so through and permanent as to withstand all temptations to swerve into compromise. To fail in one point is to fail in all, and to admit, under stress, a compromise with falsehood, howsoever necessary and insignificant it may appear, is to throw down the shield of integrity, and to stand exposed to the onslaughts of evil.

The man who works as carefully and conscientiously when his employer is away as when his eye is upon him, will not long remain in an inferior position. Such integrity in duty, in performing the details of his work, will quickly lead him into the fertile regions of prosperity.

The shirker, on the other hand – he who does not scruple to neglect his work when his employer is not about, thereby robbing his employer of the time and labour for which he is paid – will quickly come to the barren region of unemployment, and will look in vain for needful labour.

There will come a time, too, to the man who is not deeply rooted in integrity, when it will seem necessary to his prospects and prosperity that he should tell a lie or do a dishonest thing – I say, to the man who is not deeply rooted in this principle, for a man of fixed and enlightened integrity knows that lying and dishonesty can never under any circumstance be necessary, and therefore he neither needs to be tempted in this particular, nor can he possibly be tempted but the one so tempted must be able to cast aside the subtle insinuation of falsehood which, in a time of indecision and perplexity, arises within him, and he must stand firmly by the principle, being willing to lose and suffer rather than sink into obliquity. In this way only can he become enlightened concerning this moral principle, and discover the glad truth that integrity does not lead to loss and suffering, but to gain and joy; that honesty and deprivation are not, and cannot be, related as cause and effect.

It is this willingness to sacrifice rather than be untrue that leads to enlightenment in all spheres of life; and the man who, rather than sacrifice some selfish aim, will lie or deceive, has forfeited his right to moral enlightenment, and takes his place lower down among the devotees of deceit, among the doers of shady transactions, than men of no character and no reputation.

A man is not truly armoured with integrity until he has become incapable of lying or deceiving either by gesture, word, or act; until he sees, clearly, openly, and freed from all doubt, the deadly effects of such moral turpitude. The man so enlightened is protect from all quarters, and can no more be undermined by dishonest men than the sun can be pulled down from heaven by madmen, and the arrows of selfishness and treachery that may be poured upon him will rebound from the strong armour of his integrity and the bright shield of his righteousness, leaving him unharmed and untouched.

A lying tradesman will tell you that no man can thrive and be honest in these days of keen competition. How can such a man know this, seeing that he has never tried honest? Moreover, such a man has no knowledge of honesty, and his statement is therefore, a statement of ignorance, and ignorance and falsehood so blind a man that he foolishly imagines all are as ignorant and false as himself. I have known such tradesmen, and have seen them come to ruin. I once heard a businessman make the following statement in a public meeting:—"No man can be entirely honest in business; he can only be approximately honest." He imagined that his statement revealed the condition of the business world; it did not, it revealed his own condition. He was merely telling his audience that he was a dishonest man, but his ignorance, moral ignorance, prevented him from seeing this. Approximate honesty is only another term for dishonesty. The man who deviated a little from the straight path, will deviate more. He has no fixed principle of right and is only thinking of his own advantage. That he persuades himself that his particular dishonesty is of a white and harmless kind, and that he is not so bad as his neighbour, is only of the many forms of self delusion which ignorance of moral principles creates.

Right doing between man and main in the varied relations and transactions of life is the very soul of integrity. It includes, but is more than, honesty. It is the backbone of human society, and the support of human institutions.

Without it there would be no trust, no confidence between men, and the business world would topple to its fall.

As the liar thinks all men are liars, and treats them as such, so the man of integrity treats all men with confidence. He trusts them, and they trust him. His clear eye and open hand shame the creeping fraud so that he cannot practice his fraud on him. As Emerson has so finely put it – "Trust men and they will be true to you, even though they make an exception in your favor to al their rules of trade."

The upright man by his very presence commands the morality of those about him making them better than they were. Men are powerfully influenced by one another, and, as good is more powerful than evil, the strong and good man both shames and elevates, by his contact, the weak and bad.

The man of integrity carries about with him an unconscious grandeur which both awes and inspires. Having lifted himself above the petty, the mean, and the false, those coward vices slink from his presence in confusion. The highest intellectual gift cannot compare with this lofty moral grandeur. In the memory of men and the estimation of the world the man of integrity occupies a higher place than the man of genius. Buckminster says, "The moral grandeur of an independent integrity is the sublimest thing in nature." It is the quality in man which produces heroes. The man of unswerving rectitude is, intrinsically, always a hero. It only needs the occasion to bring out the heroic element. He is always, too, possessed a permanent happiness. The man of genius may be very unhappy, but not to the man of integrity. Nothing nor sickness, nor calamity, nor death – can deprive him of that permanent satisfaction which inheres in uprightness.

Rectitude leads straight to prosperity by four successive steps. First, the upright man wins the confidence of others. Second, having gained their confidence, they put trust in him. Third, this trust, never being violated, produces a good reputation; and fourth, a good reputation spreads further and further, and so bring about success.

Dishonesty has the reverse effect. By destroying the confidence of others, it produces in them suspicion and mistrust, and these bring about a bad reputation, which culminates in failure.

The Pillar of Integrity is held together by these four virile elements:

1. Honesty
2. Fearlessness
3. Purposefulness
4. Invincibility

Honesty is the surest way to success. The day at last comes when the dishonest man repents in sorrow and suffering: but not man ever needs to repent of having been honest. Even when the honest man fails – as he does sometimes, through lacking other of these pillars, such as energy, economy, or system his failure is not the grievous thing it is to the dishonest man, for he can always rejoice in the fact that he has never defrauded a fellow being. Even in his darkest hour he finds repose in a clear conscience.

Ignorant men imagine that dishonesty is a short cut to prosperity. This is why they practice it. The dishonest man is morally short sighted. Like the drunkard who sees the immediate pleasure of his habit, but not the ultimate degradation, he sees the immediate effect of a dishonest act – a larger profit but not its ultimate outcome; he does not see that an accumulated number of such acts must inevitably undermine his character, and bring his business toppling about his ears in ruin. While pocketing his gains, and thinking how cleverly and successfully he is imposing on others, he is all the time imposing on himself, and every coin thus gained must be paid back with added interest, and from this just retribution there is no possible loophole of escape. This moral gravitation is an sure and unvarying as the physical gravitation of a stone to the earth.

The tradesman who demands of his assistants that they shall be, and misrepresents his goods to customers, is surrounding himself on all hands with suspicion, mistrust, and hatred. Even the moral weaklings who carry out his instructions, despise him while defiling themselves with his unclean work. How can success thrive in such a poisonous atmosphere? The spirit of ruin is already in such a business, and the day of his fall is ordained.

An honest man may fail, but not because he is honest, and his failure will be honourable, and will not injure his character and reputation. His failure, too, resulting doubtless from his incapacity in the particular direction of his failure, will be a means of leading him into something more suited to his talents, and thus to ultimate success.

Fearlessness accompanies honesty. The honest man has a clear eye and an unflinching gaze. He looks his fellowmen in the face, and his speech is direct and convincing. The liar and cheat hangs his head; his eye is muddy and his gaze oblique. He cannot look another man in the eye, and his speech arouses mistrust, for it is ambiguous and unconvincing.

When a man has fulfilled his obligations, he has nothing to fear. All his business relations are safe and secure. His methods and actions will endure the light of day. Should he pass through a difficult time, and, get into debt, everybody will trust him and be willing to wait for payment, and all his debts will be paid. Dishonest people try to avoid paying their debts, and they live in fear; but the honest man tries to avoid getting into debt, but when debt overtakes him, he does not fear, but, redoubling his exertions, his debts are paid.

The dishonest are always in fear. They do not fear debt, but fear that they will have to pay their debts. They fear their fellow-men, fear the established authorities, fear the results of all that they do, and they are in constant fear of their misdeeds being revealed, and of the consequences which may at any moment overtake them.

The honest man is rid of all this burden of fear. He is light hearted, and walks erect among his fellows; not assuming a part, and skulking and cringing, but being himself, and meeting eye to eye. Not deceiving or injuring any, there are none to fear, and anything and against him can only rebound to his advantage.

And this fearlessness is, in itself, a tower to strength in a man's life, supporting him through all emergencies, enabling him to battle manfully with difficulties, and in the end securing for him that success of which he cannot be dispossessed.

Purposefulness is the direct outcome of that strength of character which integrity fosters. The man of integrity is the man of direct aims and strong and intelligent purposes. He does not guess, and work in the dark. All his plans have in them some of that moral fiber of which his character is wrought. A man's work will always in some way reflect himself, and the man of sound integrity is the man of sound plan. He weights and considers and looks ahead, and so is less likely to make serious mistakes, or to bungle into a dilemma from which it is difficult to escape. Taking a moral view of all things, and always considering moral consequences, he stands on a firmer and more exalted ground than the man of mere policy and expedience; and while commanding a more extended view of any situation, he wields the greater power which a more comprehensive grasp of details with the principles involved, confers upon him. Morality always has the advantage of expediency. Its purposes always reach down far below the surface, and are therefore more firm and secure, more strong and lasting. There is a native directness, too, about integrity, which enables the man to get straight to the mark in whatever he does, and which makes failure almost impossible.

Strong men have strong purposes, and strong purposes lead to strong achievements. The man of integrity is above all men strong, and his strength is manifested in that thoroughness with which he does the business of his life; thoroughness which commands respect, admiration, and success.

Invincibility is a glorious protector, but it only envelopes the man whose integrity is perfectly pure and unassailable. Never to violate, even in the most insignificant particular, the principle of integrity, is to be invincible against all the assaults of innuendo, slander, and misrepresentation. The man who has failed in one point is vulnerable, and the shaft of evil, entering that point, will lay him low, like the arrow in the heel of Achilles. Pure and perfect integrity is proof against all attack and injury, enabling its possessor to meet all opposition and persecution with dauntless courage and sublime equanimity. No amount of talent, intellect, or business acumen can give a man that power of mind and peace of heart which come from an enlightened acceptance and observance of lofty moral principles. Moral force is the greatest power. Let the seeker for a true prosperity discover this force, let him foster and develop it in his mind and in his deeds, and as he succeeds he will take his place among the strong leaders of the earth.

Such is the strong and adamantine Pillar of integrity. Blessed and prosperous above all men will be he who builds its incorruptible masonry into the temple of his life.

Fourth Pillar – System

System is that principle of order by which confusion is rendered impossible. In the natural and universal order everything is in its place, so that the vast universe runs more perfectly than the most perfect machine. Disorder in space would mean the destruction of the universe; and disorder in a man's affairs destroys his work and his prosperity.

All complex organizations are built up by system. No business or society can develop into large dimensions apart from system, and this principle is preeminently the instrument of the merchant, the business man, and the organizer of institutions.

There are many departments in which a disorderly man may succeed – although attention to order would increase his success but he will not succeed in business unless he can place the business entirely in the hands of a systematic manager, who will thereby remedy his own defect.

All large business concerns have been evolved along definitely drawn systematic lines, any violation of which would be disastrous to the efficiency and welfare of the business. Complex business or other organizations are built up like complex bodies in nature, by scrupulous attention to details. The disorderly man thinks he can be careless about every thing but the main end, but by ignoring the means he frustrates the end. By the disarrangement of details, organisms perish, and by the careless neglect of details, the growth of any work or concern is prevented.

Disorderly people waste an enormous amount of time and energy. The time frittered away in hunting for things is sufficient, were if conserved by order, to enable them to achieve any success, for slovenly people never have a place for anything, and have to hunt, frequently for a long time, for any article which they require. In the irritation, bad humour, and chagrin which this daily hunting for things brings about, as much energy is dissipated as would be required to build up a big business, or scale the highest heights of achievement in any direction.

Orderly people conserve both their time and energy. They never lose anything, and therefore never have to find anything. Everything is in its place, and the hand can be at once placed upon it, though it be in the dark. They can well afford to be cool and deliberate and so use their mental energies in something more profitable than irritation, bad temper and accusing others for their own lack of order.

There is a kind of genius in system which can perform apparent wonders with ease. A systematic man can get through so great a quantity of work in such a short time, and with such freedom from such exhaustion, as to appear almost miraculous. He scale the heights of success while his slovenly competitor is wallowing hopelessly in the bogs of confusion. His strict observance of the law of order enables him to reach his ends, swiftly and smoothly, without friction or loss of time.

The demands of system, in all departments of the business world, are as rigid and exacting as the holy vows of a saint, and cannot be violated in the smallest particular but at the risk of one's financial prospects. In the financial world, the law of order is an iron necessity, and he who faultlessly observes it, saves time, temper, and money.

Every enduring achievement in human society rests upon a basis of system; so true is this, that were system withdrawn, progress would cease. Think, for instance, of the vast achievements of literature the works of classic authors and of great geniuses; the great poems, the innumerable prose works, the monumental histories, the soul – stirring orations; think also the social intercourse of human society, of it religions, its legal statutes, and its vast fund of book knowledge think of all these wonderful resources and achieve- ments of language, and then reflect that they all depend for their origin, growth, and continuance on the systematic arrangements of twenty six letters, an arrangement having inexhaustible and illimitable results by the fact of its rigid limitation within certain fixed rules.

Again; all the wonderful achievements of mathematics have come from the systematic arrangement of ten figures; while the most complex piece of machinery, with its thousands of parts working together smoothly and almost noiselessly to the achievement of the end for which it was designed, was brought forth by the systematic observance of a few mechanical laws.

Herein we see how system simplifies that is complex: how it makes easy that which was difficult; how it relates an infinite variety of details of the one central law or order, and so enables them to be dealt with and accounted for with perfect regularity, and with an entire absence of confusion.

The scientist names and classifies the myriad details of the universe, from the microscopic rotifer to the telescopic star, by his observance of the principle of system, so that out of many millions of objects, reference can be made to any one object in, at most, a few minutes. It is this faculty of speedy references and swift dispatch which is of such overwhelming importance in every department of knowledge and industry, and the amount of time and labour thus saved to humanity is so vast as to be incompatible. We speak of religious, political, and business systems; and so on, indicating that all things in human society are welded together by the adhesive qualities of order.

System is, indeed, one of the great fundamental principles in progress, and in the binding together, in one complete whole, of the world's millions of human beings while they are at the same time each striving for a place and are competing with one another in opposing aims and interest.

We see here how system is allied with greatness, for the many separate units whose minds are untrained to the discipline of system, are kept in their places by the organizing power of the comparatively few who perceive the urgent, the inescapable, necessity for the establishment of fixed and inviolable rules, whether in business, law, religion, science, or politics in fact, in every sphere of human activity for immediately two human beings meet together, they need some common ground of understanding for the avoidance of confusion; in a word, some system to regulate their actions.

Life is too short for confusion; and knowledge grows and progress proceeds along avenues of system which prevent retardation and retrogression, so that he who systematizes his knowledge or business, simplifies and enhances it for his successor, enabling him to begin, with a free mind, where he left off.

Every large business has its system which renders its vast machinery workable, enabling it to run like a well balanced and well oiled machine. A remarkable business man, a friend of mine, once told me that he could have his huge business for twelve months, and it would run on without hitch till his return; and he does occasionally leave it for several months, while travelling, and on his return, every man, boy and girl; every tool, book, and machine; every detail down to the smallest, is in its place doing its work as when he left; and no trouble, no difficulty, no confusion has arisen.

There can be no marked success part from a love of regularity and discipline, and the avoidance of friction, along with the restfulness and efficiency of mind which spring from such regularity. People who abhor discipline, whose minds are ungoverned and anarchic, and who are careless and irregular in their thinking, their habits and the management of their affairs, cannot be highly successful and prosperous, and they fill their lives with numerous worries, troubles, difficulties, and petty annoyances, all of which would disappear under a proper regulation of their lives.

An unsystematic mind is an untrained mind and it can no more cope with well disciplined minds in the race of life than an untrained athlete can successfully complete with a carefully trained competitor in athletic competitor in athletic races. The ill disciplined mind, that thinks anything will do, rapidly falls behind the well disciplined minds who are convinced that only the best will do in the strenuous race for the prizes of life, whether they be material, mental, or moral prizes. The man who, when he comes to do his work, is unable to find his tools, or to balance his figures, or to find the key of his desk, or the key to his thoughtless, will be struggling in his self made toils while his methodical neighbor will be freely and joyfully scaling the invigorating heights of successful achievement. The business man whose method is slovenly, or cumbersome, or behind the most recent developments of skilled minds, should only blame himself as his prospects are decadent, and should wake up to the necessity for more highly specialized and effective methods in his concern. He should seize upon every thing – every invention and idea – that will enable him to economize time and labour, and aid him in thoroughness, deliberation and dispatch.

System is the law by which everything – every organism, business, character, nation, empire – is built. By adding cell to cell, department to department, thought to thought, law to law, and colony to colony in orderly sequence and classification, all things, concerns and institutions grow in magnitude, and evolve to completeness. The man who is continually improving his methods, is gaining in building power; it therefore behoves the business man to be resourceful and inventive in the improvement of his methods, for the builders – whether of cathedrals or characters, business or religions – are the strong ones of the earth, and the protectors and pioneers of humanity. The systematic builder is a creator and preserver, while the man of disorder demolishes and destroys, and no limit can be set to the growth of a man's powers, the completeness of his character, the influence of his organization, or the extent of his business, if he but preserve intact the discipline of order, and have every detail in its place, keep every department to its special task, and tabulate and classify with such efficiency and perfection as to enable him at any moment to bring under examination or into requisition to the remotest detail in connection with his special work.

In system is contained these four ingredients:

1. Readiness
2. Reccuracy
3. Utility
4. Comprehensiveness

Readiness is aliveness. It is that spirit of alertness by which a situation is immediately grasped and dealt with. The observance of system fosters and develops this spirit. The successful General must have the power of readily meeting any new and unlooked for move on the part of the enemy; so every business man must have the readiness to deal with any unexpected develop-ment affecting his line of trade; and so also must the man of thought be able to deal with the details of any new problems which may arise. Dilatoriness is a vice that is fatal to prosperity, for it leads to incapability and stupidity. The men of ready hands, ready hearts, and ready brains, who know what they are doing, and do it methodically, skillfully, and with smooth yet consummate despatch are the men who need to think little of prosperity as an end, for it comes to them whether they seek it or not; success runs after them, and knocks at their door; and they unconsciously command it by the superb excellence of their faculties and methods.

Accuracy is of supreme importance in all commercial concerns and enterprises, but there can be no accuracy apart from system, and a system which is more or less imperfect will involve its originator in mistakes more or less disastrous until he improves it.

Inaccuracy is one of the commonest failings, because accuracy is closely allied to self-discipline, and self-discipline, along with that glad subjection to external discipline which it involves, is an indication of high moral culture to which the majority have not yet attained. If the inaccurate man will not willingly subject himself to the discipline of his employer or instructor, but thinks he knows better, his failing can never be remedied, and he will thereby bind himself down to an inferior position, if in the business world; or to imperfect knowledge, if in the world of thought.

The prevalence of the vice of inaccuracy (and in view of its disastrous effect it must be regarded as a vice, though perhaps one of the lesser vices) is patent to every observe in the way in which the majority of people relate a circumstance or repeat a simple statement of fact. It is nearly always made untrue by more or less marked inaccuracies. Few people, perhaps (not reckoning those who deliberately lie), have trained themselves to be accurate in what they say, or are so careful as to admit and state their liability to error, and from this common form of inaccuracy many untruths and misunderstand-ings arise.

More people take pains to be accurate in what they do than in what they say, but even here inaccuracy is very common, rendering many inefficient and incompetent, and unfitting them for any strenuous and well sustained endeavour. The man who habitually uses up a portion of his own or his employer's time in trying to correct his errors, or for the correction of whose mistakes another has to be employed, is not the man to maintain any position in the work a day world; much less to reach a place among the ranks of the prosperous.

There never yet lived a man who did not make some mistakes on his way to his particular success, but he is the capable and right minded man who perceives his mistakes and quickly remedies them, and who is glad when they are pointed out to him. It is habitual and persistent; inaccuracy which is a vice; and he is the incapable and wrong minded man who will not see or admit his mistakes, and who takes offence when they are pointed out to him.

The progressive man learns by his own mistakes as well as by the mistakes of others. He is always ready to test good advice by practice, and aims at greater and ever greater accuracy in his methods, which means higher and higher perfection, for accuracy is perfect, and the measure of a man's accuracy will be the measure of his uniqueness and perfection.

Utility or usefulness, is the direct result of method in one's work. Labour arrives at fruitful and profitable ends when it is systematically pursued. If the gardener is to gather in the best produce, he must not only sow and plant, but he must sow and plant at the right time; and if any work is to be fruitful in results, it must be done seasonably, and the time for doing a thing must not be allowed to pass by.

Utility considers the practical end; and employs the best means to reach that end. It avoids side issues, dispenses with theories, and retains its hold only on those things which can appropriated to good uses in the economy of life.

Unpractical people burden their minds with useless and unverifiable theories, and court failure by entertaining speculations which, by their very nature, cannot be applied in practice. The man whose powers are shown in what he does, and not in mere talking are arguing, avoids metaphysical quibbling and quandaries, and applies himself to the accomplishment of some good and useful end.

That which cannot be reduced to practice should not be allowed to hamper the mind. It should be thrown aside, abandoned, and ignored. A man recently told me that if his theory should be proved to have no useful end, he should still retain his hold upon it as a beautiful theory. If a man chooses to cling to so-called "beautiful" theories which are proved to have no use in life, and no substantial basis of reality, he must not be surprised if he fails in his wordly undertakings, for he is an unpractical man.

When the powers of the mind are diverted from speculative theorizing to practical doing, whether in material or moral directions, skill, power, knowledge, and prosperity increase. A man's prosperity is measured by his usefulness to the community, and a man is useful in accordance with that he does, and not because of the theories which he entertains.

The carpenter fashions a chair; the builder erects a house; the mechanic produces a machine; and the wise man moulds a perfect character. Not the schismatic, the theorists and the controversialists, but the workers, the makers, and the doers are the salt of the earth.

Let a man turn away from the mirages of intellectual speculation, and begin to do something, and to do it with all his might, and he will thereby gain a special knowledge, wield a special power, and reach his own unique position and prosperity among his fellows.

Comprehensiveness is that quality of mind which enables a man to deal with a large number of related details, to grasp them in their entirety, along with the single principle which governs them and binds them together. It is a masterly quality, giving organizing and governing power, and is developed by systematic attention to details. The successful merchant holds in his mind, as it were, all the details of his business, and regulates them by a system adapted to his particular form of trade. The inventor has in his mind all the details of his machine, along with their relation to a central mechanical principle, and so perfects his invention. The author of a great poem or story relates all his characters and incidents to a central plot, and so produces a composite and enduring literary work. Comprehensiveness is analytic and synthetic capacity combined in the same individual. A capacious and well ordered mind, which holds within its silent depths an army of details in their proper arrangement and true working order, is the mind that is near to genius, even if it has not already arrived. Every man cannot be a genius nor does he need to be, but he can be gradually evolving his mental capacity by careful attention to system in his thoughts and business, and as his intellect depends and broadens his powers will be intensified and his prosperity accentuated.

Such, then, are four corner pillars in the Temple of Prosperity, and of themselves they are sufficient to permanently sustain it without the addition of the remaining four. The man who perfects himself in Energy, Economy, Integrity, and System will achieve an enduring success in the work of his life, no matter what the nature of that work may be. It is impossible for one to fail who is full of energy, who carefully economizes his time and money, and virtuously husbands his vitality, who practices unswerving integrity, and who systematizes his work by first systematizing his mind.

Such a man's efforts will be rightly directed, and that, too, with concentrated power, so that they will be effective and fruitful. In addition he will reach a manliness and an independent dignity which will unconsciously command respect and success, and will strengthen weaker ones by its very presence in their midst. "Seest thou a man diligent in business; he shall stand before kings, he shall not stand before mean men," says Scripture of such a one. He will not beg, or whimper, or complain, or cynically blame others, but will be too strong and pure and upright a man to sink himself so low. And so standing high in the nobility and integrity of his character, he will fill a high place in the world and in the estimation of men. His success will be certain and his prosperity will endure. "He will stand and not fall in the battle of life."

Fifth Pillar – Sympathy

The remaining pillars are the four central pillars in the Temple of Prosperity. They gave it greater strength and stability, and add both to its beauty and utility. They contribute greatly to its attractiveness, for they belong to the highest moral sphere, and therefore to great beauty and nobility of character. They, indeed, make a man great, and place him among the comparatively few whose minds are rare, and that shine apart in sparkling purity and bright intelligence.

Sympathy should not be confounded with that maudlin and superficial sentiment which, like a pretty flower without root, presently perishes and leaves behind neither seed nor fruit. To fall into hysterical some suffering abroad, is not sympathy. Neither are bursts of violent indignation against the cruelties and injustices of others nor any indication of a sympathetic mind. If one is cruel at home – if he badgers his wife, or beats his children, or abuses his servants, or stabs his neighbors with shafts of bitter sarcasm what hypocrisy is in his profession of love for suffering people who are outside the immediate range of his influence! What shallow sentiment informs his bursts of indignation against the injustice and hard heartedness in the world around him.

Says Emerson of such – "Go, love they infant; love thy wood chopper; be good natured and modest; have that grace; and never varnish your hard uncharitable ambition with this incredible tenderness for black folk a thousand miles off. They love afar is spite at home." The test of a man is in his immediate acts, and not in ultra sentiments; and if those acts are consistently informed with selfishness and bitterness, if those at home hear his steps with dread, and feel a joyful relief on his departure, how empty are his expressions of sympathy for the suffering or down trodden how futile his membership of a philanthropic society.

Though the well of sympathy may feed the spring of tears, that spring more often draws its supply from the dark pool of selfishness, for when selfishness is thwarted it spends itself in tears.

Sympathy is a deep, silent, inexpressible tenderness which is shown in a consistently self forgetful gentle character. Sympathetic people are not gushing and spasmodic, but are permanently self restrained, firm, quiet, unassuming and gracious. Their undisturbed demeanour, where the suffering of others is concerned, is frequently mistaken for indifference by shallow minds, but the sympathetic and discerning eye recognizes, in their quiet strength and their swiftness to aid while others are sweeping, and wronging their hands, the deepest, soundest sympathy.

Lack of sympathy is shown in cynicism, illnatured sarcasm, bitter ridicule, taunting and mockery, and anger and condemnation, as well as in that morbid and false sentiment which is a theoretical and assumed sympathy, having no basis in practice.

Lack of sympathy arises in egotism; sympathy arises in love. Egotism is involved in ignorance; love is allied to knowledge. It is common with men to imagine themselves as separate from their fellows, with separate aims and interests; and to regard themselves as right and others wrong in their respective ways. Sympathy lifts a man above this separate and self centred life and enables him to live in the hearts of his fellows, and to think and feel with them. He puts himself in their place, and becomes, for the time being, as they are. As Whitman, the hospital hero, expresses it – "I do not ask the wounded person." It is a kind of impertinence to question a suffering creature. Suffering calls for aid and tenderness, and not for curiosity; and the sympathetic man or woman feels the suffering, and ministers to its alleviation.

Nor can sympathy boast, and wherever self praise enters in, sympathy passes out. If one speaks of his many deeds of kindness, and complains of the ill treatment he has received in return, he has not done kindly deeds, but has yet to reach that self forgetful modest which is the sweetness of sympathy.

Sympathy, in its real and profound sense, is oneness with others in their strivings and sufferings, so that the man of sympathy is a composite being; he is, as it were, a number of men, and he views a thing from a number of different sides, and not from one side only, and that his own particular side. He sees with the others men's eyes, hears with their ears, thinks with their minds, and feels with their hearts. He is thus able to understand men who are vastly different from himself; the meaning of their lives is revealed to him, and he is united to them in the spirit of goodwill. Said Balzac – "The poor fascinate me; their hunger is my hunger; I am with them in their homes; their privations I suffer; I feel the beggar's rags upon my back; I for the time being become the poor and despised man." It reminds us of the saying of One greater than Balzac, that a deed done for a suffering little one was done for him.

And so it is; sympathy leads us to the hearts of all men, so that we become spiritually united to them, and when they suffer we feel the pain; when they are glad we rejoice with them; when they are despised and persecuted, we spiritually descend with them into the depths, and take into our hearts their humiliation and distress; and he who has this binding, uniting spirit of sympathy, can never be cynical and condemnatory can never pass thoughtless and cruel judgements upon his fellows; because in his tenderness of heart he is ever with them in their pain.

But to have reached this ripened sympathy, it must needs be that one has loved much, suffered much and sounded the dark depths of sorrow. It springs from acquaintance with the profoundest experiences, so that a man has ad conceit, thoughtlessness, and selfishness burnt out of his heart. No man can have true sympathy who has not been, in some measure at least, "a man of sorrows, and acquainted with grief," but the sorrow and grief must have passed, must have ripened into a fixed kindness and habitual calm.

To have suffered so much in a certain direction that the suffering is finished, and only its particular wisdom remains, enables one, wherever that suffering presents itself, to understand and deal with it by pure sympathy; and when one has been "perfected by suffering" in many directions, he becomes a centre of rest and healing for the sorrowing and broken hearted who are afflicted with the affections which he has experienced and conquered. As a mother feels the anguish of her suffering child, so the man of sympathy feels the anguish of suffering men.

Such is the highest and holiest sympathy, but a sympathy much less perfect is a great power for good in human life and a measure of it is everywhere and every day needed. While rejoicing in the fact that in every walk in life there are truly sympathetic people, one also perceives that harshness, resentment, and cruelty are all too common. These hard qualities bring their own sufferings, and there are those who fail in their business, or particular work, entirely because of the harshness of their disposition. A man who is fiery and resentful, or who is hard, cold and calculating, with the springs of sympathy dried up within him, even though he be otherwise an able man, will, in the end scarcely avoid disaster in his affairs. His heated folly in the one case, or cold cruelty in the other, will gradually isolate him from his fellows and from those who are immediately related to him in his particular avocation, so that the elements of prosperity will be eliminated from his life, leaving him with a lonely failure, and perhaps a hopeless despair.

Even in ordinary business transactions, sympathy is an important factor, for people will always be attracted to those who are of a kindly and genial nature, preferring to deal with them rather than with those who are hard and forbidding. In all spheres where direct personal contact plays an important part, the sympathetic man with average ability will always take precedence of the man of greater ability but who is unsympathetic.

If a man be a minister or a clergyman, a cruel laugh or an unkind sentence from him will seriously injure his reputation and influence, but particularly his influence, for even they who admire his good qualities will, through his unkindness, unconsciously have a lower regard for him in their personal esteem.

If a business man profess religion, people will expect to see the good influence of that religion on his business transactions. To profess to be a worshipper of the gentle Jesus on Sunday, and all the rest of the wee be a hard, grasping worshipper of mammon, will injure his trade, and detract considerably from his prosperity.

Sympathy is a universal spiritual language which all, even the animals, instinctively understand and appreciate, for all beings and creatures are subject to suffering, and this sameness of painful experience leads to that unity of feeling which we call sympathy.

Selfishness impels men to protect themselves at the expense of others; but sympathy impels them to protect others by the sacrifice of self; and in this sacrifice of self there is no real and ultimate loss, for while the pleasure of selfishness are small and few, the blessings of sympathy are great and manifold.

It may be asked, "How can a business man; whose object is to develop his own trade, practice self-sacrifice?" Even man can practice self sacrifice just where he is, and in the measure that he is capable of understand it. If one contends that he cannot practice a virtue it, for were his circumstances different, he would still have the same excuse. Diligence in business is not incompatible with self sacrifice, for devotion to duty, even though that duty be trade, is not selfishness, but may be an unselfish devotion. I know a business man who, when a competitor who had tried to 'cut him out' in business, cut himself out and failed, set that same competitor up in business again. Truly a beautiful act of self sacrifice; and the man that did it is, today, one of the most successful and prosperous of business men.

The most prosperous commercial traveler I have ever known, was overflowing with exuberant kindness and geniality. He was as innocent of all "tricks of trade" as a new born infant, but his great heart and manly uprightness won for him fast friends wherever he went. Men were glad to see him come into their office or shop or mill, and not alone for the good and bracing influence he brought with him, but also because his business was sound and trustworthy. This man was successful through sheer sympathy, but sympathy so pure and free from policy, that he himself would probably have denied that his success could be attributed to it. Sympathy can never hinder success. It is selfishness that blights and destroys. As goodwill increases, man's prosperity will increase. All interests are mutual, and stand or fall together, and as sympathy expands the heart, it extends the circle of influence, making blessings, both spiritual and material, to more greatly abound.

Fourfold are the qualities which make up the great virtue of sympathy, namely:—

1. Kindness
2. Generosity
3. Gentleness
4. Insight

Kindness, when fully developed, is not a passing impulse but a permanent quality. An intermittent and unreliable impulse is not kindness, though it often goes under that name. There is no kindness in praise if it be followed by abuse. The love which seems to prompt the spontaneous kiss will be of little account if it be associated with a spontaneous spite. The gift which seemed so gracious will lose its value should the giver afterwards wish its value in return. To have one's feelings aroused to do a kind action towards another by some external stimulus pleasing to one's self, and shortly afterwards to be swayed to the other extreme towards the same person by an external event unpleasing to one's self, should be regarded as weakness of character; and it is also a selfish condition, us, and when he pleases us, to be thinking of one's self only. A true kindness is unchangeable, and needs no external stimulus to force it into action. It is a well from which thirsty souls can always drink, and it never runs dry. Kindness, when it is a strong virtue, is bestowed not only on those who please us, but also upon those whose actions go contrary to our wish and will, and it is a constant and never – varying glow of genial warmth.

There are some actions of which men repent; such are all unkind actions. There are other actions of which men do not repent, and such are all kind actions. The day comes when men are sorry for the cruel things they said and did; but the day of gladness is always with them for the kindly things they have said and done.

Unkindness mars a man's character, it mars his face as time goes on, and it mars that perfection of success which he would otherwise reach.

Kindness beautifies the character, it beautifies the face with the growth of the years, and it enables a man to reach that perfection of success to which his intellectual abilities entitle him. A man's prosperity is mellowed and enriched by the kindness of his disposition.

Generosity goes with a larger hearted kindness. If kindness be the gentle sister, Generosity is the strong brother. A free, open handed, and magnanimous character is always attractive and influential. Stringiness and meanness always repel; they are dark, cramped, narrow, and cold. Kindness and generosity always attack; they are sunny, genial, open, and warm. That which repels makes for isolation and failure; that which attracts makes for union and success.

Giving is as important a duty as getting; and he who gets all he can, and refuses to give, will at last be unable to get; for it is as much a spiritual law that we cannot get unless we give, as that we cannot give unless we get.

Giving has always been taught as a great and important duty by all the religious teachers. This is because giving is one of the highways of personal growth and progress. It is a means by which we attain to greater and greater unselfishness, and by which we prevent the falling back into selfishness. It implies that we recognize our spiritual and social kinship with our fellow-men, and are willing to part with a portion of that we have earned or possess, for man who, the more he gets, hungers for more still, and refuses to loosen his grasp upon his accumulating store, like a wild beast with its prey, is retrogressing; he is shutting himself out from all the higher and joy giving qualities, and from free and life giving communion with unselfish, happy human hearts. Dickens's Scrooge in "A Christmas Carol" represents the condition of such a man with graphic vividness and dramatic force.

Our public men in England to-day (probably also in America) are nearly all (I think I might say all, for I have not yet met an exception) great givers. These men – Lord Mayors, Mayors, Magistrates, Town and City Councillors, and all men filling responsible public offices – being men who have been singularly successful in the management of their own private affairs, are considered the best men for the management of public affairs, and numerous noble institutions throughout the land are perpetual witnesses to the munificence of their gifts. Nor have I been able to find any substantial truth in the accusation, so often hurled against such men by the envious and unsuccessful, that their riches are made unjustly. Without being perfect men, they are an honourable class of manly, vigorous, generous, and successful men, who have acquired riches and honour by sheer industry, ability and uprightness.

Let a man beware of greed, of meanness, of envy, of jealousy, of suspicion, for these things, if harboured, will rob him of all that is best in life, aye, even all that is best in material things, as well as all that is best in character and happiness. Let him be liberal of heart and generous of hand, magnanimous and trusting, not only giving cheerfully and often of his substance, but allowing his friends and fellow-men freedom of thought and action – let him be thus, and honour, plenty, and prosperity will come knocking at the door for admittance as his friends and guests.

Gentleness is akin to divinity. Perhaps no quality is so far removed from all that is coarse, brutal and selfish as gentleness, so that when one is becoming gentle, he is becoming divine. It can only be acquired after much experience and through great self-discipline. It only becomes established in a man's heart when he has controlled and brought into subjection his animal voice, a distinct, firm, but quiet enunciation, and freedom from excitement, vehemence, or resentment in peculiarly aggravating circumstances.

If there is one quality which, above all others, should distinguish the religious man, it is the quality of gentleness, for it is the hall mark of spiritual culture. The rudely aggressive man is an affront to cultivated minds and unselfish hearts. Our word gentlemen has not altogether departed from its original meaning. It is still applied to one who is modest and self-restrained, and is considerate for the feelings and welfare of others. A gentle man one whose good behavior is prompted by thoughtfulness and kindliness is always loved, whatever may be his origin. Quarrelsome people make a display in their bickering and recriminations – of their ignorance and lack of culture. The man who has perfected himself in gentleness never quarrels. He never returns the hard word; he leaves it alone, or meets it with a gentle word which is far more powerful than wrath. Gentleness is wedded to wisdom, and the wise man has overcome all anger in himself, and so understands how to overcome it in others. The gentleman is saved from most of the disturbances and turmoil's with which uncontrolled men afflict themselves. While they are wearing themselves out with wasteful and needless strain, he is quiet and composed, and such quietness and composure are strong to win in the battle of life.

Insight is the gift of sympathy. The sympathetic mind is the profoundly perceiving mind. We understand by experience, and not by argument. Before we can know a thing or being, our life must touch its or his life. Argument analyzes the outer skin, but sympathy reaches to the heart. The cynic sees the hat and coat, and thinks he sees the man. The sympathetic seer sees the man, and is not concerned with the hat and coat. In all kinds of hatred there is a separation by which each misjudges the other. In all kinds of love there is a mystic union by which each knows the other. Sympathy, being the purest form of this the greatest poet because he has the largest heart. No other figure in all literature has shown such a profound knowledge of the human heart, and of nature both animate and inanimate. The personal Shakespeare is not to be found in his works; he is merged, by sympathy, into his characters. The wise man and the philosopher; the madman and the fool; the drunkard and the harlot – these he, for the time into their particular experiences and knew them better than they knew themselves. Shakespeare has no partiality, no prejudice; his sympathy embraces all, from the lowest to the highest.

Prejudice is the great barrier to sympathy and knowledge. It is impossible to understand those against whom one harbours a prejudice. We only see men and things as they are when we divest our minds of partial judgements. We become seers as we become sympathizers. Sympathy has knowledge for her companion.

Inseparable are the feeling heart and the seeing eye. The man of pity is the man of prophecy. He whose heart beats in tune with all hearts, to him the contents of all hearts are revealed. Nor are past and future any longer insoluble mysteries to the man of sympathy. His moral insight apprehends the perfect round of human life.

Sympathetic insight lifts a man into the consciousness of freedom, gladness and power. His spirit inhales joy as his lungs inhale air. There are no longer any fears of his fellow-men of competition, hard times, enemies, and the like. These grovelling illusion have disappeared, and there has opened up before his awakened vision a realm of greatness and grandeur.

Sixth Pillar – Sincerity

Human society is held together by its sincerity. A universal falseness would beget a universal mistrust which would bring about a universal separation, if not destruction. Life is made sane, wholesome, and happy, by our deep rooted belief in one another. If we did not trust men, we could not transact business with them, could not even associate with them. Shakespeare's "Timon" shows us the wretched condition of a man who, through his own folly, has lost all faith in the sincerity of human nature. He cuts himself off from the company of all men, and finally commits suicide. Emerson has something to the effect that if the trust system were withdrawn from commerce, society would fall to pieces; that system being an indication of the universal confidence men place in each other. Business, commonly supposed by the shortsighted and foolish to be all fraud and deception is based on a great trust – a trust that men will meet and fulfil their obligations. Payment is not asked until the goods are delivered; and the fact of the continuance of this system for ages, proves that most men do pay their debts, and have no wish to avoid such payment.

Back of all its shortcomings, human society rests on a strong basis of truth. Its fundamental note in sincerity. Its great leaders are all men of superlative sincerity; and their names and achievements are not allowed to perish – a proof that the virtue of sincerity is admired by all the race.

It is easy for the insincere to imagine that everybody is like themselves, and to speak of the "rottenness of society," — though a rotten thing could endure age after age, for is not everything yellow to the jaundiced eye? People who cannot see anything good in the constitution of human society, should overhaul themselves. Their trouble is near home. They call good, evil. They have dwelt cynically and peevishly on evil till they cannot see good, and everything and everybody appears evil. "Society is rotten from top to bottom," I heard a man say recently; and he asked me if I did not think so. I replied that I should be sorry to think so; that while society had many blemishes, it was sound at the core, and contained within itself the seeds of perfection.

Society, indeed is so sound that the man who is playing a part for the accomplishment of entirely selfish ends cannot long prosper, and cannot fill any place as an influence. He is soon unmasked and disagreed; and the fact that such a man can, for even a brief period, batten on human credulity, speaks well for the trustfulness of men, if it reveals their lack of wisdom.

An accomplished actor on the stage is admired, but the designing actor on the stage of life brings himself down to ignominy and contempt. In striving to appear what he is not, he becomes as one having no individuality, no character, and he is deprived of all influence, all power, all success.

A man of profound sincerity is a great moral force, and there is no force – not even the highest intellectual force – that can compare with it. Men are powerful in influence according to the soundness and perfection of their sincerity. Morality and sincerity are so closely bound up together, that where sincerity is lacking, morality, as a power, is lacking also, for insincerity undermines all the other virtues, so that they crumble away and become of no account. Even a little insincerity robs a character of all its nobility, and makes it common and contemptible. Falseness is so despicable a vice and no man of moral weight can afford to dally with pretty complements, or play the fool with trivial and howsoever light, in order to please, and he is no longer strong and admirable, but is become a shallow weakling whose mind has no deep well of power from which men can draw, and no satisfying richness to stir in them a worshipful regard.

Even they who are for the moment flattered with the painted lie, or pleased with the deftly woven deception, will not escape those permanent under currents of influence which move the heart and shape the judgement to fixed and final issues, while these designed delusions create but momentary ripples on the surface of the mind.

"I am very pleased with his attentions," said a woman of an acquaintance, "but I would not marry him." "Why not?" she was asked. "He doesn't ring true," was the reply.

Ring true, a term full of meaning. It has reference to the coin which, when tested by its ring, emits a sound which reveals the sterling metal throughout, without the admixture of any base material. It comes up to the standard, and will pass anywhere and everywhere for its full value.

So with men. Their words and actions emit their own peculiar influence. There is in them an inaudible sound which all other men inwardly hear and instinctively detect. They know the false ring from the true, yet know not how they know. As the outer ear can make the most delicate distinctions in sounds, so the inner ear can make equally subtle distinctions between souls. None are ultimately deceived but the deceiver. It is the blind folly of the insincere that, while flattering themselves upon their successful simulations, they are deceiving none but themselves. Their actions are laid bare before all hearts. There is at the hear of man a tribunal whose judgements do not miscarry. If the senses faultlessly detect, shall not the soul infallibly know! This inner infallibility is shown in the collective judgement of the race. This judgement is perfect; so perfect than in literature, art, science, invention, religion – in every department of knowledge – it divides the good from the bad, the worthy from the unworthy, the true from the false, zealously guarding and preserving the former, and allowing the latter to perish. The works, words, and deeds of great men are the heirlooms of the race, and the race is not careless of their value. A thousand men write a book, and one only is a work of original genius, yet the race singles out that one, elevates and preserves it, while it consigns the nine hundred and ninety nine copyists to oblivion. Ten thousand men utter a sentence under a similar circumstance, and one only is a sentence of divine wisdom, yet the race singles out that saying for the guidance of posterity, while the other sentences are heard no more. It is true that the race slays its prophets, but even that slaying becomes a test which reveals the true ring, and men detect its tureens. The slain one has come up to the standard, and the deed of his slaying is preserved as furnishing infallible proof of his greatness.

As the counterfeit coin is detected, and cast back into the melting pot, while the sterling coin circulates among all men, and is valued for its worth, so the counterfeit word, deed, or character is perceived, and is left to fall back into the nothingness from which it emerged, a thing unreal, powerless, dead.

Spurious things have no value, whether they be bric-a-brac or men. We are ashamed of imitations that try to pass for the genuine article. Falseness is cheap. The masquerader becomes a byword; he is less than a man; he is a shadow, a spook, a mere mask. Trueness is valuable. The sound hearted man becomes an exemplar; he is more than a man; he is a reality; a force, a moulding principle, by falseness all is lost – even individuality dissolves for falseness is nonentity, nothingness. By trueness everything is gained, for trueness is fixed, permanent, real.

It is all important that we be real; that we harbour no wish to appear other than what we are; that we simulate no virtue, assume no excellency, adopt no disguise. The hypocrite thinks he can hood wink the world and the eternal law of the world. There is but one person that he hoodwinks, and that is himself, and for that the law of the world inflicts its righteous penalty. There is an old theory that the excessively wicked are annihilated. I think to be a pretender is to come as near to annihilation as a man can get, for there is a sense in which the man is gone, and in his place there is but a mirage of shams. The hell of annihilation which so many dread, he has descended into; and to think that such a man can prosper is to think that shadows can do the work of entities, and displace real men.

If any man thinks he can build up a successful career on pretences and appearances, let him pause before sinking into the abyss of shadows; for in insincerity there is no solid ground, no substance, no reality; there is nothing on which anything can stand, and no material with which to build; but there are loneliness, poverty, shame, confusion, fears, suspicions, weeping, groaning, and lamentations; for if there is one hell lower, darker, fouler than all others, it is the hell of insincerity.

Four beautiful traits adorn the mind of the sincere man; they are:—

1. Simplicity
2. Attractiveness
3. Penetration
4. Power

Simplicity is naturalness. It is simple being, without fake or foreign adornment. Why are all things in nature so beautiful? Because they are natural. We see them as they are, no task they might wish to appear, for in sooth they have no wish to appear, for in sooth they have no wish to appear otherwise. There is no hypocrisy in the world of nature outside of human nature. The flower which is so beautiful in all eyes would lose its beautify in all eyes would nature we look upon reality, and its beauty and perfection gladden and amaze us. We cannot find anywhere a flaw, and are conscious of our incapacity to improve upon anything, even to the most insignificant. Everything ha sits own peculiar perfection, and shines in the beauty of unconscious simplicity.

One of the modern social cries is, "Back to nature." It is generally understood to mean a cottage in the country, and a piece of land to cultivate. It will be of little use to go into the country if we take our shams with us; and any veneer which may cling to us can as well be washed off just where we are. It is good that they who feel burdened with the conventions of society should fly to the country, and court the quiet of nature, but it will fail if it by anything but a means to that inward redemption which will restore us to the simple and the true.

But though humanity has wandered from the natural simplicity of the animal world, it is moving towards a higher, a divine simplicity. Men of great genius are such because of their spontaneous simplicity. They do not foreign; they are. Lesser minds study style and effect. They wish to cut a striking figure on the stage of the world, and by that unholy wish they are doomed to mediocrity. Said a man to me recently, "I would give twenty years of my life to be able to write an immortal hymn." With such an ambition a man cannot write a hymn. He wants to pose. He is thinking of himself, of his own glory. Before a man can writer an immortal hymn, or create any immortal work he must give, not twenty years of his life to ambition but his can do anything great, and must sing, paint, write, out of ten thousand bitter experiences, ten thousand failures, ten thousand conquests, ten thousand joys. He must know Gethsemane; he must work with blood and tears.

Retaining his intellect and moral powers, and returning to simplicity, a man becomes great. He forfeits nothing real. Only the shams are cast aside, revealing the standard gold of character. Where there is sincerity there will always be simplicity – a simplicity of the kind that we see in nature, the beautiful simplicity of truth.

Attractiveness is the direct outcome of simplicity. This is seen in the attractiveness of all natural objects; to which we have referred, but in human nature it is manifested as personal influence. Of recent years certain pseudomystics have been advertising to sell the secret of "personal magnetism" for so many dollars, by which they purport to show vain people how they can make themselves attractive to others by certain "occult" means as though attractiveness can be brought and sold, and put on and off like powder and paint. Nor are people who are anxious to be thought attractive, likely to become so, for their vanity is a barrier to it. The very desire to be thought attractive is, in itself, a deception, and it leads to the practice of numerous deceptions. It infers, too, that such people are conscious of lacking the genuine attractions and graces of character, and are on the look out for a substitute; but there is no substitute for beauty of mind and strength of character. Attractiveness, like genius, is lost by being coveted, and possessed by those who are too solid and sincere of character to desire it. There is nothing in human nature – nor talent, nor intellect, nor affection, nor beauty of features that can compare in attractive power with that soundness of mind and wholeness of heart which we call sincerity. There is a perennial charm about a sincere man or woman, and they draw about themselves the best specimens of human nature. There can be no personal charm apart from sincerity. Infatuation there may be, and is, but this is a kind of disease, and is vastly different from the indissoluble bond by which sincere people are attached. Infatuation ends in painful disillusion, but as there is nothing hidden between sincere souls, and they stand upon that solid ground of reality, there is no illusion to be displayed.

Leaders among men attract by the power of their sincerity, and the measures of their sincerity is the measure of their sincerity is the great may be a man's intellect he can never be a permanent leader and guide of men unless he be sincere. For a time he may sail jauntily upon the stream of popularity, and believe himself secure, but it is only that he may shortly fall the lower in popular odium. He cannot long deceive the people with his painted front. They will soon look behind, and find of what spurious stuff he is made. He is like a woman with a painted face. She thinks she is admired for her complexion, but all know it is paint, and despise her for it. she has one admirer – herself, and the hell of limitation to which all the insincere commit themselves is the hell of self admiration.

Sincere people do not think of themselves, of their talent, their genius, their virtue, their beautify and because they are so unconscious of themselves, they attract all, and win their confidence, affection, and esteem.

Penetration belongs to the sincere. All shams are unveiled in their presence. All simulators are transparent to the searching eye of the sincere man. With one clear glance he sees through all their flimsy pretences. Tricksters with under his strong gaze, and want to get away from it. He who has rid his heart of all falseness, and entertains only that which is true, has gained the power to distinguish the false from the true in others. He is not deceived who is not self deceived.

As men, looking around on the objects of nature, infallibly distinguish them such as a snake, a bird, a horse, a tree, a rose, and so on – so the sincere man distinguishes between the variety of characters. He perceives in a movement, a look, a word, an act, the nature of the man, and acts accordingly. He is on his guard without being suspicious. He is prepared for the pretender without being mistrustful. He acts from positive knowledge, and not from negative suspicion. Men are open to him, and he reads their contents. His penetrative judgement pierces to the centre of actions. His direct and unequivocal conduct strengthens in others the good, and shames the bad, and he is a staff of strength to those who have not yet attained to his soundness of heart and head.

Power goes with penetration. An understanding of the nature of actions is accompanied with the power to meet and deal with all actions in the right and best way. Knowledge is always power, but knowledge of the nature of actions is superlative power, and he who possesses it becomes a Presence to all hearts, and modifies their actions for good. Long after his bodily presence has passed away, he is still a moulding force in the world and is a spiritual reality working subtly in the minds of men, and shaping them towards sublime ends. At first his power local and limited, but the circle of righteousness which he has set moving, continues to extend and extended till it embraces the whole world, and all men are influenced by it.

The sincere man stamps his character upon all that he does, and also upon all people with whom he comes in contact. He speaks a word in season, and some one is impressed; the influence is communicated to another, and another, and presently some despairing soul ten thousand miles away hears it and is restored. Such a power is prosperity in itself, and its worth is not to be valued in coin. Money cannot purchase the priceless jewels of character, but labour in right doing can, and he who makes himself sincere, who acquires a robust soundness throughout his entire being, will become a man of singular success and rare power.

Such is the strong pillar of sincerity. It supporting power is to great that, one it is completely erected, the Temple of Prosperity is secure. Its walls will not crumble; its rafters will not decay; its roof will not fall in. It will stand while the man lives, and when has passed away it will continue to afford a shelter and a home for others through many generation.

Seventh Pillar – Impartiality

To get rid of prejudice is a great achievement. Prejudices piles obstacles in a man's way – obstacles to health, success, happiness, and prosperity, so that he is continually running up against imaginary enemies, who, when prejudice is removed, are seen to be friend. Life, indeed, a sort of obstacle race to the man of prejudice, a race wherein the obstacles cannot be negotiated and the goal is not reached; whereas to the impartial man life is a day's walk in a pleasant country, with refreshment and rest at the end of the day.

To acquire impartiality, a man must remove that innate egotism which prevents him from seeing any thing from any point of view other than this own. A great task, truly; but a notable, and one that can be well begun now, even if it cannot be finished. Truth can "remove mountains," and prejudice is a range of mental mountains beyond which the partisan does not see, and of which he does not believe there is any beyond. These mountains removed, however, there opens to the view the unending vista of mental variety blended in one glorious picture of light and shade, of colour and tone, gladdening beholding eyes.

By clinging to stubborn prejudice what joys are missed, what friends are sacrificed, what happiness is destroyed, and what prospects are blighted! And yet freedom from prejudice is a rare thing. There are few men who are not prejudiced partisans upon the subjects which are of interest to them. One rarely meets a man that will dispassionately discuss his subject from both sides, considering all the facts and weighing all the evidence so as to arrive at truth on the matter. Each partisan has his own case to make out. He is not searching for truth, for he is already convinced that his own conclusion is the truth, and that all else is error; but he is defending his own case, and striving for victory. Neither does he attempt to prove that he has the truth by a calm array of facts and evidence, but defends his position with more or less heat and agitation.

Prejudice causes a man to form a conclusion, sometimes without any basis of fact or knowledge, and then to refuse to consider anything which does not support that conclusion; and in this way prejudice is a complete barrier to the attainment of knowledge. It binds a man down to darkness and ignorance, and prevents the development of his mind in the highest and noblest directions. More than this, it also shuts him out from communion with the best minds, and confines him to the dark and solitary cell of his own egotism.

Prejudice is a shutting up of the mind against the entrance of new light, against the perception of more beauty, against the hearing of diviner music. The partisan clings to his little, fleeting, flimsy opinion, and thinks it the greatest thing in the world. He is so in love with his own conclusion (which is only a form of self love), that he thinks all men ought to agree with him, and he regards men as more or less stupid who do not see as he sees, while he praises the good judgement of those who are one with him in his view. Such a man cannot have knowledge, cannot have truth. He is confined to the sphere of opinion (to his own self created illusions) which is outside the realm of reality. He moves in a kind of self infatuation which prevents him from seeing the commonest facts of life, while his own theories – usually more or less groundless – assume, in his mind, overpowering proportions. He fondly imagines that there is but one side to everything, and that side is his own. There are at least two sides to everything, and he it is who finds the truth in a matter who carefully examines both sides with all freedom from excitement, and without any desire for the predominance of one side over another.

In its divisions and controversies the world at large is like two lawyers defending a case. The counsel for the prosecution presents all the facts which prove his side, while counsel for the defense presents all the facts which support his contention, and each belittles or ignores, or tries to reason away, the facts of the other. The Judge in the case, however, is like the impartial thinker among men: having listened to all the evidence on both sides, he compares and sifts it so as to form an impartial summing up in the cause of justice.

Not that this universal partiality is a bad thing, nor as in all other extremes, nature here reduces the oppositions of conflicting parties to a perfect balance; moreover, it is a factor in evolution; it stimulates men to think who have not yet developed the power to rouse up vigorous thought at will, and it is a phase through which all men have to pass. But it is only byway – and a tangled, confused and painful one – towards the great highway of Truth. It is the are of which impartiality is the perfect round. The partisan sees a portion of the truth, and thinks it the whole, but the impartial thinker sees the whole truth which includes all sides. It is necessary that we find see truth in sections, as it were, until, having gathered up all the parts, we may piece them together and form the perfect circle, and the forming of such circle is the attainment of impartiality.

The impartial man examines, weighs, and considers, with freedom from prejudice and from likes and dislikes. His one wish is to discover the truth. He abolishes preconceived opinions, and lets facts and evidence speak for themselves. He has no case to make out for himself, for he knows that truth is unalterable, that his opinions can make no difference to it, and that it can be investigated and discovered. He thereby escapes a vast amount of friction and nervous wear and tear to which the feverish partisan is subject; and in addition, he looks directly upon the face of Reality, and so becomes tranquil and peaceful.

So rare is freedom from prejudice that wherever the impartial thinker may be, he is sure, sooner or later, to occupy a very high position in the estimation of the world, and in the guidance of its destiny. Not necessarily an office in worldly affairs, for that is improbable, but an exalted position in the sphere of influence. There may be such a one now, and he may be a carpenter, a weaver, a clerk; he may be in poverty or in the home of a millionaire; he may be short or tall, or of any complexion, but whatever and wherever he may be, he has, though unknown, already begun to move the world, and will one day be universally recognized at a new force and creative centre in evolution.

There was one such some nineteen hundred years ago. He was only a poor, unlettered carpenter; He was regarded as a madman by His own relatives, and he came to an ignominious end in the eyes of His countrymen, but He sowed the seeds of an influence which has altered the whole world.

There was another such in India some twenty five centuries ago. He was accomplished, highly educated, and was the son of a capitalist and landed proprietor a petty king. He became a penniless, homeless mendicant, and to day one third of the human race worship at his shrine, and are restrained and elevated by his influence.

"Beware when the great God lets loose a thinker on this plane," says Emerson; and a man is not a thinker who is bound by prejudice; he is merely the strenuous upholder of an opinion. Every idea must pass through the medium of his particular prejudice, and receive its colour, so that dispassionate thinking and impartial judgement are rendered impossible. Such a man sees everything only in its relation, or imagined relation, to his opinion, whereas the thinker sees things as they are. The man who has so purified his mind of prejudice and of all the imperfections of egotism as to be able to look directly upon reality, has reached the acme of power; he holds in his hands, as it were, the vastest influence, and he will wield this power whether he knows it or not; it will be inseparable from his life, and will go from him as perfume from the flower. It will be in his words, his deeds, in his bodily postures and the motions of his mind, even in his silence and the stillness of his frame. Wherever he goes, even though he should fly to the desert, he will not escape this lofty destiny, for a great thinker is the centre of the world; by him all men are held in their orbits and all thought gravitates towards him.

The true thinker lives above and beyond the seething whirlpool of passion in which mankind is engulfed. He is not swayed by personal consideration, for he has grasped the importance of impersonal principles, and being thus a noncombatant in the clashing warfare of egotistic desires, he can, from the vantage ground of an impartial but not indifferent watcher, see both sides equally, and grasp the cause and meaning of the fray.

Not only the Great Teachers, but the greatest figures in literature, are those who are free from prejudice, who, like true mirrors, effect things impartially. Such are Whitman, Shakespeare, Balzac, Emerson, Homer. These minds are not local, but universal. Their attitude is cosmic and not personal.

They contain within themselves all things and beings all worlds and laws. They are the gods who guide the race, and who will bring it at last out of its fever of passion into their own serene land.

The true thinker is the greatest of men, and his destiny is the most exalted. The altogether impartial mind has reached the divine, and it basks in the full daylight of Reality.

The four great elements of impartiality are

1. Justice
2. Patience
3. Calmness
4. Wisdom

Justice is the giving and receiving of equal values. What is called "striking a hard bargain" is a kind of theft. It means that the purchaser gives value for only a portion of his purchase, the remainder being appropriated as clear gain. The seller also encourages it by closing the bargain.

The just man does not try to gain an advantage; he considers the true values of things, and moulds his transactions in accordance therewith. He does not let "what will pay" come before "what is right," for he knows that the right pays best in the end. He does not seek his own benefit to the disadvantage of another, for he knows that a just action benefits, equally and fully, both parties to a transaction. If "one man's loss is another man's gain," it is only that the balance may be adjusted later on. Unjust gains cannot lead to prosperity, but are sure to bring failure. A just man could no more take from another an unjust gain by what is called a "smart transaction" that he could take it by picking his pocket. He would regard the one as dishonest as the other.

The bargaining spirit in business is not the true spirit of commerce. It is the selfish and thieving spirit which wants to get something for nothing. The upright man purges his business of all bargaining, and builds it one the more dignified basis of justice. He supplies "a good article" at its right price, and does not alter. He does not soil his hands with any business which is tainted with fraud. His goods are genuine and they are properly priced.

Customers who try to "beat down" a tradesman in their purchases are degrading themselves. Their practice assumes one or both of two things, namely, that either the tradesman is dishonest and is overcharging (a low, suspicious attitude of mind), or that they are eager to cajole him out of his profit (an equally base attitude), and so benefit by his loss. The practice of "bearing down" is altogether a dishonest one, and the people who pursue it most assiduously are those who complain most of being "imposed on" and this is not surprising, seeing that they themselves are all the time trying to impose upon others.

On the other hand, the tradesman who is anxious to get all he can out of his customers, irrespective of justice and the right values of things, is a kind of robber, and is slowly poisoning his success, for his deeds will assuredly come home to him in the form of financial ruin.

Said a man of fifty to me other day, "I have just discovered that all my life I have been paying fifty percent, more for everything than I ought to." A just man cannot feel that he has ever paid too much for anything, for he does not close with any transaction which he considers unjust; but if a man is eager to get everything at half price, them he will be always meanly and miserably mourning that he is paying double for everything. The just man is glad to pay full value for everything, whether in giving or receiving and his mind is untroubled and his days are full of peace.

Let a man above all avoid meanness, and strive to be ever more and more perfectly just, for if not just, he can be neither honest, nor generous, nor manly, but is a kind of disguised thief trying to get all he can, and give back as little as possible. Et him eschew all bargaining, and teach bargainers a better way by conducting his business with that exalted dignity which commands a large and meritorious success.

Patience is the brightest jewel in the character of the impartial man. Not a particular patience with a particular thing – like a girl with her needlework, or a boy building his toy engine but on unswerving considerateness, a sweetness of disposition at all times and under the most trying circumstances, an unchangeable and gentle strength which no trial can mar and no persecution can break. A rare possession, it is true, and one not to be expected for a long time yet from the bulk of mankind, but a virtue that can be reached by degree, and even a partial patience will work wonders in a man's life and affairs, as a confirmed impatience all work devastation. The irascible man is courting speedy disaster, for who will care to deal with a man who continually going off like ground powder when some small spark of complaint or criticism falls upon him! Even his friends will one by one desert him, for who would court the company of a man who rudely assaults him with an impatient and fiery tongue over every little difference or misunderstanding.

A man must begin to wisely control himself, and to learn the beautiful lessons of patience, if he is to be highly prosperous, if he is to be a man of use and power. He must learn to think of others, to act for their good, and not alone for himself; to be considerate, for bearing, and long suffering. He must study how to have a heart at peace with men who differ from him on those things which he regards as most vital. He must avoid quarrelling as he would avoid drinking a deadly poison. Discords from without will be continually overtaking him, but he must fortify himself against them; he must study how to bring harmonies out of them by the exercise of patience.

Strife is common: it pains the heart and distorts the mind. Patience is rare, it enriches the heart and beautifies the mind. Every cat can spit and fume; it requires no effort, but only a looseness of behavior. It takes a man to keep his mornings through all events, and to be painstaking and patient with the shortcomings of humanity. But patience wins. As soft water wears away the hardest rock, so patience overcomes all opposition. It gains the hearts of men. It conquers and controls.

Calmness accompanies patience. It is a great and glorious quality. It is the peaceful haven of emancipated souls after their long wanderings on the tempest riven ocean of passion. It makes the man who has suffered much, endured much, experienced much, and has finally conquered.

A man cannot be impartial who is not calm. Excitement, prejudice, and partiality spring from disturbed passions. When personal feeling is thwarted, it rises and seethes like a stream of water that is dammed. The calm man avoids this disturbance by directing his feeling from the personal to the impersonal channel. He thinks and feels for others as well as for himself. He sets the same value on other men's opinions as on his own. If he regards his on work as important, he sees also that the work of other men is equally important. He does not content for the merit of his own against the demerit of that of others. He is not overthrown, like Humptydumpty, with a sense of self importance. He has put aside egotism for truth, and he perceives the right relations of things. He has conquered irritability, and has come to see that there is nothing in itself that should cause irritation. As well be irritable with a pansy because it is not a rose, as a with a man because he does not see as you see. Minds differ, and the calm man recognizes the differences as facts in human nature.

The calm, impartial man, is not only the happiest man, he also has all his powers at his command. He is sure, deliberate, executive, and swiftly and easily accomplishes in silence what the irritable men slowly and laboriously toils through with much nice. His mind is purified, poised, concentrated, and is ready at any moment to be directed upon a given work with unerring power. In the calm mind all contradictions are reconciled, and there is radiant gladness and perpetual peace. As Emerson puts it: "Calmness is joy fixed and habitual."

One should not confound indifference with calmness, for it is at the opposite extreme. Indifference is lifelines, while calmness is glowing life and full orbed power. The calm man has partly or entirely conquered self, and having successfully battled with the selfishness within, he knows how to meet and overcome it successfully in others. In any moral content the calm man is always the victor. So long as he remains calm, defeat is impossible.

Self control is better than riches and calmness is a perpetual benediction.

Wisdom abides with the impartial man. Her counsels guide him; her wings shield him; she leads him along pleasant ways to happy destinations.

Wisdom is many sided. The wise man adapts himself to others. He acts for their good, yet never violates the moral virtues or the principles of right conduct. The foolish man cannot adapt himself to others; he acts for himself only, and continually violates the moral virtues and the principles of right conduct. There is a degree of wisdom in every act of impartiality, and once a man has touched and experience the impartial zone, he can recover it again and again until he finally establishes himself in it.

Every thought, word, and act of wisdom tells on the world at large, for it is fraught with greatness. Wisdom is a well of knowledge and a spring of power. It is profound and comprehensive, and is so exact and all inclusive as to embrace the smallest details. In its spacious greatness it does not overlook the small. The wise mind is like the world, it contains all things in their proper place and order, and is not burdened thereby. Like the world also, it is free, and unconscious of any restrictions; yet it is never loose, never erring, never inful and repentant. Wisdom is the steady, grown up being of whom folly was the crying infant. It was outgrown the weakness and dependence, the errors and punishments of infantile ignorance, and is erect, poised, strong, and serene.

The understanding mind needs no external support. It stands of itself on the firm ground of knowledge; not book-knowledge, but ripened experience. It has passed through all minds, and therefore knows them. It has traveled with all hearts, and knows their journeying in joy and sorrow.

When wisdom touches a man, he is lifted up and transfigured. He becomes a new being with new aims and powers, and he inhabits a new universe in which to accomplish a new and glorious destiny.

Such is the Pillar of impartiality which adds its massive strength and incomparable grace to support and beautify the Temple of Prosperity.

Eighth Pillar – Self-reliance

Every young man ought to read Emerson's essay on 'Self Reliance'. It is the manliest, most virile essay that was ever penned. It is calculated to cure alike those two mental maladies common to youth, namely, self depreciation and self conceit. It is almost as sure to reveal to the prig the smallness and emptiness of his vanity, as it is to show the bashful man the weakness and ineffectuality of his dividence. It is a new revelation of manly dignity; as much a revelation as any that was vouchsafed to ancient seer and prophet, and perhaps a more practical, eminently suited to his mechanic age, coming, as it does from a modern prophet of a new type and called in a new race, and its chief merit is its powerfully tonic quality.

Let not self-reliance be confounded with self conceit, for as high and excellent as is the one, just so low and worthless is other. There cannot be anything mean in self reliance, while in self conceit there cannot be anything great.

The man that never says "no" when questioned on subjects of which he is entirely ignorant, to avoid, as he imagines, being thought ignorant, but confidently puts forward guesses and assumptions as knowledge, will be known for his ignorance, and ill esteemed for his added conceit. An honest confession of ignorance will command respect where a conceited assumption of knowledge will elicit contempt.

The timid, apologetic man who seems almost afraid to live, who fears that he will do something not in the approved way, and will subject himself to ridicule, is not a full man. He must needs imitate others, and have no independent action. He needs that self reliance which will compel him to fall back on his own initiative, and so become a new example instead of the slavish follower of an old one. As for ridicule he who is hurt by it is no man. The shafts or mockery and sarcasm cannot pierce the strong armour of the self reliant man. They cannot reach the invincible citadel of his honest heart to sting or wound it. The sharp arrows of irony may rain upon him, but he laughs as they are deflected by the strong breast plate of his confidence, and fall harmless about him.

"Trust thyself," says Emerson, 'every heart vibrates to that iron string." Throughout the ages men have so far leaned, and do still lean, upon external makeshifts instead of standing upon their own native simplicity and original dignity. The few who have had the courage to so stand, have been singled out and elevated as heroes; and he is indeed the true hero who has the hardihood to let his nature speak for itself, who has that strong metal which enables him to stand upon his own intrinsic worth.

It is true that the candidate for such heroism must endure the test of strength. He must not be shamed from his ground by the bugbears of an initiate conventionalist. He must not fear for his reputation or position, or for his standing in the church or his prestige in local society. He must learn to act and live as independently of these consideration as he does of the current fashions in the antipodes. Yet when he has endured this test, and stander and odium have failed to move or afflict him, he has become a man indeed, one that society will have to reckon with, and finally accept on his own terms.

Sooner or later all men will turn or guidance to the self reliant man, and while the best minds do not make a prop of him, they respect and value his work and worth, and recognize his place among the goods that have gone before.

It must not be thought an indication of self reliance to scorn to learn. Such an attitude is born of a stubborn superciliousness which has the elements of weakness, and is prophetic of a fall, rather than the elements of strength and the promise of high achievement which are characteristic of self – reliance. Pride and vanity must not be associated with self rests upon incidentals and appurtenances – on money, clothing, property, prestige, position and these lost, all is lost. Self reliance rests upon essentials and principles on worth, probity, purity, sincerity, character, truth and whatever may be lost is of little account, for these are never lost. Pride tries to hide its ignorance by ostentation and assumption, and is unwilling to be thought a learner in any direction. It stands, during its little fleeting day, on ignorance and appearance, and the higher it is lifted up today the lower it will be cast down tomorrow. Self reliance has nothing to hide, and is willing to learn; and while there can be no humility where pride is, self reliance and humility are compatible, nay more, they are complementary, and the sublimes form of self reliance is only found associated with the profoundest humility. "Extremes meet" says Emerson "and there is no better example than the haughtiness of humility. No aristocrat, no prince born to the purple, can begin to compare with the self respect of the saint. Why is he so lowly, but that he knows that he can well afford it, resting on the largeness of God in him?" It was Buddha who, I this particular, said; — "Those who, either now or after I am dead, shall be a lamp unto themselves, relying upon them selves only and not relying upon any external help, but holding fast to the truth as their lamp, and seeking their salvation in the truth alone, shall not look for assistance to any one beside themselves, it is they, among my disciples, who shall reach the very top mist height. But they must be willing to learn." In this saying, the repeated insistence on the necessity for relying upon one's self alone, coupled with the final exhortation to be eager to learn, is the wisest utterance on self reliance that I know. In it, the Great Teacher comprehends that perfect balance between self trust and humility which the man of truth must acquire.

"Self – trust is the essence of heroism." All great men are self reliant, and we should use them as teachers and exemplars and not as props and perambulators. A great man comes who leans upon no one, but stands alone in the solitary dignity of truth, and straightway the world begins to lean upon him, begins to make him an excuse for spiritual indolence and a destructive self-abasement. Better than cradling our vices in the strength of the great would it be to newly light our virtues at their luminous lamp. If we rely upon the light of another, darkness will over take us, but if we rely upon our own light we have but to keep it burning. We may both draw light from another and communicate it, but to think it sufficient while our own lamp is rusting in neglect, is shortly to find ourselves abandoned in darkness. Our own inner light is the light which never fails us.

What is the "inner light" of the Quakers but another name for self reliance? We should stand upon what we are, not upon what another is. "But I am so small and poor," you say: well, stand upon that smallness, and presently it will become great. A babe must needs suckle and cling, but not so man. Henceforth he goes upon his own limbs. Men pray to God to put into their hands that which they are framed to reach out for; to put into their mouth the food for which they should strenuously labour. But men will outgrow this spiritual infancy. The time will come when men will no more pay a priest to pray for them and preach to them.

Man's chief trouble is a mistrust of himself, so that the self trusting man becomes a rare and singular spectacle. If a man look upon himself as a "worm," what can come out of him but an ineffectual wriggling. Truly, "He that humbleth shall be exalted," but not he that degardeth himself. A man should see himself as he is, and if there is any unworthiness in him, he should get rid of it, and retain and rely upon that which is of worth. A man is only debased when he debases himself; he is exalted when he lives an exalted life.

Why should a man, with ceaseless iterations, draw attention to his fallen nature? There is a false humility which takes a sort of pride in vice. If one has fallen, it is that he may rise and be the wiser for it. if a man falls into a ditch, he does not lie there and call upon every passer by to mark his fallen state, he gets up and goes on his way with greater care. So if one has fallen into the ditch of vice, let him rise and be cleansed, and go on his way rejoicing.

There is not a sphere in life wherein a man's influence and prosperity will not be considerably increased by even a measure of self reliance, and to the teacher – whether secular or religious to organizers, managers, overseers, and in all positions of control and command, it is an indispensable equipment.

The four grand qualities of self reliance are:—

1. Decision
2. Steadfastness
3. Dignity
4. Independence

Decision makes a man strong. The wearer is the weakling. A man who is to play a speaking part, however small, in the drama of life must be decisive and know what he is about. Whatever he doubts, he must not doubt his power to act. He must know his part in life, and put all his energy into it. He must have some solid ground of knowledge from which to work, and stand securely on that. It may be only the price and quality of stock, but he must know his work thoroughly, and know that he knows it. he must be ready at any time to answer for himself when his duty is impugned. He should be so well grounded upon his particular practice as not to be affected with hesitation on any point or in any emergence. It is a true saying that "the man that hesitates is lost." No one believes in him who does not believe in himself, who doubts, halts, and wavers, and cannot extricate himself from the tangled threads of two courses. Who would deal with a tradesman who did not know the price of his own goods, or was not sure where to find them? A man must know his business. If he does not know his own, who shall instruct him? He must be able to give a good report of the truth that is in him, must have that deceive touch which skill and knowledge only can impart.

Certainty is a great element in self reliance. To have weight, a man must have some truth to impart, and all skill is a communication of truth. He must "speak with authority, and not as the scribes." He must master something, and know that he has mastered it, so as to deal with it lucidly and under-standingly, in the way of a master, and not to remain always an apprentice.

Indecision is a disintegrating factor. A minute's faltering may turn back the current of success. Men who are afraid to decide quickly for fear of making a mistake, nearly always makes a mistake when they do act. The quickest, in thought and action, are less liable to blunder, and it is better to act with decision and make a mistake than to act with indecision and make a mistake than to act with indecision and make a mistake, for in the former case there is but error, but in the latter, weakness is added to error.

A man should be decided always, both where he knows and where he does not know. He should be as ready to say "no" as "yes," as quick to acknowledge his ignorance as to impart his knowledge. If he stands upon fact, and acts from the simple truth, he will find no room for halting between two opinions.

Make up your mind quickly, and act decisively. Better still, have a mind that is already made up and then decision will be instinctive and spontaneous.

Steadfastness arises in the mind that is quick to decide. It is indeed a final decision upon the best course of conduct and the best path in life. It is the vow of the soul to stand firmly by its principles whatever betide. It is neither necessary nor unnecessary that there by any written or spoken vow, for unswerving loyalty to a fixed principle is the spirit of all vows.

The man without fixed principles will not accomplish much. Expediency is a quagmire and a thorny waste, in which a man is continually sticking in the shifting mud of his own moral looseness, and is pricked and scratched with the thorns of his self created disappointments.

One must have some solid ground on which to stand among one's fellows. He cannot stand on the bog of concession. Shiftiness is a vice of weakness, and the vices of weakness do more to undermine character and influence than the vices of strength. The man that is vicious through excess of animal strength takes a shorter cut to truth – when his mind is made up that he who is vicious through lack of virility, and whose chief vice consists in not having a mind of his own upon anything. When one understands that power is adaptable to both good and bad ends, it will not surprise him that the drunkards and harlots should reach the kingdom of heaven before the diplomatic religionists. They are at least through in the course which they have adopted, vile though it be, and thoroughness is strength. It only needs that strength to be turned from bad to good, and lo! The loathed sinner has become the lofty saint!

A man should have a firm, fixed, determined mind. He should decide upon those principles which are best to stand by in all issues, and which will most safely guide him through the maze of conflicting opinions, and inspire him with unflinching courage in the battle of life. Having adopted his principles, they should be more to him than gain or happiness, more even than life itself, and if he never deserts them he will find that they will never desert him; they will defend him from all enemies, deliver him safely from all dangers, light up his pathway through all darkness and difficulties. They will be to him a light in darkness, a resting place from sorrow, and a refuge from the conflicts of the world.

Dignity clothes, as with a majestic garment, the steadfast mind. He who is as unyielding as a bar of steel when he is expected to compromise with evil, and as supple as a willow wand in adapting himself to that which is good, carries about with him a dignity that calms and uplifts others by its presence.

The unsteady mind, the mind that is not anchored to any fixed principles, that is stubborn where its own desires are threatened, and yielding where its own moral welfare is at stake, has no gravity, no balance, no calm composure.

The man of dignity cannot be down-trodden and enslaved, because he has ceased to tread upon and enslave himself. He at once disarms, with a look, a word, a wise and suggestive silence, any attempt to demean him. His mere presence is a wholesome reproof to the flippant and the unseemly, while it is a rock of strength to the lover of the good.

But the chief reason why the dignified man commands respect is, not only that he is supremely self respecting, but that he graciously treats all others with a due esteem. Pride loves itself, and treats those beneath it with supercilious contempt, for love of self and contempt for others are always found together in equal degrees, so that the greater the self love, the greater the arrogance. True dignity arises, not from self love, but from self sacrifice that is, from unbiased adherence to a fixed central principle. The dignity of the Judge arises from the fact that in the performance of his duty he sets aside all personal consideration, and stands solely upon the law; his little personality, impermanent and fleeting' becomes nothing, while the law, enduring and majestic, becomes all. Should a Judge, in deciding a case, forget the law, and fall into personal feeling and prejudice, his dignity would be gone. So with the man of stately purity of character, he stands upon the divine law, and not upon personal feeling, for immediately a man gives way to passion he has sacrificed dignity, and takes his place as one of the multitude of the unwise and uncontrolled.

Every man will have composure and dignity in the measure that he acts from a fixed principle. It only needs that the principle be right, and therefore unassailable. So long as man abides by such a principle, and does not waver or descend into the personal element, attacking passions, prejudices and interests, however powerful, will be weak and ineffectual before the

unconquerable strength of an incorruptible principle, and will at last yield
their combined and unseemly confusion to his single and majestic right.

Independence is the birthright of the strong and well controlled man. All
men love and strive for liberty. All men aspire to some sort of freedom.

A man should labour for himself or for the community. Unless he is a
cripple, a chronic invalid, or is mentally irresponsible, he should be ashamed
to depend upon others for all he has, giving nothing in return. If one imagines
that such a condition is freedom, let him know that it is one of the lowest
forms of slavery. The time will come when, to be a drone in the human hive,
even (as matters are now) a respectable drone and not a poor tramp, will be
a public disgrace, and will be no longer respectable.

Independence, freedom, glorious liberty, come through labour and not from
idleness, and the self reliant man is too strong, too honourable, too upright
to depend upon others, like a sucking babe, for his support. He earns, with
hand or brain, the right to live as becomes a man and a citizen; and this he
does whether born rich or poor, for riches are no excuse for idleness; rather
are they an opportunity to labour, with the rare facilities which they afford,
for the good of the community.

Only he who is self supporting is free, self reliant, independent.

Thus is the nature of the Eight Pillars explained. On what foundation they
rest, the manner of their building, their ingredients, the fourfold nature of the
material of which each is composed, what positions they occupy, and how
they support the Temple, all may now build; and he who knew but imper-
fectly may know more perfectly; and he who knew perfectly may rejoice in
this systematization and simplification of the moral order in Prosperity. Let
us now consider the Temple itself, that we may know the might of its Pillars,
the strength of its walls, the endurance of its roof, and the architectural
beauty and perfection of the whole.

The Temple of Prosperity

The reader who has followed the course of this book with a view to obtaining information on the details of money making, business transactions, profit and loss in various undertakings, prices, markets, agreements, contracts, and other matters connected with the achievement of prosperity, will have noted an entire absence of any instruction on these matters of detail. The reason for this is fourfold, namely:—

First. Details cannot stand alone, but are powerless to build up anything unless intelligently related to principles.

Second. Details are infinite, and are ceaselessly changing, while principles are few, and are eternal and unchangeable.

Third. Principles are the coherent factors in all details, regulating and harmonizing them, so that to have right principles is to be right in all the subsidiary details.

Fourth. A teacher of truth in any direction must adhere rigidly to principles, and must not allow himself to be drawn away from them into the ever-changing maze of private particulars and personal details, because such particulars and details have only a local right, and are only necessary for certain individuals, while principles are universally right and are necessary for all men.

He who grasps the principles of this book so as to be able to intelligently practice them, will be able to reach the heart of this fourfold reason. The details of a man's affairs are important, but they are his details or the details of his particular branch of industry, and all outside that branch are not concerned with them, but moral principles are the same for all men; they are applicable to all conditions, and govern all particulars.

The man who works from fixed principles does not need to harass himself over the complications of numerous details. He will grasp, as it were, the entire details in one single thought, and will see them through and through, illumined by the light of the principle to which they stand related, and this without friction, and with freedom from anxiety and strain.

Until principles are grasped, details are regarded, and dealt with, as primary matters, and so viewed they lead to innumerable complications and confused issues. In the light of principles, they are seen to be secondary facts, and so seen, all difficulties connected with them are at once overcome and annulled by a reference to principles.

He who is involved in numerous details without the regulating and synthesizing element of principles is like one lost in a forest, with no direct path along which to walk amid the mass of objects. He is swelled up by the details, while the man of principles contains all details within himself; he stands outside them, as it were, and grasps them in their entirety, while the other man can only see the few that are nearest to him at the time.

All things are contained in principles. They are the laws of things, and all things observe their own law. It is an error to view things apart from their nature. Details are the letter of which principles are the spirit. It is as true in art, science, literature, commerce, as in religion, that "the letter killeth, the spirit of giveth life." The body of a man, with its wonderful combination of parts, is important, but only in its relation to the spirit. The spirit being withdrawn, the body is useless and is put away. The body of a business, with all its complicated details is important, but only in its relation to the vivifying principles by which it is controlled. These withdrawn, the business will perish.

To have the body of prosperity – its material presentation – we must first have the spirit of prosperity, and the spirit of prosperity is the quick spirit of moral virtue. Moral blindness prevails. Men see money, property, pleasure, leisure, etc., and, mistaking them for prosperity, strive to get them for their own enjoyment, but, when obtained, they find no enjoyment in them.

Prosperity is at first a spirit, an attitude of mind, a moral power, a life, which manifests outwardly in the form of plenty, happiness, joy. Just as a man cannot become a genius by writing poems, essay as plays, but must develop and acquire the soul of genius – when the writing will follow as effect to cause — so one cannot become prosperous by hoarding up money, and by gaining property and possessions, but must develop and acquire the soul of virtue, when the material accessories will follow as effect to cause, for the spirit of virtue is the spirit of joy, and it contains within itself all abundance, all satisfaction, all fullness of life.

There is no joy in money, there is no joy in property, there is no joy in material accumulations or in any material things of itself. These things are dead and lifeless. The spirit of joy must be in the man or it is nowhere. He must have within him the capacity for happiness. He must have the wisdom to know how to use these things, and not merely hoard them. He must possess them, and not be possessed by them. They must be dependent upon him, and not he upon them. They must be dependent upon him, and not he upon them. They must follow him, and not be for ever be running after them; and they will inevitably follow him, if he has the moral elements within to which they are related.

Nothing is absent from the Kingdom of heaven; it contains all good, true, and necessary things, and "the Kingdom of God is within you." I know rich people who are supremely happy, because they are generous, magnanimous, pure and joyful; but I also know rich people who are very miserable, and these are they who looked to money and possessions for their happiness, and have not developed the spirit of good and of joy within themselves.

How can it be said of a wretched man that he is "prosperous," even if his income be ten thousand pounds a year? There must be fitness, and harmony, and satisfaction in a true prosperity. When a rich man is happy, it is that he brought the spirit of happiness to his riches, and not that the riches brought happiness to him. He is a full man with full material advantages and responsibilities, while the miserable rich man is an empty man looking to riches for that fullness of life which can only be evolved from within.

Thus prosperity resolves itself into a moral capacity, and in the wisdom to rightfully use and lawfully enjoy the material things which are inseparable from our earthly life. If one would be free without, let him first be free within, for if he be bound in a spirit by weakness, selfishness, or vice, how can the possession of money liberate him! Will it not rather become, in his hands, a ready instrument by which to further enslave himself?

The visible effects of prosperity, then, must not be considered alone, but in their relation to the mental and moral cause. There is a hidden foundation to every building; the fact that it continues to stands is proof of that. There is a hidden foundation to every from of established success; its permanence proves that it is so. Prosperity stands on the foundation of character, and there is not, in all the wide universe, any other foundation. True wealth is weal, welfare, well being, soundness, wholeness, and happiness. The wretched rich are not truly wealthy. They are merely encumbered with money, luxury, and leisure, as instruments of self torture. By their possessions they are self cursed.

The moral man is ever blessed, ever happy, and his life, viewed as a whole, is always a success. To these there is no exception, for whatever failures he may have in detail, the finished work of his life will be sound, whole, complete; and through all he will have a quiet conscience, an honorable name, and all manifold blessings which are inseparable from richness of character, and without this moral richness, financial riches will not avail or satisfy.

Let us briefly recapitulate, and again view the Eight Pillars in their strength and splendour.

Energy – Rousing one's self up to strenuous and unremitting exertion in the accomplishment of one's task.

Economy – Concentration of power, the conservation of both capital and character, the latter being mental capital, and therefore of the utmost importance.

Integrity – Unswerving honesty; keeping inviolate all promises, agreements, and contracts, apart from all considerations of loss or gain.

System – Making all details, subservient to order, and thereby relieving the memory and the mind of superfluous work and strain by reducing many to one.

Sympathy – Magnanimity, generosity, gentleness, and tenderness; being open handed, free, and kind.

Sincerity – Being sound and whole, robust and true; and therefore not being one person in public and another in private, and not assuming good actions openly while doing bad actions in secret.

Impartiality – Justice; not striving for self, but weighing both sides, and acting in accordance with equity.

Self – Reliance – Looking to one's self only for strength and support by standing on principles which are fixed and invincible, and not relying upon outward things which at any moment may be snatched away.

How can any life be other than successful which is built on these Eight Pillars? Their strength is such that no physical or intellectual strength can compare with it; and to have built all the eight perfectly would render a man invincible. It will be found, however, that men are often strong in one or several of these qualities, and weak in others, and it is this weak element that invites failure. It is foolish, for instance, to attribute a man's failure in business to his honest. It is impossible for honesty to produce failure. The cause of failure must be looked for in some other direction – in the lack, and not the possession, of some good necessary quality. Moreover, such attribution of failure to honesty is a slur on the integrity of commerce; and a false indict-ment of those men, numerous enough, who are honourably engaged in trade. A man may be strong in Energy, Economy, and System, but comparatively weak in the other five. Such a man will just fail of complete success by lacking one of the four corner pillars, namely, Integrity. His temple will give way at that weak corner, for the first four Pillars must be well built before the

Temple of Prosperity can stand secure. They are the first qualities to be acquired in a man's moral evolution, and without them the second four cannot be possessed. Again, if a man be strong in the first three, and lack the fourth, the absence of order will invite confusion and disaster into his affairs; and so on with any partial combination of these qualities, especially of the first four, for the second four are of so lofty a character that at present men can but possess them, with rare exceptions, in a more or less imperfect form. The man of the world, then, who wishes to secure an abiding success in any branch of commerce, or in one of the many lines of industry in which men are commonly engaged, must build into his character, by practice, the first four moral Pillars. By these fixed principles he must regulate his thought, his conduct, and his affairs; consulting them in every difficulty, making every detail serve them, and above all, never deserting them under any circumstance to gain some personal advantage or to save some personal trouble, for to so desert them is to make one's self vulnerable to the disintegrating elements of evil, and to become assailable to accusations from others. He who so abides by these four principles will achieve a full measure of success in his own particular work, whatever it may be; his Temple of Prosperity will be well built and well supported, and it will stand secure. The perfect practice of these four principles is within the scope of all men who are willing to study them with that object in view, for they are so simple and plain that a child could grasp their meaning, and their perfection in conduct does not call for an unusual degree of self sacrifice, though it demands some self denial and personal discipline without which there can be no success in this world of action. The second four pillars, however, are principles of a more profound nature, are more difficult to understand and practice, and call from the highest degree of self sacrifice and self effacement. Few, at present, can reach that detachment from the personal element which their perfect practice demands, but the few who accomplish this in any marked degree will vastly enlarge their powers and enrich their life, and will adorn their Temple of Prosperity with a singular and attractive beauty which will gladden and elevate all beholders long after they have passed away.

But those who are beginning to build their Temple of Prosperity in accordance with the teaching of this book, must bear in mind that a building requires time to erect, and it must be patiently raised up, brick upon brick and stone upon stone, and the Pillars must be firmly fixed and cemented, and labour and care will be needed to make the whole complete. And the building of this inner mental Temple is none the less real and substantial because invisible and noiseless, for in the raising up of his, as of Solomon's Temple which was "seven years in building" – it can be said, "there was neither hammer nor axe nor any tool of iron heard in the house, while it was in the building."

Even so, oh reader construct thy character, raise up the house of thy life, build up thy Temple of Prosperity. Be not as the foolish who rise and fall upon the uncertain flux of selfish desires: but be at peace in thy labour, crown thy career with completeness, and so be numbered among the wise who, without uncertainty, build upon a fixed and secure foundation – even upon the Principles of Truth which endure for ever.

Foundation Stones to Happiness and Success

Table of Contents

Editor's Preface. 84

Foreword. 85

Right Principles. 86

Sound Methods. 89

True Actions. 92

True Speech. 95

Equal-Mindedness. 98

Good Results. 100

Editor's Preface

This is one of the last MSS. written by James Allen. Like all his works it is eminently practical. He never wrote theories, or for the sake of writing, or to add another to his many books; but he wrote when he had a message, and it became a message only when he had lived it out in his own life, and knew that it was good. Thus he wrote facts, which he had proven by practice.

To live out the teaching of this book faithfully in every detail of life will lead one to more than happiness and success — even to Blessedness, Satisfaction and Peace.

LILY L. ALLEN

Foreword

How does a man begin the building of a house? He first secures a plan of the proposed edifice, and then proceeds to build according to the plan, scrupulously following it in every detail, beginning with the foundation. Should he neglect the beginning — the beginning on a mathematical plan — his labour would be wasted, and his building, should it reach completion without tumbling to pieces, would be insecure and worthless. The same law holds good in any important work; the right beginning and first essential is a definite mental plan on which to build.

Nature will have no slipshod work, no slovenliness and she annihilates confusion, or rather, confusion is in itself annihilated. Order, definiteness, purpose, eternally prevail, and he who in his operations ignores these mathematical elements at once deprives himself of substantiality, completeness, happiness and success.

JAMES ALLEN

Right Principles

It is wise to know what comes first, and what to do first. To begin anything in the middle or at the end is to make a muddle of it. The athlete who began by breaking the tape would not receive the prize. He must begin by facing the starter and toeing the mark, and even then a good start is important if he is to win. The pupil does not begin with algebra and literature, but with counting and ABC. So in life – the businessmen who begin at the bottom achieve the more enduring success; and the religious men who reach the highest heights of spiritual knowledge and wisdom are they who have stooped to serve a patient apprenticeship to the humbler tasks, and have not scorned the common experiences of humanity, or overlooked the lessons to be learned from them.

The first things in a sound life — and therefore, in a truly happy and successful life — are right principles. Without right principles to begin with, there will be wrong practices to follow with, and a bungled and wretched life to end with. All the infinite variety of calculations which tabulate the commerce and science of the world, come out of the ten figures; all the hundreds of thousands of books which constitute the literature of the world, and perpetuate its thought and genius, are built up from the twenty-six letters. The greatest astronomer cannot ignore the ten simple figures. The profoundest man of genius cannot dispense with the twenty-six simple characters. The fundamentals in all things are few and simple: yet without them there is no knowledge and no achievement. The fundamentals — the basic principles — in life, or true living, are also few and simple, and to learn them thoroughly, and study how to apply them to all the details of life, is to avoid confusion, and to secure a substantial foundation for the orderly building up of an invincible character and a permanent success; and to succeed in comprehending those principles in their innumerable ramifications in the labyrinth of conduct, is to become a Master of Life.

The first principles in life are principles of conduct. To name them is easy. As mere words they are on all men's lips, but as fixed sources of action, admitting of no compromise, few have learned them. In this short talk I will deal with five only of these principles. These five are among the simplest of the root principles of life, but they are those that come nearest to the everyday life, for they touch the artisan the businessman, the householder, the citizen at every point. Not one of them can be dispensed with but at severe cost, and he who perfects himself in their application will rise superior to many of the troubles and failures of life, and will come into these springs and currents of thought which flow harmoniously towards the regions of enduring success. The first of these principles is —

DUTY — A much-hackneyed word, I know, but it contains a rare jewel for him who will seek it by assiduous application. The principle of duty means strict adherence to one's own business, and just as strict non-interference in the business of others. The man who is continually instructing others, gratis, how to manage their affairs, is the one who most mismanages his own. Duty also means undivided attention to the matter in hand, intelligent concentration of the mind on the work to be done; it includes all that is meant by thoroughness, exactness, and efficiency. The details of duties differ with individuals, and each man should know his own duty better then he knows his neighbour's, and better than his neighbour knows his; but although the working details differ, the principle is always the same. Who has mastered the demands of duty?

HONESTY is the next principle. It means not cheating or overcharging another. It involves the absence of all trickery, lying, and deception by word, look, or gesture. It includes sincerity, the saying what you mean, and the meaning what you say. It scorns cringing policy and shining compliment. It builds up good reputations, and good reputations build up good businesses, and bright joy accompanies well-earned success. Who has scaled the heights of Honesty?

ECONOMY is the third principle. The conservation of one's financial resources is merely the vestibule leading towards the more spacious chambers of true economy. It means, as well, the husbanding of one's physical vitality and mental resources. It demands the conservation of energy by the avoidance of enervating self-indulgences and sensual habits. It holds for its follower strength, endurance, vigilance, and capacity to achieve. It bestows great power on him who learns it well. Who has realized the supreme strength of Economy?

LIBERALITY follows economy. It is not opposed to it. Only the man of economy can afford to be generous. The spendthrift, whether in money, vitality, or mental energy, wasted so much on his own miserable pleasures as to have none left to bestow upon others. The giving of money is the smallest part of liberality. There is a giving of thoughts, and deeds, and sympathy, the bestowing of goodwill, the being generous towards calumniators and opponents. It is a principle that begets a noble, far-reaching influence. It brings loving friends and staunch comrades, and is the foe of loneliness and despair. Who has measured the breadth of Liberality?

SELF–CONTROL is the last of these five principles, yet the most important. Its neglect is the cause of vast misery, innumerable failures, and tens of thousands of financial, physical, and mental wrecks. Show me the businessman who loses his temper with a customer over some trivial matter, and I will show you a man who, by that condition of mind, is doomed to failure. If all men practised even the initial stages of self-control, anger, with its consuming and destroying fire, would be unknown. The lessons of patience, purity, gentleness, kindness, and steadfastness, which are contained in the principle of self-control, are slowly learned by men, yet until they are truly learned a man's character and success are uncertain and insecure. Where is the man who has perfected himself in Self-Control? Where he may be, he is a master indeed.

The five principles are five practices, five avenues to achievement, and five source of knowledge. It is an old saying and a good rule that "Practice makes perfect," and he who would make his own the wisdom which is inherent in those principles, must not merely have them on his lips, they must be established in his heart. To know them and receive what they alone can bring, he must do them, and give them out in his actions.

Sound Methods

From the five foregoing Right Principles, when they are truly apprehended and practised, will issue Sound Methods. Right principles are manifested in harmonious action, and method is to life what law is to the universe. Everywhere in the universe there is the harmonious adjustment of parts, and it is this symmetry and harmony that reveals a cosmos, as distinguished from chaos. So in human life, the difference between a true life and a false, between one purposeful and effective and one purposeless and weak, is one of method. The false life is an incoherent jumble of thoughts, passions, and actions; the true life is an orderly adjustment of all its parts. It is all the difference between a mass of lumber and a smoothly working efficient machine. A piece of machinery in perfect working order is not only a useful, but an admirable and attractive thing; but when its parts are all out of gear, and refuse to be readjusted, its usefulness and attractiveness are gone, and it is thrown on the scrap-heap. Likewise a life perfectly adjusted in all its parts so as to achieve the highest point of efficiency, is not only a powerful, but an excellent and beautiful thing; whereas a life confused, inconsistent, discordant, is a deplorable exhibition of wasted energy.

If life is to be truly lived, method must enter into, and regulate, every detail of it, as it enters and regulates every detail of the wondrous universe of which we form a part. One of the distinguishing differences between a wise man and a foolish is, that the wise man pays careful attention to the smallest things, while the foolish man slurs over them, or neglects them altogether. Wisdom consists in maintaining things on their right relations, in keeping all things, the smallest as well as the greatest, in their proper places and times. To violate order is to produce confusion and discord, and unhappiness is but another name for discord.

The good businessman knows that system is three parts of success, and that disorder means failure. The wise man knows that disciplined, methodical living is three parts of happiness, and that looseness means misery. What is a fool but one who thinks carelessly, acts rashly, and lives loosely? What is a wise man but one who thinks carefully, acts calmly, and lives consistently?

The true method does not end with the orderly arrangement of the material things and external relations of life; this is but its beginning; it enters into the adjustment of the mind — the discipline of the passions, the elimination and choice of words in speech, the logical arrangement of the thoughts, and the selection of right actions.

To achieve a life rendered sound, successful, and sweet by the pursuance of sound methods, one must begin, not by neglect of the little everyday things, but by assiduous attention to them. Thus the hour of rising is important, and its regularity significant; as also are the timing of retiring to rest, and the number of hours given to sleep. Between the regularity and irregularity of meals, and the care and carelessness with which they are eaten, is all the difference between a good and bad digestion (with all that this applies) and an irritable or comfortable frame of mind, with its train of good or bad consequences, for, attaching to these meal-times and meal-ways are matters of both physiological and psychological significance. The due division of hours for business and for play, not confusing the two, the orderly fitting in of all the details of one's business, times for solitude, for silent thought and for effective action, for eating and for abstinence — all these things must have their lawful place in the life of him whose "daily round" is to proceed with the minimum degree of friction, who is to get the most of usefulness, influence, and joy out of life.

But all this is but the beginning of that comprehensive method which embraces the whole life and being. When this smooth order and logical consistency is extended to the words and actions, to the thoughts and desires, then wisdom emerges from folly, and out of weakness comes power sublime. When a man so orders his mind as to produce a beautiful working harmony between all its parts, then he reaches the highest wisdom, the highest efficiency, the highest happiness.

But this is the end; and he who would reach the end must begin at the beginning. He must systematise and render logical and smooth the smallest details of his life, proceeding step by step towards the finished accomplishment. But each step will yield its own particular measure of strength and gladness.

To sum up, method produces that smoothness which goes with strength and efficiency. Discipline is method applied to the mind. It produces that calmness which goes with power and happiness. Method is working by rule; discipline is living by rule. But working and living are not separate; they are but two aspects of character, of life.

Therefore, be orderly in work; be accurate in speech, be logical in thought. Between these and slovenliness, inaccuracy and confusion, is the difference between success and failure, music and discord, happiness and misery.

The adoption of sound methods of working, acting, thinking – in a word, of living, is the surest and safest foundation for sound health, sound success, sound peace of mind. The foundation of unsound methods will be found to be unstable, and to yield fear and unrest even while it appears to succeed, and when its time of failure comes, it is grievous indeed.

True Actions

Following on Right Principles and Methods come True Actions. One who is striving to grasp true principles and work with sound methods will soon come to perceive that details of conduct cannot be overlooked — that, indeed, those details are fundamentally distinctive or creative, according to their nature, and are, therefore, of deep significance and comprehensive importance; and this perception and knowledge of the nature and power of passing actions will gradually open and grow within him as an added vision, a new revelation. As he acquires this insight his progress will be more rapid, his pathway in life more sure, his days more serene and peaceful; in all things he will go the true and direct way, unswayed and untroubled by the external forces that play around and about him. Not that he will be indifferent to the welfare and happiness of those about him; that is quite another thing; but he will be indifferent to their opinions, to their ignorance, to their ungoverned passions. By True Actions, indeed, is meant acting rightly towards others, and the right-doer knows that actions in accordance with truth are but for the happiness of those about him, and he will do them even though an occasion may arise when some one near to him may advise or implore him to do otherwise.

True actions may easily be distinguished from false by all who wish so to distinguish in order that they may avoid false action, and adopt true. As in the material world we distinguish things by their form, colour, size, etc., choosing those things which we require, and putting by those things which are not useful to us, so in the spiritual world of deeds, we can distinguish between those that are bad and those that are good by their nature, their aim, and their effect and can choose and adopt those that are good, and ignore those that are bad.

In all forms of progress, avoidance of the bad always precedes acceptance and knowledge of the good, just as a child at school learns to do its lessons right by having repeatedly pointed out to it how it has done them wrong. If one does not know what is wrong and how to avoid it, how can he know what is right and how to practise it? Bad, or untrue, actions are those that spring from a consideration of one's own happiness only, and ignore the happiness of others, that arise in violent disturbances of the mind and unlawful desires, or that call for concealment in order to avoid undesirable complications. Good or true actions are those that spring from a consideration for others, that arise in calm reason and harmonious thought framed on moral principles or that will not involve the doer in shameful consequences if brought into the full light of day.

The right-doer will avoid those acts of personal pleasure and gratification which by their nature bring annoyance, pain, or suffering to others, no matter how insignificant those actions may appear to be. He will begin by putting away these; he will gain a knowledge of the unselfish and true by first sacrificing the selfish and untrue. He will learn not to speak or act in anger, or envy, or resentment, but will study how to control his mind, and will restore it to calmness before acting; and, most important of all, he will avoid, as he would the drinking of deadly poison, those acts of trickery, deceit, double-dealing, in order to gain some personal profit of advantage, and which lead, sooner or later, to exposure and shame for the doer of them. If a man is prompted to do a thing which he needs to conceal, and which he would not lawfully and frankly defend if it were examined of witness, he should know by that that it is a wrong act and therefore to be abandoned without a further moment's consideration.

The carrying out of this principle of honesty and sincerity of action, too, will further lead him into such a path of thoughtfulness in right-doing as will enable him to avoid doing those things which would involve him in the deceptive practices of other people. Before signing papers, or entering into verbal or written arrangements, or engaging himself to others in any way at their request, particularly if they be strangers, he will first inquire into the nature of the work or undertaking, and so, enlightened, he will know exactly what to do, and will be fully aware of the import of his action. To the right-doer thoughtlessness is a crime. Thousands of actions done with good intent lead to disastrous consequences because they are acts of thoughtlessness, and it is well said "that the way to hell is paved with good intentions." The man of true actions is, above all things, thoughtful:— "Be ye therefore wise as serpents and harmless as doves."

The term Thoughtlessness covers a wide field in the realm of deeds. It is only by increasing in thoughtfulness that a man can come to understand the nature of actions, and can, thereby, acquire the power of always doing that which is right. It is impossible for a man to be thoughtful and act foolishly. Thoughtfulness embraces wisdom.

It is not enough that an action is prompted by a good impulse or intention; it must arise in thoughtful consideration if it is to be a true action; and the man who wishes to be permanently happy in himself and a power for good to others must concern himself only with true actions. "I did it with the best of intentions," is a poor excuse from one who has thoughtlessly involved himself in the wrong-doing of others. His bitter experience should teach him to act more thoughtfully in the future.

True actions can only spring from a true mind, and therefore while a man is learning to distinguish and choose between the false and the true, he is correcting and perfecting his mind, and is thereby rendering it more harmonious and felicitous, more efficient and powerful. As he acquires the "inner eye" to clearly distinguish the right in all the details of life, and the faith and knowledge to do it, he will realise that he is building the house of his character and life upon a rock which the winds of failure and the storms of persecution can never undermine.

True Speech

Truth is known by practice only. Without sincerity there can be no knowledge of Truth; and true speech is the beginning of all sincerity. Truth in all its native beauty and original simplicity consists in abandoning and not doing all those things which are untrue, and in embracing and doing all those things which are true. True speech is therefore one of the elementary beginnings in the life of Truth. Falsehood, and all forms of deception; slander and all forms of evil-speaking — these must be totally abandoned and abolished before the mind can receive even a small degree of spiritual enlightenment. The liar and slanderer is lost in darkness; so deep is his darkness that he cannot distinguish between good and evil, and he persuades himself that his lying and evil-speaking are necessary and good, that he is thereby protecting himself and other people.

Let the would-be student of "higher things" look to himself and beware of self-delusion. If he is given to uttering words that deceive, or to speaking evil of others – if he speaks in insincerity, envy, or malice — then he has not yet begun to study higher things. He may be studying metaphysics, or miracles, or psychic phenomena, or astral wonders – he may be studying how to commune with invisible beings, to travel invisibly during sleep, or to produce curious phenomena — he may even study spirituality theoretically and as a mere book study, but if he is a deceiver and a backbiter, the higher life is hidden from him. For the higher things are these – uprightness, sincerity, innocence, purity, kindness, gentleness, faithfulness, humility, patience, pity, sympathy, self-sacrifice, joy, goodwill, love – and he who would study them, know them, and make them his own, must practice them, there is no other way.

Lying and evil-speaking belong to the lowest forms of spiritual ignorance, and there can be no such thing as spiritual enlightenment while they are practised. Their parents are selfishness and hatred.

Slander is akin to lying, but it is even more subtle, as it is frequently associated with indignation, and by assuming more successfully the appearance of truth, it ensnares many who would not tell a deliberate falsehood. For there are two sides to slander — there is the making of repeating of it, and there is the listening to it and acting upon it. The slanderer would be powerless without a listener. Evil words require an ear that is receptive to evil in which they may fall, before they can flourish; therefore he who listens to a slanderer, who believes it, and allows himself to be influenced against the person whose character and reputation are defamed, is in the same position as the one who framed or repeated the evil report. The evil-speaker is a positive slanderer; the evil-listener is a passive slanderer. The two are co-operators in the propagation of evil.

Slander is a common vice and a dark and deadly one. An evil report begins in ignorance, and pursues its blind way in darkness. It generally takes its rise in a misunderstanding. Some one feels that he or she has been badly treated, and, filled with indignation and resentment, unburdens himself to his friends and others in vehement language, exaggerating the enormity of the supposed offence on account of the feeling of injury by which he is possessed; he is listened to and sympathised with; the listeners, without hearing the other person's version of what has taken place, and on no other proof than the violent words of an angry man or woman, become cold in their attitude towards the one spoken against, and repeat to others what they have been told, and as such repetition is always more or less inaccurate, a distorted and altogether untrue report is soon passing from mouth to mouth.

It is because slander is such a common vice that it can work the suffering and injury that it does. It is because so many (not deliberate wrong-doers, and unconscious of the nature of the evil into which they so easily fall) are ready to allow themselves to be influenced against one whom they have hitherto regarded as honourable, that an evil report can do its deadly work. Yet its work is only amongst those who have not altogether acquired the virtue of true speech, the cause of which is a truth-loving mind. When one who has not entirely freed himself from repeating or believing an evil report about another, hears of an evil report about himself, his mind becomes aflame with burning resentment, his sleep is broken and his peace of mind is destroyed. He thinks the cause of all his suffering is in the other man and what that man has said about him, and is ignorant of the truth that the root and cause of his suffering lies in his own readiness to believe an evil report about another. The virtuous man — he who has attained to true speech, and whose mind is sealed against even the appearance of evil-speaking — cannot be injured and disturbed about any evil reports concerning himself; and although his reputation may for a time be stained in the minds of those who are prone to suggestions of evil, his integrity remains untouched and his character unsoiled; for no one can be stained by the evil deeds of another, but only by his own wrongdoing. And so, through all misrepresentation, misunderstanding, and contumely, he is untroubled and unrevengeful; his sleep is undisturbed, and his mind remains in peace.

True speech is the beginning of a pure, wise and well-ordered life. If one would attain to purity of life, if he would lessen the evil and suffering of the world, let him abandon falsehood and slander in thought and word, let him avoid even the appearance of these things, for there are no lies and slanders so deadly as those which are half-truths, and let him not be a participant in evil-speaking by listening to it. Let him also have compassion on the evil-speaker, knowing how such a one is binding himself to suffering and unrest; for no liar can know the bliss of Truth; no slanderer can enter the kingdom of peace.

By the words which he utters is a man's spiritual condition declared; by these also is he finally and infallibly adjudged, for as the Divine Master of the Christian world has declared, "By thy words shalt thou be justified, and by thy words shalt thou be condemned."

Equal-Mindedness

To be equally-minded is to be peacefully-minded, for a man cannot be said to have arrived at peace who allows his mind to be disturbed and thrown off the balance by occurrences.

The man of wisdom is dispassionate, and meets all things with the calmness of a mind in repose and free from prejudice. He is not a partisan, having put away passion, and he is always at peace with himself and the world, not taking sides nor defending himself, but sympathising with all.

The partisan is so convinced that his own opinion and his own side is right, and all that goes contrary to them is wrong, that he cannot think there is any good in the other opinion and the other side. He lives in a continual fever of attack and defence, and has no knowledge of the quiet peace of an equal mind.

The equal-minded man watches himself in order to check and overcome even the appearance of passion and prejudice in his mind, and by so doing he develops sympathy for others, and comes to understand their position and particular state of mind; and as he comes to understand others, he perceives the folly of condemning them and opposing himself to them. Thus there grows up in his heart a divine charity which cannot be limited, but which is extended to all things that live and strive and suffer.

When a man is under the sway of passion and prejudice he is spiritually blind. Seeing nothing but good in his own side, and nothing but evil in the other, he cannot see anything as it really is, not even his own side; and not understanding himself, he cannot understand the hearts of others, and thinks it is right that he should condemn them. Thus there grows up in his heart a dark hatred for those who refuse to see with him and who condemn him in return, he becomes separated from his fellow-men, and confines himself to a narrow torture chamber of his own making.

Sweet and peaceful are the days of the equal-minded man, fruitful in good, and rich in manifold blessings. Guided by wisdom, he avoids those pathways which lead down to hatred and sorrow and pain, and takes those which lead up to love and peace and bliss. The occurrences of life do not trouble him, nor does he grieve over those things which are regarded by mankind as grievous, but which must befall all men in the ordinary course of nature. He is neither elated by success nor cast down by failure. He sees the events of his life arrayed in their proper proportions, and can find no room for selfish wishes or vain regrets, for vain anticipations and childish disappointments.

And how is this equal-mindedness — this blessed state of mind and life — acquired? Only by overcoming one's self, only by purifying one's own heart, for the purification of the heart leads to unbiased comprehension, unbiased comprehension leads to equal-mindedness, and equal-mindedness leads to peace. The impure man is swept helplessly away on the waves of passion; the pure man guides himself into the harbour of rest. The fool says, "I have an opinion;" the wise man goes about his business.

Good Results

A considerable portion of the happenings of life comes to us without any direct choosing on our part, and such happenings are generally regarded as having no relation to our will or character, but as appearing fortuitously; as occurring without a cause. Thus one is spoken of as being "lucky," and another "unlucky," the inference being that each has received something which he never earned, never caused. Deeper thought, and a clearer insight into life convinces us, however, that nothing happens without a cause, and that cause and effect are always related in perfect adjustment and harmony. This being so, every happening directly affecting us is intimately related to our own will and character, is, indeed, an effect justly related to a cause having its seat in our consciousness. In a word, involuntary happenings of life are the results of our own thoughts and deeds. This, I admit, is not apparent on the surface; but what fundamental law, even in the physical universe, is so apparent? If thought, investigation, and experiment are necessary to the discovery of the principles which relate one material atom to another, even so are they imperative to the perception and understanding of the mode of action which relate one mental condition to another; and such modes, such laws, are known by the right-doer, by him who has acquired an understanding mind by the practice of true actions.

We reap as we sow. Those things which come to us, though not by our own choosing, are by our causing. The drunkard did not choose the delirium tremens or insanity which overtook him, but he caused it by his own deeds. In this case the law is plain to all minds, but where it is not so plain, it is nonetheless true. Within ourselves is the deep-seated cause of all our sufferings, the spring of all our joys. Alter the inner world of thoughts, and the other world of events will cease to bring you sorrow; make the heart pure, and to you all things will be pure, all occurrences happy and in true order.

"Within yourselves deliverance must be sought,
Each man his prison makes.
Each hath such lordship as the loftiest ones;

Nay, for with Powers above, around, below,
As with all flesh and whatsoever lives,
Act maketh joy or woe."

Our life is good or bad, enslaved or free, according to its causation in our thoughts, for out of these thoughts spring all our deeds, and from these deeds come equitable results. We cannot seize good results violently, like a thief, and claim and enjoy them, but we can bring them to pass by setting in motion the causes within ourselves.

Men strive for money, sigh for happiness, and would gladly possess wisdom, yet fail to secure these things, while they see others to whom these blessings appear to come unbidden. The reason is that they have generated causes which prevent the fulfilment of their wishes and efforts.

Each life is a perfectly woven network of causes and effects, of efforts (or lack of efforts) and results, and good results can only be reached by initiating good efforts, good causes. The doer of true actions, who pursues sound methods, grounded on right principles will not need to strive and struggle for good results; they will be there as the effects of his righteous rule of life. He will reap the fruit of his own actions and the reaping will be in gladness and peace.

This truth of sowing and reaping in the moral sphere is a simple one, yet men are slow to understand and accept it. We have been told by a Wise One that "the children of darkness are wiser in their day than the children of light", and who would expect, in the material world, to reap and eat where he had not sown and planted? Or who would expect to reap wheat in the field where he had sown tares, and would fall to weeping and complaining if he did not? Yet this is just what men do in the spiritual field of mind and deed. They do evil, and expect to get from it good, and when the bitter harvesting comes in all its ripened fullness, they fall into despair, and bemoan the hardness and injustice of their lot, usually attributing it to the evil deeds of others, refusing even to admit the possibility of its cause being hidden in themselves, in their own thoughts and deeds. The children of light — those who are searching for the fundamental principles of right living, with a view to making themselves into wise and happy beings – must train themselves to observe this law of cause and effect in thought, word and deed, as implicitly and obediently as the gardener obeys the law of sowing and reaping. He does not even question the law; he recognises and obeys it. When the wisdom which he instinctively practices in his garden, is practiced by men in the garden of their minds – when the law of the sowing of deeds is so fully recognised that it can no longer be doubted or questioned – then it will be just as faithfully followed by the sowing of those actions which will bring about a reaping of happiness and well-being for all. As the children of matter obey the laws of matter, so let the children of spirit obey the laws of spirit, for the law of matter and the law of spirit are one; they are but two aspects of one thing; the out-working of one principle in opposite directions.

If we observe right principles, or causes, wrong effects cannot possibly accrue. If we pursue sound methods, no shoddy thread can find its way into the web of our life, no rotten brick enter into the building of our character to render it insecure; and if we do true actions, what but good results can come to pass; for to say that good causes can produce bad effects is to say that nettles can be reaped from a sowing of corn.

He who orders his life along the moral lines thus briefly enunciated, will attain to such a state of insight and equilibrium as to render him permanently happy and perennially glad; all his efforts will be seasonally planted; all the issues of his life will be good, and though he may not become a millionaire as indeed he will have no desire to become such – he will acquire the gift of peace, and true success will wait upon him as its commanding master.

The Shining Gateway

Table of Contents

Editor's Foreword. 104

The Shining Gateway of Meditation. 105

Temptation. 110

Regeneration. 115

Actions and Motives. 119

Morality and Religion. 123

Memory, Repetition, and Habit. 125

Words and Wisdom. 129

Truth Made Manifest. 132

Spiritual Humility. 134

Spiritual Strength. 137

Editor's Foreword

Students of the works of James Allen all over the world will welcome with joy another book from his able pen. In this work we find the Prophet of Meditation in one of his deepest and yet most lucid expositions. How wonderfully he deals with fundamental principles! Here the reader will find no vague statement of generalities, for the writer enters with tender reverence into every detail of human experience. It is as though he came back to The Shining Gate, and, standing there, he reviewed all the way up which his own feet have travelled, passing over no temptation that is common to man; knowing that the obstacles that barred his ascending pathway, or the clouds that at times obscured his vision, are the common experiences of all those who have set their faces towards the heights of Blessed Vision. As we read his words now, he seems to stand and beckon to us, saying, "Come on, my fellow Pilgrims; it is straight ahead to the Shining Gateway; I have blazed the track for you." In sending forth this, another posthumous volume from his pen, we have no doubt but that it will help many and many an aspiring soul up to the heights, until at last they too stand within The shining Gateway.

Lily L. Allen

Behold the Shining Gateway
He who attaineth unto Purity
The faultless Parthenon of Truth doth use
Awake! Disperse the dreams of self and sin?
Behold the Shining Gateway! Enter in!

The Shining Gateway of Meditation

Be watchful, fearless, faithful, patient, pure:
By earnest meditation sound the depths
Profound of life, and scale the heights sublime
Of Love and Wisdom. He who does not find
The Way of Meditation cannot reach
Emancipation and enlightenment.

The unregenerate man is subject to these three things —
Desire, Passion, Sorrow. He lives habitually in these conditions, and neither
questions nor examines them. He regards them as his life itself, and cannot
conceive of any life apart from them. To-day he desires, to-morrow he
indulges his passions, and the third day he grieves; by these three things
(which are always found together) he is impelled, and does not know why he
is so impelled; the inner forces of desire and passion arise, almost automatically, within him, and he gratifies their demands Sans question; led on blindly
by his blind desires, he falls, periodically, into the ditches of remorse and
sorrow. His condition is not merely unintelligible to him, it is unperceived: for
so immersed is he in the desire (or self) consciousness that he cannot step
outside of it, as it were, to examine it.

To such a man the idea of rising above desire and suffering into a new life
where such things do not obtain seems ridiculous. He associates all life with
the pleasurable gratification of desire, and so, by the law of reaction, he also
lives in the misery of afflictions, fluctuating ceaselessly between pleasure and
pain.

When reflection dawns in the mind, there arises a sense (dim and
uncertain at first) of a calmer, wiser, and loftier life; and as the stages of
introspection and self-analysis are reached, this sense increases in clearness
and intensity, so that by the time the first three stages are fully completed, a
conviction of the reality of such a life and of the possibility of attaining it is
firmly fixed in the mind.

Such conviction, which consists of a steadfast belief in the supremacy of purity and goodness over desire and passion, is called faith. Such faith is the stay, support and comfort of the man who, while yet in the darkness, is searching earnestly for the Light which breaks upon him for the first time in all its dazzling splendour and ineffable majesty when he enters the Shining Gateway of Meditation. Without such faith he could not stand for a single day against the trials, failures, and difficulties which beset him continually, much less could be courageously fight and overcome them, and his final conquest and salvation would be impossible.

Upon entering the stage of meditation, faith gradually ripens into knowledge, and the new regenerate life begins to be realised in its quiet wisdom, calm beauty, and ordered strength, and day by day its joy and splendour increase.

The final conquest over sin is now assured. Lust, hatred, anger, covetousness, pride and vanity, desire for pleasure, wealth, and fame, worldly honour and power —all these have become dead things, shortly to pass away for ever; there is no more life nor happiness in them; they have no part in the life of the regenerate one, who knows that he can never again go back to them, for now the "Old man" of self and sin is dead, and the "new man" of Love and Purity is born within him. He has become (or becomes, as the process of meditation ripens and bears fruit) a new being, one in whom Purity, Love, Wisdom, and Peacefulness are the ruling qualities, and wherein strifes, envies, suspicions, hatreds, and jealousies cannot find lodgment. "Old things have passed away, and, behold, all things have become new"; men and things are seen in a different light, and a new universe is unveiled; there is no confusion; as out of the inner chaos of conflicting desires, passions, and sufferings the new being arises, there arises in the outer world of apparently irreconcilable conditions a new Cosmos, ordered, sequential, harmonious, ineffably glorious, faultless in equity.

Meditation is a process both of Purification and Adjustment. Aspiration is the purifying element, and the harmonising power resides in the intellectual train of thought involved.

When the stage of meditation is reached and entered upon, two distinct processes of spiritual transmutation is reached and entered upon, two distinct processes of spiritual transmutation begin to take place, namely:

1.   Transmutation of passion.
2.   Transmutation of affliction.

The two conditions proceed simultaneously, as they are interdependent, and act and react one upon the other. Passion and affliction, or sin and suffering, are two aspects of one thing, namely, the Self in man, that self which is the source of all the troubles which afflict mankind. They represent Power, but power wrongly used. Passion is a lower manifestation of a divine energy which possesses a higher use and application. Affliction is the limitation and negation of that energy, and is therefore a means of restoring harmony. It says, in effect to the self-bound man, 'Thus far shalt thou go and no farther.' The man of meditation transfers the passional energy from the realm of evil (Self-following) to the realm, of good (self-overcoming). To-day he reflects, tomorrow he overcomes his passions, and the third day he rejoices. The mind is drawn from its downward tendency, and is directed upwards. The base metal of error is transmuted into the pure gold of Truth. Lust, hatred, and selfishness disappear; and purity, love, and goodwill take their place. As the stage proceeds, the mind becomes more and more firmly fixed in the higher manifestations, and it becomes increasingly difficult for it to think and act in the lower; and just in the measure that the mind is freed from the lower, violent, and inharmonious activities, just so much is passion transmuted into power, and affliction into bliss.

This means that there is no such thing as affliction to the sinless man. When sin is put away, affliction disappears.

Selfhood is the source of suffering; Truth is the source of bliss.

When the unregenerate man is abused, or slandered, misunderstood, or persecuted, it causes him intense suffering; but when these things are brought to bear on the regenerate man, there arises in him the rapture of heavenly bliss. None but he who has put away the great enemy, self, under his feet can fully enter into and understand the saying.:

Blessed are ye, when men shall revile you, and persecute you, and shall say all manner of evil against you falsely, for my sake. Rejoice, and be exceeding glad.

And why does the righteous (regenerate) man rejoice under those conditions which cause such misery to the unrighteous (unregenerate) man? It is because, having overcome the evil in himself, he ceases to see evil without. To the good man all things are good, and he utilises everything for the good of the world. To him persecution is not an evil, it is a good. Having acquired insight, knowledge, and power, he, by meeting that persecution in a loving spirit, helps and uplifts his persecutors, and accelerates their spiritual progress, though they themselves know it not at the time. Thus he is filled with unspeakable bliss because he has conquered the forces of evil; because, instead of succumbing to those forces, he has learned how to use and direct them for the good and gain of mankind. He is blessed because he is at one with all men, because he is reconciled to the universe, and has brought himself into harmony with the Cosmic Order.

The following symbol will perhaps help the mind of the reader to more readily grasp what has been explained.

LOVE, LIGHT, AND LIFE

KNOWLEDGE

A

S

P

I

R

A

T

I

O

N

PASSION AFFLICTION

D

E

S

I

R

E

IGNORANCE

LUST, DARKNESS AND DEATH

There is at first the underworld of lust, darkness, and death which is associated with ignorance; rooted in this is the foot of the cross—desire; in the body of the cross, desire branches out into two arms— the right (active or positive) are, passion, being equalised and balanced by the left (passive or negative) arm of affliction; uniting these, and rising out of them at the head of the cross, is aspiration; here, wounded and bleeding, rests the thorn-crowned head, of humanity; at the end of this, and right at the summit of the cross, is knowledge, which, while being at the apex of the self-life, is the base of the Truth-life; and above rises the heavenly world of Love, Light, and Life.

In this supremely beautiful world the regenerate man lives, even while living on this earth. He has reached Nirvana, the Kingdom of Heaven. He has taken up his cross, and there is no more sin and sufferings desire and passion and affliction are passed away. Harmony is restored, and all is bliss and peace.

The cross is the symbol of pain. Desire is painful, passion is painful, affliction is painful, and. aspiration is painful; this is why these things are symbolised by a cross which has two pairs of conflicting poles. Affliction is the harmonising and purifying element in passion; aspiration is the harmonising and purifying element in desire. Where the one is, the other must be also. Take away the one, and the other disappears. Suffering, or affliction, is necessary to counteract passion; aspiration, or prayer, is necessary to purge away desire; but for the regenerate man all these things are ended; he has-risen into a new life and a new order of things—the consciousness of purity; lacking nothing and being at one with all things, he does not need to pray for anything; redeemed and reconciled, contented and ill peace, he finds nothing in the universe to hate or fear, and his is both the duty and the power to work without ceasing for the present good and the ultimate salvation of mankind.

Temptation

I know that sorrow follows passion; know
That grief and emptiness and heartache wait
Upon all earthly joys; so am I sad;
Yet Truth must be, and being, can be found;
And though I am in sorrow, this I know—
I shall be glad when I have found the Truth.

The only external tempters of man are The objects of Sensation. These, however, are powerless in themselves until they are reflected in his mind as desirable objects to possess. His only enemy, therefore, is his coveting of the objects of sensation. By ceasing to covet objects of sensation, temptation and the painful fighting against impure desires pass away. This ceasing to covet objects of sensation is called the relinquishing of desire; it is the renunciation of the inner defilement, by which a man ceases to be the slave of outward things, and becomes their master.

Temptation is a growth, a process more or less slow, the duration of which can be measured by the sage who has gained accurate knowledge of the nature of his thoughts and acts and the laws governing them, by virtue of having subjected himself to a long course of training in mental discipline and self-control. It has its five stages, which can be clearly defined, and their development traced with precision. But the man who is still immersed in temptation has, as yet, little or no knowledge of the nature of his thoughts and acts and the laws governing them. He has lived so long in outward things—in the objects of sensation—and has given so little time to introspection and the cleansing of his heart, that he lives in almost total ignorance of the real nature of his thoughts and acts which he thinks and commits every day. To him, temptation seems to be instantaneous, and his powerlessness to combat the sudden and, apparently, unaccountable on slaught, causes him to regard it as a mystery, and mystery being the mother of superstition, he may and usually does fall back upon some speculative belief to account for his trouble, such as the belief in an invisible Evil Being, or power, outside himself who suddenly, and without warning, attacks and torments him. Such a superstition renders him more powerless still, for he has sufficient knowledge to understand that he cannot hope to successfully cope with a being more powerful than himself, and of whose whereabouts and tactics he is altogether unacquainted; and so he introduces other beliefs and superstitions which his dilemma seems to necessitate, until at last; in addition to all his sins and sufferings, he becomes burdened with a mass of supernatural beliefs which engross his attention, and take him farther and farther away from the real cause of his difficulty. Meantime he continues to be tempted and to fall, and must do so until by self-subjugation and self-purification he has acquired the ability to trace the relation between cause and effect in his spiritual nature, when, with purified and enlightened vision, he will see that the moment of temptation is but the fulfilment of those impure desires which he secretly harbours in his own heart. And, later, with a still purer heart, and when he has gained sufficient control over his wandering thoughts to be able to analyse and understand them, he will see that the actual moment of temptation itself has its inception, its growth, and its fruition.

What, then, are the stages in temptation? And how is the process of temptation born in the mind? How does it grow and bear its bitter fruit? The stages are five, and are as follows .

1. PERCEPTION
2. COGITATION
3. CONCEPTION
4. ATTRACTION
and
5. DESIRE

The first stage is that in which objects of sensation are perceived as objects. This is pure perception, and is without sin or defilement. The second stage is that in which objects of sensation are considered as objects of personal pleasure. This is a brooding of the mind upon objects, with an undefined groping for pleasurable sensation, and is the beginning of defilement and sin. In the third stage objects of sensation are conceived as objects of pleasure. In this stage the objects are associated with certain pleasurable sensations, and these sensations are conceived and called up vividly in the mind. In the fourth stage objects of sensation are perceived as objects of pleasure. At this stage the pleasure as connected with the object is distinctly defined, yet there is a confusion of pleasure and object, so that the two appear as one, and a wish to possess the object arises in the mind; there is also a going out of the mind towards the object. The fifth and last stage is an intense desire, a coveting and lusting to possess the object in order to experience the pleasure and gratification which it will afford. With every repetition, in the mind, of the first four stages, this desire is added to, as fuel is added to fire, and it increases in intensity and ardour until at last the whole being is aflame with a burning passion which is blind to everything but its own immediate pleasure and gratification. And when this painful fruition of thought is reached, a man is said to be tempted. There is a still further stage of Action, which is merely the doing of the thing desired, the outworking of the sin already committed in the mind. From desire to action is but a short step.

The following table will better enable the mind of the reader to grasp the process and principle involved.

Inaction — Holiness; Rest.

1. Perception. Objects of Sensation Perceived as such.

2. Cogitation.   Objects of Sensation Considered as a source of pleasure.

3. Conception. Objects of Sensation Conceived as affording pleasure.

4. Attraction. Objects of Sensation Perceived as pleasurable in possession.

5.   Desire. Objects of Sensation Coveted as such: i.e., desired for personal delight and pleasure.

Action—Sin; Unrest.

Every time a man is tempted, he passes, from inaction, though all the five stages in succession, and his fall is a passing on into Action. The process varies greatly in duration according to the nature of the temptation and the character of the tempted; but after much yielding and many falls, the mind becomes so familiar with the transition that it passes through all the stages with such rapidity as to make the temptation appear as an instantaneous, indivisible experience.

The sage, however, never loses sight of the duration of time occupied in the process of temptation, but watches its growth and transition; and just as the scientist can measure the time occupied in the transition of sensation from the brain to the bodily extremities, or from the extremities to the brain, which, ordinarily, appears not to occupy duration, so the sage measures (though by a different method) the passage from pure perception to inflamed desire in a sudden experience of temptation.

This knowledge of the nature of temptation destroys its power, or rather its apparent power, for power exists in holiness only. Ignorance is at the root of all sin, and it fades away when knowledge is admitted into the mind. Just as darkness and the effects of darkness disappear when light is introduced, so sin and its effects are dispersed when knowledge of one's spiritual nature is acquired and embraced.

How, then, does the sage avoid sin and remain in peace? Knowing the nature of sinful acts—how they are the result of temptation; knowing also the nature of temptation—how it is the end—and fruition of a particular train of thought, he cuts off that train of thought at its commencement, not allowing his mind to go out into the world of sensation, which is the world of pain and sorrow. He stands over his mind,, eternally vigilant, and does not allow his thoughts to pass beyond the safe gates of pure perception. To him "all things are pure" because his mind is pure—He sees all objects, whether material or mental, as they are, and not as the pleasure-seeker sees them —as objects of personal enjoyment; nor as the tempted one sees them—as sources of evil and pain. His normal sphere, however, is that of Inaction, which is perfect holiness and rest. This is a position of entire indifference to considerations of pleasure and pain, regarding all things from the standpoint of right, and not from that of enjoyment. Is, then, the sage, the sinless one, deprived of all enjoyment? Is his life a dead monotony of inaction—inertia? Truly, he is delivered from all those sensory excitement which the world calls "pleasure", but which conceals, as a mask, the drawn features of pain; and, being released from the bondage of cravings and pleasures, he lives without ceasing in the divine, abidingjoy which the pleasure-seeker and the wanderer in sin can neither know nor understand; but inaction in this particular means inaction as regards sin; inaction in the lower animal activities which, being cut off, their energy is transferred to the higher intellectual and moral activities, releasing their power, and giving them untrammelled scope and freedom.

Thus the sage avoids sin by extracting its root within himself, not allowing it to grow into attraction, to blossom into desire, and to bear the bitter fruits of sinful actions. The unwise man, however, allows the thought of pleasure to take root in his mind, where its growth, evokes sensations which are pleasant to him, and on these sensations he dwells with enjoyment, thinking in his heart, "So long as I do not commit the sinful act, I am free from sin." He does not know that his thoughts are causes the effects of which are actions, and that there is no escape from sinful acts for him who dwells in sinful thoughts. And so the process develops in his mind and blossoms into desire, and in the final moment of temptation (which is but the moment of opportunity brought into prominence by that desire), with the coveted object at his unreserved command, the fall of the man into sinful action is swift and certain.

Regeneration

Submit to naught but nobleness; rejoice
Like a strong athlete straining for the prize,
When thy full strength is tried; be not the slave
Of lusts and cravings and indulgences,
Of disappointments, miseries, and griefs,
Fears, doubts, and lamentations, but control
Thyself with calmness; master, that in thee
Which masters others, and which heretofore
Has mastered thee; let not thy passions rule,
But rule thy passions; subjugate thyself Till
passion is transmuted into peace,
And wisdom crown thee; so shalt thou attain
And, by attaining, know.

Having considered and examined the nature of temptation in its five interdependent stages, let us now turn to the process of regeneration, and also consider its nature, so that the reader who has already received some measure of enlightenment may be still further guided in his strenuous climbing towards the Perfect Life.

The five stages in regeneration (already enumerated) are:—1. Reflection; 2. Introspection; 3. Self-analysis; 4. Meditation; and 5. Pure Perception.

The first stage in a pure and true life is that of thoughtfulness. The thoughtless cannot enter the right way in life. Only the reflective mind can acquire wisdom. When a man, ceasing to go after enjoyment, brings himself to a standstill in order to examine his position, and to reflect upon the condition of the world and the meaning of life, then he has entered upon the first stage of regeneration. When a man begins to think seriously, and with a deep and noble purpose in view, he has stepped out of the broad way where the thoughtless and the frivolous clutch at the bubbles of pleasure, and has entered the narrow way where the thoughtful and the wise comprehend eternal verities. Such a man's liberation from sin and suffering is already assured; for though he is, as yet, surrounded by much uncertainty, he is already realising a foretaste of the peace which awaits him; his passions, though still strong, are quieter; his mind is calmer and clearer; his intercourse with others is purer and graver; and in his moments of deepest thought he sees, as in a vision, the strength and calmness and wisdom which he knows will one day be his well-earned possessions.

Thus he passes on to the second stage.

Reflecting day by day, with ever-increasing earnestness upon life in all its phases, he comes to perceive the passions and desires in which men are involved, and realises the sorrows which are connected with their strangely ephemeral existence. He sees the burning fevers of lusts and ambitions and cravings for pleasure, and the chilling agues of anxieties and fears, and the uncertainty of slowly approaching death, and he aspires to know the meaning of it all; is eager to find the source and cause of that seems so sorrowful and inexplicable. Recognising himself as a unit in humanity, as one involved in like passions and sorrows with all other men, he vaguely understands that somehow the secret of all life is inevitably bound up with the neophyte, with mind purified, calmed, and his own existence, and so, unsatisfied with the surface theories which are based on observation only, and which still leave him subject to passions and sorrows, and the prey of anxieties and fears, he turns his thoughts inwardly upon his own mind, thinking, perchance, that the wished for revelation of wisdom and peace awaits him there. Thus he becomes introspective, and so he passes on to the third stage.

When the introspective habit is fully ripened and acquired, there is called up in the mind a subtle process of inductive thought by the aid of which the innermost recesses of the man's nature, and, therefore, of all humanity, begin to unveil themselves, and yield up their secrets to the penetrating insight of the patient searcher who, unravelling now the tangled threads of thought, and tracing out the warp and woof of the web of life as it is woven in the mental processes and by the swift-flying shuttle of thought, begins, for the first time, to somewhat clearly comprehend the inner causes of human deeds and the meaning and purpose of existence. As this process of thought is proceeded with, the desires and passions are purified away from the mind; the calmness necessary to a right perception of Truth is acquired; and gradually the fixed principles of things are presented to the comprehension and the eternal laws of life are coherently grasped by the understanding.

And now, quietly, and almost as imperceptibly as the soft light of dawn stealing upon the sleeping world, controlled, passes into the fourth stage, and opens his long-sleeping eyes upon the rising light of Truth. He becomes habitually meditative, and in meditation he finds the master-key which unlocks the Door of Knowledge. It is at this advanced stage in the process of regeneration that the sinner becomes the saint, and the pupil is transformed into the master; for here the process of transmutation, hitherto slow and painful, is greatly accelerated, so that the spiritual forces formerly spent in pleasures, gratifications, passions, and afflictions are now conserved, controlled, and turned into channels of productive and reproductive thought, and so wisdom is born in the mind, and bliss, and peace.

As skill and power are acquired in meditation, the fifth and last stage is reached, where the perfect insight of the seer and the sage is evolved, so that the facts of life are grasped, and the laws and principles of things stand revealed. Here the man is altogether regenerated, is purified and perfected; all human passions are conquered, and human sorrows transcended. Here things are seen as they are; all the intricacies of life stand out naked in the light of Truth, and there is no more doubt and perplexity, no more sin and anguish; for he whose pure and enlightened eyes perceive the hidden causes and effects which operate infallibly in human life—he who knows how the bitter fruits of passion ripen, and where the dark waters of sorrow spring—he it is who no more sins and no more sorrows. Lo! he has come to peace.

The five stages so passed through may be thus presented:
Ignorance—Sin; Suffering.
1. Reflection. Deep and earnest thought on the nature and meaning of life.
2. Introspection. Looking inwardly, for the causes and effects which operate in life.
3. Self-analysis. Searching the springs of thought and purifying the motives in order to find the truth of life.
4. Meditation. Pure and discriminative thought on the facts and principles of life.
5. Pure Perception. Insight. Direct knowledge of the laws of life.
Enlightenment—Purity; Peace.

The whole process of regeneration may be likened to the growth of a plant. At first the small seed of reflection is cast into the dark soil of ignorance; then the little rootlets come forth and grope about for light and sustenance (introspection); next the strenuous self-examination is as the plant reaching upwards toward the light; and then the development of the bud and opening flower of meditation, ending at last in that pure and wise insight which is the spiritual glory of the sage, the perfect flower of enlightenment.

Thus beginning in sin and suffering, and passing through thoughtfulness, self-searching, self-purification, meditation, and insight, the seeker after the pure life and the divine wisdom reaches at last the undented habitation of a spotless life, and so passes beyond the dark halls of suffering, knowing the perfect Law.

Actions and Motives

Obey the Right,
And wrong shall ne'er again assail thy peace,
Nor error hurt thee more: attune thy heart
To Purity, and thou shalt reach the
Place Where sorrow is not, and all evil ends.

It has been said that "the way to hell is paved with good intentions," and one frequently hears sin excused on the ground that it was done with a "good motive."

There are actions which are bad-in-themselves, and there are actions which are good-in-themselves, and good intentions cannot make the former good— selfish intentions cannot make the latter bad. Foremost among actions which are bad-in- themselves are those which are classified as "criminal" by all civilised communities. Thus murder, theft, adultery, libel, etc, are always bad, and it is not necessary to inquire into the motive which prompts them. Black and white remain black and white to all eternity, and are not altered by specious argumentations. A lie is eternally a lie, and no number of good intentions can turn it into a truth. If a man tell a lie with a good intention, he has none the less uttered a lie; if a man speak the truth with a selfish intention, he has none the less spoken the truth.

Beside those actions above mentioned, there are others which, while not classified by the law of the land as criminal, are yet recognised as wrong by nearly all intelligent people-actions pertaining to social and family life, and to our everyday relations with our fellowmen. Thus when a child wilfully violates its duty to its parents, the father does not stop to inquire into the motives of the child, but metes out the due correction, because the act of disobedience is wrong-in-itself.

The reader may here ask, "In being taught, then, to regard the motive, the condition of heart, as all important, and the act as secondary, have we been taught wrongly?" No, you have not. The motive is all important, for it determines the nature of the act, and here we must distinguish between intentions and motives. When people speak of good and bad motives, they nearly always mean good or bad intentions— that is, the action is done with a certain object, good or bad, in view. The motive is the deeply seated cause in the mind, the habitual condition of heart; the intention is the purpose in view. Thus an act may spring from an impure motive, yet be done with the best intention. It is possible for one to be involved in wrong motives, and yet at the same time to be so charged with good intentions as to be continually intruding himself on other people, and interfering in their business and their lives under the delusion that they "need his help."

Intentions are more or less superficial, and are largely matters of impulse, while motives are more deeply seated, and are concerned with a man's fixed moral condition. A man may do an action to-day with a good intention, and in a few weeks' time do the same action with a bad intention; but in both instances the motive underlying the action will be the same.

In reality a wrong act cannot spring from a right motive, although it may be guided by a good intention. A man who can resort, whether habitually or under stress of temptation, to murder, theft, lying or other actions known as bad, is in a dark, confused condition of mind, and is not capable of acting from right motives. Such acts can only spring from an impure source; and this is why the Great Teachers rarely refer to motives , but always refer to actions. In their precepts they tell us what actions are bad and what are good, without any reference to motive, for the bad and good acts-in-themselves are the fruits of bad and good motives. "By their fruits you shall know them."

In being exhorted to "judge not," we are not taught to persuade ourselves that grapes are figs and figs grapes, but must employ our judgment in clearly distinguishing between the two; so in like manner must we distinguish with unmistakable clearness between bad actions and good actions, so as to avoid the former and embrace the latter; for only in this way can one purify his heart and render himself capable of acting from right motives. A clear perception of what is bad or good, both in ourselves and others, is not false judgment, it is wisdom. It is only when one harbours groundless suspicion about others, and reads into their actions bad and selfish intentions, that he falls into that judging against which we are warned, and which is so pernicious.

There is no need to doubt the good intentions of those about us, while, at the same time, being fully alive to a knowledge of those bad actions which were better left undone, and those good actions which were better done; taking care not to do the former, and to do the latter ourselves, thus teaching by our lives instead of accusing and condemning others. Numberless wrong actions are committed every day with good intentions; and this is why so many good purposes are frustrated and end in disappointment, because the underlying motive is impure, and the good fruit which is sought does not appear; the act is out of harmony with the good intent; the means are not adapted to the end. Bad actions, bring forth bitter fruit; good actions bring forth sweet fruit.

The law runs, "Thou shalt not kill; thou shalt not steal; thou shalt not commit adultery"; not "Thou shalt not kill, steal or commit adultery with a bad motive."

Wrong actions are always accompanied with self-delusion, and the chief form which such self-delusion assumes is that of self-justification. If a man flatter himself that he can commit a sinful act, and yet be free from sin because he is prompted by a "pure motive," no limit can be set to the evil which he may commit.

It will be found that bad actions, in the majority of instances, arc accompanied with good intentions. The object of the slanderer generally is to protect his fellow-men from one another. Troubled with foolish suspicions, or smarting under the thought of injury, he warns men against each other, speaking only of their bad qualities, and, in his eagerness, distorting the truth. His intention is good, namely, to protect his neighbours; but his motive is bad, namely, hatred of those whom he slanders. Such a man's good intention is frustrated by his bad action, and he at last only succeeds in separating himself from all truth-loving people.

The sore of a bad action is not cured by plastering it over with good intentions, nor is the cause of the defilement removed from the heart.

Men who are involved in bad actions cannot work from pure motives. An issue of foul water always proceeds from an impure source; and an issue of impure actions proceeds from a heart that is defiled.

It greatly simplifies life, and solves all complex problems of conduct, when certain actions are recognised as eternally bad, and others as eternally good, and the bad are for ever abandoned, and final refuge is taken in the good.

The wise and good perform good actions; and motive, act, and intention being harmoniously adjusted, their lives are powerful for good, and free from disappointment, and the good fruit of their efforts appears in due season. They do not need to defend their actions by subtle and specious arguments, not to enter into interminable metaphysical speculations concerning motives; but are content to act and to leave their actions to bear their own fruit.

Let us not try to persuade ourselves that our good intentions will wipe out the results of our bad actions; but let us resort to the practice of good actions; for only in this way can we acquire goodness; only thus can the life be established on fixed principles, and the mind be rendered capable of comprehending, and working from, pure motives.

Morality and Religion

The Wise Man
By adding thought to thought and deed to deed
In ways of good, buildeth his character.
Little by little he accomplishes
His noble ends; in quiet patience works
Diligently.

Daily he builds into his heart and mind
Pure thoughts, high aspirations, selfless deeds.
Until at last the edifice of Truth
Is finished, and behold! there rises and appears
The Temple of Perfection.

There is no surer indication of confusion and decadence in spiritual matters than the severance of morality from religion. "He is a highly moral man, but he is not religious"; "He is exceptionally good and virtuous, but is not at all spiritual," are common expressions on the lips of large numbers of people who thus regard religion as something quite distinct from goodness, purity, and right-living.

If religion be regarded merely and only as worship combined with adherence to a particular form of faith, then it would be correct to say, "He is a very good man, but is not religious," in some instances, just as it would be equally correct to say, "He is an immoral man, but is very religious," in other instances, for murderers, thieves, and other evil-doers are sometimes devout worshippers and zealous adherents to a creed.

Such a narrowing down of religion, however, would' render much of the Sermon on the Mount superfluous, from a religious point of view, and would lead to the confounding of the means of religion with its end, the idolising of the letter of religion to the exclusion of the spirit; and this is what actually occurs when morality is severed from religion, and is regarded as something alien and distinct from it.

Religion, however, has a broader significance than this, and the most obscure creed embodies in its ritual some longing human cry for that goodness, that virtue, that morality, which many, with thoughtless judgement, divorce from religion. And is not a life of moral excellence, of good and noble character, of pure-heartedness, the very end and object of religion? Is it not the substance and spirit, of which worship and adherence to a form of faith are but the shadow and letter?

In religion, as in other things, there are the means and the end, the methods and the attainment. Worship, beliefs about God, adherence to creeds—these are some of the means; goodness, virtue, morality—these are the end. The methods are many and Various, and they are embodied in countless forms of faith; but the end is one—it is moral grandeur!

Thus the moral man, far from being irreligious because he. may not openly profess some form of worship, possesses the substance of religion, diffuses its spirit, has attained its end; and when the sweet Kernel of religion is found and enjoyed, the shell, protective and necessary in its place, has served its purpose, and may be dispensed with.

Let not this, however, be misunderstood. The "moral" man does not refer to one who has only the outward form of morality, appearing moral in the eyes of the world, but keeping his vices secret; nor does it refer to him whose morality extends only to legal limits; nor to those who are proud of their morality—for pride is the reverse of moral—but to those who delight in purity, who are gracious, gentle, unselfish, and thoughtful, who, being good at heart, pour forth the fragrance of pure thoughts and good deeds. By the "moral" is meant the good, the pure, the noble, and the true-hearted.

A man may call himself Christian, Jew, Buddhist, Mohammedan, Hindu—or by any other name—and be immoral; but if one is pure-hearted, if he is true and noble and beautiful in character—in a word, if he is moral—then he is an inhabitant of the "Holy City" in which, there is "no temple"; he is, by example and influence, a regenerator of mankind; he is one of the company of the Children of Light.

Memory, Repetition, and Habit

I shall gain.
By purity and strong self-mastery,
The awakened vision that doth set men free
From painful slumber and the night of grief.

When a particular combination of words has been repeated a number of times, it is said to have been committed to memory—that is, it can then be repeated without visual reference to the words themselves, and without pause or effort; indeed, the words have then a tendency to repeat themselves in the mind, and sometimes people are troubled with the ringing of a refrain, or the repetition of a sentence in the mind, which they find it very difficult to get rid of and forget.

There is a sense in which the whole of life is a process of committing to memory. At first there is act, from act springs experience, from experience arises recollection, from recollection repetition, and from repetition is formed habit; hence proceeds impulse, faculty, character, individualised existence.

Life is a repetition of the same things over again. There is very little difference between the days and years in the life of a man; one is almost entirely a repetition of the other. Every being is an accumulation of experiences gathered, learnt, and woven into the life by a ceaseless series of repetitions extending over an incalculable number of lives which thread their way through eons of time.

The life of a man, from the germ-cell to maturity, is a repetition, in synthesis, of the entire process of evolution. There is a cosmic memory at the root of all growth and progress, which is an informing and sustaining principle in the process of evolution.

The sensuous memory of man is fickle and ephemeral, but the supersensuous memory which is inherent in all matter, building up forms and faculty is infallible in its reproduction of experiences.

Life is ceaseless reiteration. Nature ever travels over old and familiar ground. Man is daily repeating that which he has learnt though: the schools of experience in which the lessons were acquired may be long forgotten; but the acquired habit is not forgotten; it is carried forward and continues to act. The unconscious and automatic ease which marks the play of faculty is not the ready-made mechanism of an arbitrary creator; it is skill acquired by practice; it is the consummation of millions of repetitions of. the same thought and act.

Thoughts and deeds long persisted in become at last spontaneous impulses.

It is a profound truth that "there is nothing new under the sun." It is possible and highly probable that, in the round of eternity, even all our modern inventions and mechanical marvels have been produced innumerable times on this or other worlds. In this world, new combinations of matter appear from time to time, but are they new in the universe? Who dare say that, in the mind which overarches eternity, the cosmic memory is not reproducing things long since fashioned out of itself?

Nothing can be added to, or taken from, the universe. Its matter can neither be increased nor decreased. Chemical combinations of matter vary, but matter itself cannot vary. Life likewise does not change. In the forms of life there is continuous flux, but in the principle of life there is no increase or diminution. Forms come forth only to retreat and disappear; but that which disappears is not lost; the memory of it is retained, and it continues to be repeated. Eternal disintegration is balanced by eternal restitution.

The mind of man is not separate from the Eternal Mind; in its daily repetitions is indelibly written the record of all its past. Character is an accumulation of deeds. Each man is the last reckoning in the long sum of evolution, and there is no falsification of the account. The mind continues to automatically perform the habit which encloses a million repetitions of the same deed. Compared with this ineffaceable, unconscious memory, the memory of three score years and ten is as a fading vapour to an Egyptian Pyramid. The tendencies, impulses, and habits of which a man is a victim are the repetitions of his accumulated deeds. They enfold the destiny which he has wrought. The grace, goodness, and genius which a man exhibits without conscious effort are the fruits of the accumulated labours of his mind. He repeats with ease that which was learned by painful labour. The wise man sees a reflection of himself in the fate which overtakes him.

Life flows in channels. Every man is in a rut. Men tell their fellows to "get out of their ruts," but they themselves are in ruts of another kind. The flow of law, of nature, cannot be avoided, but it can be utilised. We cannot avoid ruts, but we can avoid bad ones; we can follow along good ones.

In their training and education, the children of to-day are strictly confined to ways which are worn by the feet of a thousand generations. In his fixed habits and characteristics, the man of to-day is reviving the actions of a thousand lives.

It is true that men are bound; but it is equally true that they can unbind. The law by which a man becomes the sorrowful victim of his own wrong deeds is a blessed, and not a cursed, law; for by the same law he can become the instrument of all that is good. Habits chain a man, but he himself forged the links. He whose inner eye has opened to perceive the law does not complain. The bondage of evil is a heavy slavery, but the bondage of good is a blessed service.

The will of man is powerless to alter the law of life, but it is powerful to obey it. The Great Law makes for good; it puts a heavy penalty on evil. Man can break his chains, and shake himself free; and when he enters earnestly upon the work of self-liberation, all the universe will be with him in his labour. Repetition and habit he cannot avoid, but he can set going repetitions that are harmonious, he can form habits that will crystallise into pure and noble characteristics.

In the self-built archives of the mind are stored away the entire records of man's evolution. Man is an epitomised history of the world. In his outbursts of rage we hear again the roar of the lion in the forest; in his selfish schemings to secure his coveted ends we see the tiger stalking its prey; his lusts, revenges, hatreds, and fears are the instinct born of primeval experiences. The universe does not forget; life remembers and restores.

Between the sensuous and the supersensuous worlds is the Lethean stream, the river of forgetfulness. Only he who has passed into the supersensuous world—the world of pure goodness—remembers with the Memory of Life which transcends a million deaths. Only he whose will obeys the Universal Will, whose heart is, in harmony with the Cosmic Order, receives the vision which pierces through the vale of time and matter, and sees the before and the beyond.

Man quickly forgets, and it is well that he forgets; the universe remembers and records. The repetition of an evil deed is its own retribution; the repetition of a good deed is its own reward. The deepest punishment of evil is evil; the highest reward of good is good. When a deed is done, it is not ended; it is but begun; it remains with the doer—to curse him, if evil; to bless him, if good. Deeds accumulate by repetition, and they remain as character, and in character is both curse and blessing.

Suffering inheres in the discordant repetition of evil; bliss inheres in the rhythmic repetitions of good. Seeing that we cannot escape the law of repetition, let us choose to do those things which are good; and as one establishes habits of purity, the divine memory will be awakened within him.

Words and Wisdom

I would find
Where Wisdom is, where Peace abides, where Truth,
Majestic, changeless, and eternal, stands
Untouched by the illusions of the world;
For surely there is Knowledge, Truth, and Peace
For him who seeks.

Thoughts, words, acts—these combine to make up the entire life of every individual. Words and acts are thoughts expressed. We think in words. In the process of thinking, words are stored up in the consciousness, where they await expression and use as occasion may call them forth.

Words fit the mind which received them; they are the tally of the intellect which uses them. The meaner the mind, the more meagre is the vocabulary. A limited and a capacious intellect alike expresses itself through a limited and an extensive use of words. A great mind expresses itself by the vehicle of flowing and noble language.

Words stand for conceptions. Conceptions are embodied in words. At the moment that a conception is formed in the mind, its corresponding word arises in the thought. Conceptions and words cannot be hidden away indefinitely. Sooner or later they will come forth into the outer world of expression. The matter of the universe is in ceaseless circulation. Its hidden things are continuously coming forth into open and visible life. Likewise the mental operations of men are ever in active circulation, and their hidden thoughts are daily expressing themselves in words and acts. The words and actions of every man are determined by the thoughts in which he habitually dwells.

Speech is audible thought. A man reveals him. self through his speech. Whether he is pure or impure, foolish or vice, he makes his inner condition known through his speech. The foolish man is known by the way in which he talks; the wise man is known by the purity, gravity, and excellence of his speech. "He who would gain a knowledge of men." says Confucius, "must first learn to understand the meaning of words."

All wise men, saints, and great teachers have declared that the first step in wisdom is to control the tongue. The disciple of speech is a mental disciple. When a man controls his tongue, he controls his mind; when he purifies his speech, he purifies his mind. Speech and mind cannot be separated. They are two aspects of character.

A man may read Scripture, study religions, and practise mystical arts; but if he allows his tongue to run loosely, he will be as foolish at the end of all his labours as he was at the beginning.

A man may not read Scripture, nor study religions, nor practise ascetic arts; but if he controls his tongue, and studies how to speak wisely and well, he will become wise.

Wisdom is perceived in the words which are its expression. We speak of certain men—of Shakespeare for instance—as being wise. We never saw Shakespeare, and we know very little of his life; how, then, do we know he was wise? By his words only. Where there are wise words, we know there is a wise mind. A foolish man may, like a parrot, repeat wise words, but a wise man frames wise sentences; his wisdom is shown in originally expressed language.

Why do men speak of words as being bad or good, degrading or inspiring, low or lofty, weak or strong? Is it not because they, unconsciously recognise that words cannot be dissociated from thoughts? Why do pure-minded people avoid a man who habitually uses impure language? Is is not because they know that such words proceed from an unclean mind?

It is impossible for any being to give utterance to words which are not already lodged in his mind fit the form of thought. The impure mind cannot speak pure words; the pure mind cannot speak impure words. The ignorant cannot speak learnedly, nor the learned ignorantly. The foolish man cannot speak wisely, nor the wise foolishly.

Altered speech follows an altered mind. When a man turns from evil to good, his conversation becomes cleansed. As a man increases in wisdom, he watches, modifies, and perfects his speech.

If the foolish and the wise are known by their words, what, then, is the speech of folly, and what the language of wisdom?

A man is foolish:

If he talks aimlessly and incoherently. If he engages in impure conversations.
If he utters falsehood. If he speaks ill of the absent, and carries about evil
reports concerning others.
If he frames flattering words.
If he utters violent and abusive words.
If his speech is irreverent, and
his words are directed against the great and good.
If he speaks in praise of himself.

    A man is wise:
If he talks with purpose and intelligence.
If his conversation is chaste.
If he utters words of sincerity and truth.
If he speaks well of and in defence of, the absent.
If he speaks words of virtuous reproof.
If his speech is gentle and kindly.
If he talks reverently of the great and good.
If he speaks in praise of others.

We are all, now and always, justified and condemned by our words. The
law of Truth is not held in abeyance, and every day is judgement day. For
"every idle word" which one speaks he is at once "called to account" in an
immediate and certain loss of happiness and influence. By the words which
we habitually utter we publish to the universe the degree of our intelligence
and the standard of our morality, and receive back through them the
judgement of the world. The fool thinks he is harshly judged and badly
treated by others, not knowing that his real scourge is his own ungoverned
tongue.

To control the tongue, to discipline the speech, to strive for the use of
purer and gentler words—this is a very lowly thing, and one that is much
despised; but it cannot be neglected by him who eagerly aspires to walk the
way of wisdom.

Truth Made Manifest

Upon the lofty Summits of the Truth
Where clouds and darkness are not, and where rests
Eternal Splendour; there, abiding Joy
Awaits thy coming.
Be watchful, fearless, faithful, patient, pure:
By earnest meditation sound the depths
Profound of life, and scale the heights sublime
Of Love and Wisdom.

Truth is rendered visible through the media of deeds. It is something seen and not heard. Words do not contain the Truth; they only symbolise it. Good deeds are the only vessels which contain Truth.

It has been frequently said that being must precede doing. Being always does precede doing; but being; and doing cannot be arbitrarily separated. A man's deeds are the expression of himself. Acts are the language of Reality. If a man's inner being is allied to Truth, his deeds will speak it forth; if with error, his deeds will make manifest that error.

No man can hide what he is. He must necessarily act, and every time he acts he reveals himself.

In the light of Reality no man can deceive humanity or the universe; but he can deceive himself.

Deeds of purity, love, gentleness, patience, humility, compassion, and wisdom are Truth made manifest. These qualities cannot be contained between the covers of a book, but only the words which refer to them; they are Life.

Deeds of impurity, hatred, anger, pride, vanity, and folly are error making itself known. A man's deeds are the publication of himself to the world.

Truth cannot be comprehended through reading, but only by correcting and converting one's self. Precepts are aids to the acquirement of wisdom, but wisdom is acquired only by practice.

If a man would know what measure of Truth he possesses, he should ask himself, "What am I? What are my deeds?"

Men dispute about words, thinking that Truth is heard and read. Truth is neither heard nor read; it is seen.

Good deeds are the visible embodiments of Truth; they are messengers of Knowledge; angels of Wisdom; but the eye of error is dark, and cannot see them.

Spiritual Humility

Who would be the companion of the wise,
And know the Cosmic Splendour; he must stoop
Who seeks to stand; must fall who fain would rise;
Must know the low, ascending to the high;
He who would know the Great must not disdain
To diligently wait upon the small;
He wisdom finds who finds humility,

Throughout the Sacred Scriptures of all religions there runs, like a silver thread, the teaching of Humility. Not only all the Scriptures, but the sages of all time have declared that only through the portal of humility is it possible for man to enter into the possession of the Life of Truth; and as that life is entirely of a spiritual Nature, so the humility that leads to it is purely and absolutely spiritual; and being such, it can never be materialised, can never be embodied in a dogma, or laid down as a formula. It is not an outward thing, nor does it consist of that practice of self-abasement that has usurped its name.

But priests have taught, and many have been led to believe, that self-depreciation is true humility, while in reality it is its extreme antithesis. Self-depreciation is self-degradation; may, it is even a sort of self-destruction, it is spiritual suicide. The man who believes that all his righteousness is as filthy rags, that there is no good thing in him, and that he can never rise by any effort of his own, is by that very attitude of his mind, rendering himself impotent; he is strangling the Spirit; he is undermining and disintegrating all that is highest and noblest in his character. Instead of building up his character he is engaged in despoiling it. "As a man thinketh in his heart, so is he"; what our thoughts are, such are our characters. We are in reality beings composed of thoughts; thoughts are the bricks which we are continually laying down in the building of our souls. If we put a large percentage of rotten bricks into the building, we shall build but a miserable hovel, and every self-depreciating thought is a brick that is already crumbling. It will be found to be a rule marvellously accurate in its application that those who continually live in this attitude of self-depreciation are throughout life, or, at any rate, until they strike a nobler attitude, wretched failures. I can bring to my mind many such men that I have known. How can it be otherwise? How can a man who has no faith in himself ever win the confidence of others, or accomplish anything worthy? Moreover such a man has not, cannot possibly have, any faith in human nature; despising himself, he despises all; and as a result, by the unerring law of cause and effect, all men despise him. Yet it is a strange fact that the men who maintain this faith-destroying attitude of mind invariably profess to have the greatest faith in God; yea, look upon it as an infallible witness to their superior spiritual faith. But I ask this question, Does not true faith, like true charity, begin at home? In the growth of the soul faith in one's self comes first, next faith in human nature, and finally faith in God. That faith which professes to have the latter to the exclusion of the two former is false faith, the outcome of fake humility.

Another kind of false humility is that of personal abasement to an individual or to established authority. This is humility materialised or subverted. It is the worship of Dagon, the bowing of the knee to Baal, the slavish adoration of the Golden Calf. No man can persist in it without undermining his character, and ultimately dissipating his spiritual and mental energies. Humility to man or to any temporal authority is degrading and slavish; humility to the Most High is grandly beautiful.

Spiritual humility is closely allied to faith, and the more there is of humility the more there is of faith. It is the key-note of all real greatness. In proof of this I have only to refer to the great sages, saints, and reformers of all time. The greatest of them are those who had the greatest share of spiritual humility. True humility, as distinguished from false, has a strengthening power, an upbuilding force. It inspires and invigorates the soul, spurring is to greater and ever greater endeavour.

Of what, then, does this humility consist? Is it the bending of the knee to ask personal favours of Deity? Is it the blind petitioning of God to accomplish for us our petty and narrow designs? Nay, these are its counterfeits. True humility is far above and. beyond all this. It is the deepest and holiest aspiration of the human heart, where deep within, hidden from all sacrilegious gaze, it works, a silent mighty power, purifying, transforming, the man of flesh and self; entering its solitary grandeur, the alienated soul returns to the foot-stool of its God, and bathes, in blissful rapture, in the light of His all-embracing Love. It is a state that can only be entered into by rising above one's lower self. It is in fact the submergence of the self in the non-self; the submission of passion and intellect to the Supreme; it is the attitude of a human soul adoring its highest conception.

Such humility takes its possessor above all that is mean and poor in his nature, into the very presence of God, making him calm, strong, noble, self-reliant, and Godlike. It is the Wine of Life to all aspiring souls. The soul that has not felt its power is dead.

It may sound like a paradox, but it is nevertheless true, that the more a man has of humility the more he has of independence. But the seeming paradox will be made clear if we think for a moment of the lives of such teachers of humility as Jesus, Buddha, Confucius, Socrates, Jacob Boehme, George Fox, and indeed of all the great religious reformers. These men walked erect, because, yielding themselves up to the simplicity' of humility, they walked with God.

The humility that causes a man to go, metaphorically speaking, on all fours is spurious, and is as debasing and destructive as the real humility is elevating and strengthening. Why should we go amongst our fellows like cringing, fearful beasts, calling ourselves miserable sinners? Shall we ever rise above sin by so doing? Is it possible to rise by ceaselessly contemplating our absolute unworthiness? No, we can only rise by continually contemplating the Highest. There may be much that is unworthy in a man's heart, but there is also a sacredness, a dignity, a divinity about it; let us dwell upon that. Let us continually contemplate the goodness, the purity, and the essential beauty of human nature, Let us ceaselessly search for the Divinity in our own souls, and, finding it through the door of humility, we shall then recognise the invisible God in all men. By so doing, we rise above the binding limitations of our selfish desires, and enter the larger, healthier, holier life of Love.

Spiritual Strength

All things are holy to the holy mind,
All uses are legitimate and pure,
All occupations blest and sanctified,
And every day a Sabbath.

A clear and firm head must precede and accompany a clean and gentle heart. Without the first the second is impossible, for the qualities of purity and gentleness can only be reached through a clear perception of right and wrong, and by the exercise of an irresistible will. The strength of a powerful animal, or of that animal force in man which enables him to gain the victory over others by attack and resistance, is weakness compared with that quiet, patient, invincible will by which a man overcomes himself, and tames to obedience, and trains to the service of holy purposes, the savage passions of his nature.

Every dog can bark and fight, and every foolish man can rail, abuse, fence with hard words, and give way to fits of bad temper; these things are easy and natural to him, and require no effort and no strength. But the wise man puts away all such follies, and trains himself in self-control—trains himself to act unerringly from fixed principles, and not from the fleeting impulses of an unstable nature.

He who succeeds in so training himself is able to train others, in a small degree by precept, but largely and chiefly by practice or example, for it is pre-eminently the prerogative of the wise to teach by their actions. The mockeries of Herod, the accusations of tie people, and the fanatical persecutions of the priests all failed to draw from Jesus the word of complaint, bitterness, or self-defence. Such sublime acts of silence and self-control continue to reach, for ages, both individuals and nations, with far greater power and effect than all the words and books uttered and written by the world's vast army of priests and learned commentators.

To retaliate and fight belongs to the animal in man as it belongs to the beast of the forest; but to refuse to be swayed from the practice of a divine principle by any external pressure—to stand firm and unalterable in goodness and truth alike amid blame and praise—this belongs to the divine in man and in the universe.

To alter one's conduct in order to please others, or to avoid their censure or misunderstanding can never lead to spiritual strength.

That divine kindness which always accompanies spiritual understanding and strength is something very different from merely saying pleasant words—for pleasant words are not always true words—but consist in doing what is best for the eternal welfare of the other person or persons.

The weak father, who is unfit to train children only considers how he can escape trouble with his children, and so he slurs over their acts of disobedience and selfishness, and tries to please them. But the strong father, who considers the future character and welfare of his children, knows how and when to administer a severe reproof; fully understanding that the few minutes' pain caused by his rebuke may save his child from years of suffering as a result of loose living which is fostered by parental neglect. The strong, kind, unselfish father, whose care is for his children's good, and not for his own immediate comfort, knows not only how to be tender in affection, but tender in discipline, knows how to stretch out the strong and (to the child at the time) severe arm of restraint to save his little ones when they would ignorantly wander away in wrong paths.

So the man of spiritual strength cannot be merely a weak framer of smooth words, but a doer of right actions, an utterer of words that are vital and true, and, therefore, eternally kind.

The spiritually weak man shrinks from right when it is brought (as by its nature it must be brought) in opposition to his desires, and he embraces sin because it is pleasant. The spiritually strong man shrinks from sin, more especially when it is presented to him in a pleasant garb, and embraces right, even though by so doing he will bring upon himself the odium of those who are ignorant of divine principles and their beneficent application.

The man of spiritual understanding is as unbending as a bar of steel where right is concerned, knowing that right alone is good; he is as unresisting as water where self is concerned, knowing that self alone is evil. Acting from imperishable principles and not from the fleeting desires of self, his actions partake of the imperishable nature of the principles from which they spring, and continue to afford instruction and inspiration through unnumbered generations.

It is always the portion of one who so acts to be misunderstood. The majority live in their desires and impulses, following them blindly as they are brought into operation by external stimuli, and do not understand what is meant by acting dispassionately from right and fixed principles, with entire freedom from self interest. Such will necessarily misunderstand and misjudge the right-doer, regarding him as cold and cruel in his unbending adherence to right, or as weak, cowardly in his quiet refusal to passionately defend himself. He will, therefore, "be accused of many things", but this will not cause him any suffering, nor will he be troubled or disturbed thereby, for the truth which he practises is a source of perpetual joy, and he will be at rest in the knowledge that there are those who will understand and follow,' that he is working for the ultimate good even of his accusers; and that by manifesting the truth in his daily actions, he is in the company of those divinely strong ones who are leading the world into ways of quietness and peace.

James Allen's Book of Meditations for Every Day in the Year

By Thought we rise; by Thought we fall, by Thought
We stand or go; all destiny is wrought
By its swift potency , and he who stands
Master of Thought, and his desires commands,
Willing and weaving thoughts of Love and Alight,
Shapes his high end in 'Truth's unerring Light.

He who does not find The way of Meditation cannot reach
Emancipation and enlightenment.
But thou wilt find the way of Holy Thought;
With mind made calm and steadfast, thou will see
The Permanent amid the mutable,
The Truth eternal in the things that change:
Thou wilt behold the Perfect Law: Cosmos
From Chaos rises when the conquered self
Lies underneath man's heel: Love be thy strength;
Look on the passion-tortured multitudes,
And have compassion on them; know their pain
By thy long sorrow ended. Thou wilt come
To perfect peace, and so wilt bless the world,
Leading unto the High and Holy Way
The feet of them that seek.—And now I go
To my Abode; go thou unto thy work.

Editor's Preface

James Allen may truly be called the Prophet of Meditation. In an age of strife, hurry, religious controversy, heated arguments, ritual and ceremony, he came with his message of Meditation, calling men away from the din and strife of tongues into the peaceful paths of stillness within their own souls, where the Light that lighteth every man that cometh into the world ever burns steadily and surely for all who will turn their weary eyes from the strife without to the quiet within. Many of the Meditations were written as he came down from the Cairn in the early morning, where he spent those precious hours alone with God while the world slept. Others are gleaned from his many writings, published and unpublished, and are arranged for daily readings at his request, and, we believe, under his spiritual guidance. The book must ever be a stronghold of Spiritual Truth and blessing to all who read it, and especially to those who use it for daily meditation. Its great power lies in that it is the very heart of a good man who lived every word he wrote. The beautiful half-tone portrait is a speaking likeness of the Author. It was taken only six weeks before his translation, and has not been published before.

We are indebted to Messrs. Putnam's Sons (London and New York), and to Messrs. Wm. Rider and Son, Limited (London), for their cordial expressions of pleasure that some of the Meditations should be culled from the books published by them, viz., The Mastery of Destiny, and Above Life's Turmoil (Putnam), and From Passion to Peace, and Man: King of Mind, Body, and Circumstance (Rider).

Lily L. Allen

The way from passion to peace is by overcoming one's self.

January First.

FREQUENTLY the man of passion is most eager to put others right; but the man of wisdom puts himself right. If one is anxious to reform the world, let him begin by reforming himself. The reformation of self does not end with the elimination of the sensual elements only; that is its beginning. It ends only when every vain thought and selfish aim is overcome. Short of perfect purity and wisdom, there is still some form of self-slavery or folly which needs to be conquered.

On the wings of aspiration man rises from earth to heaven, from ignorance to knowledge, from the under darkness to the upper light. Without it he remains a grovelling animal, earthly, sensual, unenlightened, and uninspired.

Aspiration is the longing for heavenly things.

Where is peace to be found! Where is the hiding-place of truth!

January Second.

LET first things be put first; work before play; duty before enjoyment; and others before self: this is an excellent rule which cannot lead astray. To make a right beginning is half-way to victory. The athlete who makes a bad start may lose his prize; the merchant who makes a false start may lose his reputation; and the Truth-seeker who makes a wrong start may forego the crown of Righteousness. To begin with pure thoughts, sterling rectitude, unselfish purpose, noble aims, and an incorruptible conscience—this is to start right * this it is to put first things first, so that all other things will follow in harmonious order, making life simple, beautiful, successful, and peaceful.

The soul will cry out for its lost heritage.

If one would find peace, he must come out of passion.

January Third.

SO long as animal conditions taste sweet to a man, lie cannot aspire: he is so far satisfied; but when their sweetness turns to bitterness, then in his sorrow he thinks of nobler tilings. When he is deprived of earthly joy, he aspires to the joy which is heavenly. It is when impurity turns to suffering that purity is sought. Truly aspiration rises, phoenix-like, from the dead ashes of repentance, but on its powerful pinions man can reach the heaven of heavens.

The man of aspiration has entered the way which leads to peace; and surely he will reach that end if he stays not nor turns back. If he constantly renews his mind with glimpses of the heavenly vision, he will reach the heavenly state.

That which can be conceived can be achieved.

Our life is what we make it by our own thoughts and deeds.
January Fourth.

MAN attains in the measure that he aspires. His longing to be is the gauge of what he can be. To fix the mind is to fore-ordain the achievement. As man can experience and know all low things, so he can experience and know all high things. As he has become human, so he can become divine. The turning of the mind in high and divine directions is the sole and needful task.

What is impurity but the impure thoughts of the thinker? What is purity but the pure thoughts of the thinker? One man does not do the thinking of another. Each man is pure or impure of himself alone. The man of aspiration sees before him the pathway up the heavenly heights, and his heart already experiences a foretaste of the final peace.

There is a life of victory over sin, and triumph over evil.

When a man wishes and wills he can find the good and the true.
January Fifth.

THE Gates of Heaven are for ever open, and no one is prevented from entering by any will or power but his own; but no one can enter the Kingdom of Heaven so long as he is enamoured of, and chooses, the seductions of hell, so long as he resigns himself to sin and sorrow.

There is a larger, higher, nobler, diviner life than that of sinning and suffering, which is so common—in which, indeed, nearly all are immersed—a life of victory over sin, and triumph over evil; a life wise and happy, benign and tranquil, virtuous and peaceful. This life can be found and lived now, and he who lives it is steadfast in the midst of change; restful among the restless; peaceful, though surrounded by strife.

Every moment is the time of choice; every hour is destiny.

The lover of the pure life renews his mind daily.
January Sixth.

As the energetic man of business is not daunted by difficulties, but studies how to overcome them, so the man of ceaseless aspiration is not crushed into submission by temptations, but meditates how he may fortify his mind; for the tempter is like a coward, he only creeps in at weak and unguarded points. The tempted one should study thoughtfully the nature and meaning of temptation, for until it is known it cannot be overcome. He who is to overcome temptation must understand how it arises in his own darkness and error, and must study, by introspection and meditation, how to disperse the darkness and supplant error by truth.

A man must know himself if he is to know truth. Self-knowledge is the handmaid of self-conquest.

Engage daily in holy meditation on Truth and its attainment.

As errors and impunities are revealed, purge them way.
January Seventh.

VERY step upward means the leaving of something behind and below. The high is reached only at the sacrifice of the low. The good is secured only by abandoning the evil. Knowledge is acquired only by the destruction of ignorance. livery acquisition has its price, which must be paid "to the uttermost farthing." Every animal, every creeping tiling, possesses some gift, so power, which man, in his upward march, has laid down, which he has exchanged for some higher gift, or power. What great good men forfeit by clinging to old selfish habits! Behind every humble sacrifice a winged angel waits to bear us up the heights of knowledge and wisdom.

Let him who has attained guard against falling back. Let him be careful in little things, and be well fortified against the entrance of sin.

Aim, with ardour, for the attainment of a perfect life.

The strife of the world in all its forms has its origin in one common cause, namely, individual selfishness.
January Eighth.

ALL the varied activities of human life are rooted in, and draw their vitality from, one common source—the human heart. The cause of all suffering and all happiness resides, not in the outer activities of human life, but in the inner activities of the heart and mind; and every external agency is sustained by the life which it derives from human conduct.

The man who cannot endure to have his errors and shortcomings brought to the surface and made known, but tries to hide them, is unfit to walk the highway of Truth. He is not properly equipped to battle with and overcome temptation. He who cannot fearlessly face his lower nature cannot climb the rugged heights of renunciation.

Each man comes under the laws of his own being, never under the laws of another.

When the soul is most tried, its need is greatest.
January Ninth.
DO not despair because of failure. From your particular failure there is a special greatness, a peculiar wisdom, to be gained; and no teacher can lead you to that greatness, that wisdom, more surely and swiftly than your experience of failure. In every mistake you make, in every fall you encounter, there is a lesson of vital import if you will but search it out; and he who will stoop to discover the good in that which appears to be disastrous will rise superior to every event, and will utilise his failures as winged steeds to bear him to a final and supreme success.

Foolish men blame others for their lapses and sins, but let the truth-lover blame only himself. Let him acknowledge his complete responsibility for his own conduct.

Where temptation is powerful, the greater and more enduring will be the victory.

The great need of the soul is the need of that permanent
January Tenth.
THE old must pass away before the new can appear. The old cottage must be demolished before the new mansion can appear upon its site. The old error must be destroyed before the new truth can come. . . . The old self must be renounced before the new man can be born. When the old self of temper, impatience, envy, pride, and impurity has perished, then in its place will appear the new man of gentleness, patience, goodwill, humility, and purity. Let the old life of sin and sorrow pass; let the new life of Righteousness and Joy come in. ... Then all that was old and ugly will be made new and beautiful.

It is in the realisation of this Principle where the Kingdom of Heaven, the abiding home of the soul, resides, and which is the source and storehouse of every permanent blessing.

A life of virtue is noble and excellent.

It matters little what is without, for it is all a reflection of your own consciousness.
January Eleventh.

THE deplorable failure of many outward and isolated reforms is traceable to the fact that their devotees pursue them as an end in themselves, failing to see that they are merely steps towards ultimate, individual perfection.

All true reform must come from within, in a changed heart and mind. The giving up of certain foods and drinks, and the breaking away from certain outward habits, are good and necessary beginnings; but they are only beginnings, and to end there is to fall far short of a true spiritual life. It is good, therefore, to cleanse the heart, to correct the mind, and to develop the understanding, for we know that the one thing needed is a regenerate heart.

It matters everything what you are within, for everything without will be mirrored and coloured accordingly.

Renew your resolution daily, and in the hour of temptation do not depart from the right path.

January Twelfth.

THE days are lengthening. Each day now the sun rises a little higher, and the light lingers a little longer. So each day we can strengthen our character; each day we can open our heart a little more to the light of Truth, and allow the Sun of Righteousness to shine more highly in our mind. The sun does not increase in volume or intensity, but the earth turns towards it, and receives more as it turns. All that there is of Truth and Good is now. It does not increase or diminish, but as we turn towards it we receive of its radiance and beneficence in ever-increasing abundance and power.

As the artisan acquires skill in fashioning the articles of his craft by daily and diligent practice with his tools, so do you acquire skill in fashioning good deeds by daily and diligent practice of the Truth.

You can acquire Truth only by practice.

The wise purify their thoughts.

January Thirteenth.

EVERYday is a new birth in time, holding out new beginnings, new possibilities, new achievements. The ages have witnessed the stars in their orbits, but this day hath no age witnessed. It is a new appearance, a new reality. It heralds a new life—yea, a new order, a new society, a new age. It holds out new hopes, new opportunities, to all men. In it you can become a new man, a new woman. For you it can be the day of regeneration, renewal, rebirth. From the old past with its mistakes, failures, and sorrows, you can rise a new being, endued with power and purpose, and radiant with the inspiration of a new ideal.

Be chaste in mind and body. Abandon sensual pleasures. Purge the mind of selfishness, and live a life of exalted purity.

Be upright, gentle, and pure-hearted.

Exert yourself ceaselessly in decreasing evil and accumulating good.
January Fourteenth.

VICTORY of all kinds is preceded by a season of preparation. It can no more appear spontaneously and erratically than can a flower or a mountain. Like them, it is the culminating point in a process of growth, in a series of causes and effects. No mere wishing, no magic word, will produce worldly success; it must be achieved by an orderly succession of well-directed efforts. No spiritual victory will be achieved by him who imagines that it does not begin until the hour of temptation arrives. All spiritual triumphs are gained in the silent hour of meditation, and through a series of successes in lesser trials. The time of great temptation is the climax of a conquest that long preparation has made certain and complete.

Fix your minds on the practice of virtue, and the comprehension and application of fixed and noble principles.

The Never-Ending Gladness awaits your Home- coming.
January Fifteenth.

AS the falling rain prepares the earth for the future crops of grain and fruit, so the rains of many sorrows showering upon the heart prepare and mellow it for the coming of that wisdom that perfects the mind and gladdens the heart. As the clouds darken the earth but to cool and fructify it, so the clouds of grief cast a shadow over the heart to prepare it for nobler things. The hour of sorrow is the hour of reverence. It puts an end to the shallow sneer, the ribald jest, the cruel calumny; it softens the heart with sympathy, and enriches the mind with thoughtfulness. Wisdom is mainly recollection of all that was learned by sorrow.

Do not think that your sorrow will remain; it will pass away like a cloud. Where self ends, grief passes away.

Live sweetly and happily, as becomes the dignity of a true manhood and womanhood.
January Sixteenth.

THERE is no greater happiness than to be occupied with good, whether it be good thoughts, good actions, or good employment; for every good thing is fraught with bliss, and evil cannot enter the heart or house that is tenanted by all that is good. The mind whose doors are guarded by good shuts out unhappiness as the well-sentried garrison shuts out the foe. Unhappiness can only enter through unguarded doors, and even then its power over the tenant is not complete unless it find him occupied with evil. Not to entertain evil thoughts; not to do bad actions; not to engage in worthless or questionable employment, but to resort to good in all things—this is the source of supreme happiness.

Pure happiness is the rightful and happy condition of the soul.

All things are orderly and sequential being governed by the law of causation.
January Seventeenth.

DO not trouble about results, or be anxious as to the future; but be troubled about personal shortcomings, and be anxious to remove them; for know this simple truth—wrong does not result from right, and a good present cannot give birth to a bad future. You are the custodian of your deeds, but not of the results which flow from them. The deeds of to-day bring the happiness or sorrow of to-morrow. Be therefore concerned about what you think and do, rather than about what may or may not come to you; for he whose deeds are good does not concern himself about results, and is freed from fear of future ill.

Verily the Law reigneth, and reigneth for ever, and Justice and Love are its eternal ministers.

Speak only words which are truthful and sincere.
January Eighteenth.

THE storm may rage without, but it cannot affect us if there is peace within. As by the fireside there is security from the fiercest storm, so the heart that is steadfast in the knowledge of Truth abides in peace, though all around be strife and perturbation. The bitter opposition of men and the unrest of the world cannot make us bitter and restless unless we enter into and co-operate with it. Rather, if we have peace in our heart, will the outer turmoil cause our peace to deepen, to take firmer root, and to show forth more abundantly in works of peace for the softening of human hearts and the enlightening of human minds.

Blessed is he who has no wrongs to remember, no injuries to forget, in whose pure heart no hateful thought about another can take root and flourish.

He who speaks evil of another cannot find the way of peace.

Purification is necessarily severe. All becoming is painful.

January Nineteenth.

WHEN a storm has subsided, and all is calm again, observe how all nature seems to pause in a restorative silence. A restful quiet pervades all things, so that even inanimate objects seem to participate in the recuperative repose. So when a too violent eagerness or a sudden burst of passion has spent itself, there comes a period of reflective thought, a time of calm, in which the mind is restored, and things are seen in their true outlines and right proportions. It is wise to take advantage of this quiet time by gaining a truer knowledge of one's self, and forming a more kindly judgment of others. The hour of calm is the hour of restoration.

Joy comes and fills the self-emptied heart; it abides with the peaceful; its reign is with the pure.

Make your every thought, word, and deed sweet and pure.

In the dark times of sorrow, men approach very near to Truth.

January Twentieth.

WHEN the tears flow, and the heart aches, remember then the sorrow of the world. When sorrow has overtaken you, remember then that it overtakes all; that none escape it; that it is the great fact in human life that makes religion a necessity. Think not that your pain is isolated and unjustly inflicted. It is but a fragment of the great pain of the world. It is the common experience of all. Perceiving this, let sorrow gently lead you into a deeper religion, a wider compassion, a tenderer regard for all men and all creatures. Let it bring you into greater love and deeper peace.

Bear well in mind that nothing can overtake you that does not belong to you, and that is not for your eternal good.

The end of sorrow is joy and peace.

The sorrowless state is reached through sorrow.

January Twenty-First

AS light displaces darkness, and quiet follows storm, so gladness displaces sorrow, and peace comes after pain. The deeper wisdom which flows from acquaintance with sorrow brings with it a holier and more abiding joy than that shallow excitement that preceded sorrow. Between the lesser joys of the senses and the greater joy of the spirit lies the dark vale of sorrow through which all earthly pilgrims pass, and having passed through it, the heavenly Joy, the Abiding Gladness, is henceforth our companion. They who have passed from the earthly to the heavenly pilgrimage have lifted the dark veil of sorrow from the radiant face of Truth.

He whose treasure is Truth, who fashions his life in accordance with Wisdom, will find the Joy which does not pass away; crossing the wide ocean of illusion, he will come to the sorrowless Shore.

All outward oppression is but the shadow and effect of the real oppression within.
January Twenty-Second.

IN happiness and unhappiness, in joy and sorrow, in success and failure, in victory and defeat; in religion, business, circumstances; in all the issues of life, the determining factor is character. In the mentality of individuals lie the hidden causes of all that pertains to their outward life. Character is both cause and effect. It is the doer of deeds and the recipient of results. Heaven, hell, purgatory, are contained within it. The character that is impure and vicious will experience a life from which the elements of happiness and beauty are lacking, wheresoever they may be placed; but a pure and virtuous character will show forth a life that is happy and beautiful. As you make your character, so will you shape your life.

To put away self and passion, and establish one's self in right doing, this is the highest wisdom.

Not departing from the path of holiness, but surmounting all difficulties and continuing to the end whosoever does this will comprehend Truth.
January Twenty-Third.

WHEN great difficulties arise, and troubles beset, regard your perplexity as a call to deeper thought and more vigorous action. Nothing will attack you that you are not capable of overcoming; no problem will vex you that you cannot solve. The greater your trial, the greater your test of strength, and the more complete and triumphant your victory. However complicated your maze of confusion may be, there is a way out of it, and the finding of that way will exercise your powers to the utmost, and will bring out all your latent skill, energy, and resource. When you have mastered that which threatens to master you, you will rejoice in a new-found strength.

Knowing the Truth by practice, and being at one with Truth, you will be invincible, for Truth cannot be confounded or overthrown.

Look not outside thee nor behind thee for the light and blessedness of Truth, but look within.

January Twenty-Fourth.

WE advance by a series of efforts. We gather strength, whether mental or physical, by a succession of strivings in given directions. Exertion, oft repeated, leads to power. It is by obeying this law that the athlete trains himself to accomplish wonderful feats of speed or endurance. When the exertion is along intellectual lines, it leads to unusual talent, or genius; and when in spiritual channels, it leads to wisdom, or transcendent greatness. We should not mourn when circumstances are driving us to greater efforts and more protracted exertion. Events are only evil to the mind that makes them so. They are good to him that accepts their discipline as salutary.

Thou wilt find Truth within the narrow sphere of thy duty, even in the humble and hidden sacrifices of thine own heart.

There is no blessedness anywhere until impatience is sacrificed.

January Twenty-Fifth.

DESPONDENCY, anxiety, worry, and irritability cannot cure the ills against which they are directed. They only add more misery to the troubles that prompt them. The cultivation of a steadfast and serene spirit cannot be overlooked if life is to yield any measure of usefulness and happiness. The trifles, and even greater troubles, which annoy would soon dissolve and disappear if confronted with a temper that refuses to be ruffled and disturbed. Personal aims, wishes, schemes, and pleasures will meet with checks, rebuffs, and obstacles; and it is in learning to meet these reverses in a wise and calm spirit that we discover the true and abiding happiness within our heart.

When impatience and irritability are put away, then is realised and enjoyed the blessedness of a strong, quiet, and peaceful mind.

The greatest blessedness comes to him who infuses into his mind the purest and noblest thoughts.

January Twenty-Sixth.

WE are becoming wise when we know and realise that happiness abides in certain habits of mind, or mental characteristics, rather than in material possessions, or in certain combinations of circumstances. It is a common delusion to imagine that if one only possessed this or that— a little more money, a little more leisure, this man's talent, or that man's opportunities; or if one had better friends, or more favourable surroundings—one would be happy with a perfect felicity. Alas! discontent and misery lie in such vain wishes. If happiness is not already found within, it will never be found without. The happiness of a wise mind abides through all vicissitudes.

Your whole life is a series of effects, having their cause in thought—in your own thought.

A sweet and happy soul is the ripened fruit of experience and wisdom,.
January Twenty-Seventh.

THERE is an infinite patience in nature which it is profitable to contemplate. A comet may take a thousand years to complete its orbit; the sea may occupy ten thousand years in wearing away the land; the complete evolution of the human race may occupy millions of years. This should make us ashamed of our hurry, fussiness, discontent, disappointments, and ridiculous self-importance over trifling things of an hour or a day. Patience is conducive to the highest greatness, the most far-reaching usefulness, and the profoundest peace. Without it, life will lose much of its power and influence, and its joy win be largely destroyed.

"So with well-ordered strenuousness Raise thou thy structure of Success."

He who fills with useful pursuits the minutes as they come and go grows old in honour and wisdom, and prosperity abides with him.

No pure thought, no unselfish deed, can fall short of its felicitous results, and every such result is a happy consummation.
January Twenty-Eighth.

IF to-day is cold and gloomy, is that a cause for despair? Do we not know that there are warm, bright days ahead? Already the birds are beginning to sing, and the tremulous trill in their little throats is prophetic of the approaching love of a new spring, and of the bounty of a summer that as yet is but a sleeping germ in the womb of this gloomy day, but whose birth is sure, and its full growth certain. No effort is vain. The spring of all your aspirations is near—very near; and the summer of your unselfish deeds will surely come to pass.

Self shall depart, and Truth shall take its place;

The Changeless One, the Indivisible, Shall take up His abode in me, and cleanse

The White Robe of the Heart Invisible.

Go to your task with love in your heart, and you will go to it light-hearted and cheerful.

All evil is corrective and remedial, and is therefore not permanent.

January Twenty-Ninth.

BY earnest self-examination strive to realise, and not merely hold as a theory, that evil is a passing phase, a self-created shadow; that all your pains, sorrows, and misfortunes have come to you by a process of undeviating and absolutely perfect law; have come to you because you deserve and require them, and that by first enduring, and then understanding them, you may be made stronger, wiser, nobler. When you have fully entered into this realisation, you will be in a position to mould your own circumstances, to transmute all evil into good, and to weave, with a master hand, the fabric of your destiny.

Cease to be a disobedient child in the school of experience, and begin to learn, with humility and patience, the lessons that are set for your ultimate perfection.

Mediation centred upon divine realities is the very essence and soul of prayer.

January Thirtieth.

TELL me what that is upon which you most frequently and intensely think, that to which, in your silent hours, your soul most naturally turns, and I will tell you to what place of pain or peace you are travelling, and whether you are growing into the likeness of the divine or the bestial. There is an unavoidable tendency to become literally the embodiment of that quality upon which one most constantly thinks. Let, therefore, the object of your meditation be above and not below, so that every time that you revert to it in thought you will be lifted up; let it be pure and unmixed with any selfish element; so shall your heart become purified and drawn nearer to Truth, and not defiled and dragged more hopelessly into error.

Meditation is the secret of all growth in spiritual life and knowledge.

If you ceaselessly think upon that which is pure and unselfish, you will surely become pure and unselfish.

January Thirty-First.

IF you are daily praying for wisdom, for peace, for loftier purity, and a fuller realisation of Truth, and that for which you pray is still far from you, it means that you are praying for one tiling, whilst living out in thought and act another. If you will cease from such waywardness, taking your mind off those things, the selfish clinging to which debars you from the possession of the stainless realities for which you pray; if you will no longer ask God to grant you that which you do not deserve, or to bestow upon you that love and compassion which you refuse to bestow upon others, but will commence to think and act in the spirit of Truth, you will day by day be growing into those realities, so that ultimately you will become one with them.

Enter the path of Meditation, and let the supreme object of your meditation be Truth.

Unrest and pain and sorrow are the shadows of life.
February First.

S there no way of escape from pain and sorrow? Are there no means by which the bonds of evil may be broken? Is permanent happiness and abiding peace a foolish dream? No, there is a way—and I speak it with gladness—by which evil may be slam for ever; there is a process by which every adverse condition or circumstance can be put on one side for ever, never to return; and there is a practice by which unbroken and unending peace and bliss can be partaken of and realised. And the beginning of the way which leads to this glorious realisation is the acquirement of a right understanding of the nature of evil. It is not sufficient to deny or ignore evil; it must be understood.

Men remain in evil because they are not willing or prepared to learn the lesson which it came to teach them.

You must get outside yourself, and must begin to examine and understand yourself.
February Second.

EVIL, when rightly understood, is found to be, not an unlimited power or principle in the universe, but a passing phase of human experience, and it therefore becomes a teacher to those who are willing to learn. Evil is not an abstract something outside yourself; it is an experience m your own heart, and by patiently examining and rectifying your heart you will be gradually led into the discovery of the origin and nature of evil, which will necessarily be followed by its complete eradication. ... There is no evil in the universe which is not the result of ignorance, and which would not, if we were ready and willing to learn its lesson, lead us to higher wisdom, and then vanish away.

Every soul attracts its own, and nothing can possibly come to it that does not belong to it.

What you are, so is your world.
February Third.

ALL that you positively know is contained in your own experience; all that you ever will know must pass through the gateway of experience, and so become part of yourself. Your own thoughts, desires, and aspirations comprise your world, and, to you, all that there is in the universe of beauty, and joy, and bliss, or 01 ugliness, and sorrow, and pain, is contained within yourself. By your own thoughts you make or mar your life, your world, your universe. As you build within by the power of thought, so will your outward life and circumstances shape themselves accordingly. Whatsoever you harbour in the inmost chambers of your heart will, sooner or later, by the inevitable law of reaction, shape itself in your outward life.

Every soul is a complex combination of gathered experiences and thoughts, and the body is but an improvised vehicle for its manifestation.

To them, that seek the highest Good All things subserve the wisest ends.
February fourth.

HE who clings to self is his own enemy, and is surrounded by enemies. He who relinquishes self is his own saviour, and is surrounded by friends like a protecting belt. Before the divine radiance of a pure heart all darkness vanishes and all clouds melt away, and he who has conquered self has conquered the universe. Come, then, out of your poverty; come out of your pain; come out of your troubles, and sighings, and complainings, and heartaches, and loneliness by coming out of yourself. Let the old tattered garment of your petty selfishness fall from you, and put on the new garment of universal Love. You will then realise the inward heaven, and it will be reflected in all your outward life.

All glory and all good await The coming of Obedient feet.

All men's accomplishments were first wrought out in thought, and then objectivised.
February Fifth.

WHEN the thought-forces are directed in harmony with the over-ruling Law, they are up-building and preservative, but when subverted they become disintegrating and self-destructive. To adjust all your thoughts to a perfect and unswerving faith in the omnipotence and supremacy of Good is to co-operate with that Good, and to realise within yourself the solution and destruction of all evil. Believe and ye shall live. And here we have the true meaning of salvation; salvation from the darkness and negation of evil, by entering into and realising the living light of the Eternal Good.

It is the silent and conquering thought-forces which bring all things into manifestation.

There is nothing that a strong faith and an unflinching purpose may not accomplish.

February Sixth.

THERE is no difficulty, however great, but will yield before a calm and powerful concentration of thought, and no legitimate object but may be speedily actualised by the intelligent use and direction of one's soul-forces.

Not until you have gone deeply and searchingly into your inner nature, and have overcome many enemies that lurk there, can you have any approximate conception of the subtle power of thought, of its inseparable relation to outward and material things, or of its magical potency, when rightly poised and directed, in re-adjusting and transforming the life-conditions. Every thought you think is a force sent out, and in accordance with its nature and intensity will it go out to seek a lodgment in minds receptive to it, and will react upon yourself for good or evil.

Think good thoughts, and they will quickly become actualised in your outward life in the form of good conditions.

He only is fitted to command and control who has succeeded in commanding and controlling himself.

February Seventh.

IF you would acquire overcoming power, you must cultivate poise and passivity. You must be able to stand alone. All power is associated with immovability. The mountain, the massive rock, the storm-tried oak, all speak to us of power, because of their combined solitary grandeur and defiant fixity; while the shifting sand, the yielding twig, and the waving reed speak to us of weakness, because they are movable and non-resistant, and are utterly useless when detached from their fellows. He is the man of power who, when all his fellows are swayed by some emotion or passion, remains calm and unmoved. The hysterical, the fearful, the thoughtless and frivolous, let such seek company, or they will fall for lack of support; but the calm, the fearless, the thoughtful and grave, let such seek solitude, and to their power more power will be added.

Be of single aim. Have a legitimate and useful purpose, and devote yourself unreservedly to it.

Self-seeking is self-destruction

February Eighth.

IF you would realise true prosperity, do not settle down, as many have done, into the belief that if you do right everything will go wrong. Do not allow the word competition to shake your faith in the supremacy of righteousness. I care not what man may say about the laws of competition, for do I not know the Unchangeable Law, which shall one day put them all to rout, and which puts them to rout even now in the heart and life of the righteous man? And knowing this Law I can contemplate all dishonesty with undisturbed repose, for I know where certain destruction awaits it. Those who have wandered from the highway of righteousness guard themselves against competition; those who always pursue the right need not to trouble about such defence.

Under all circumstances do that which you believe to be right, and trust the Law; trust the Divine Power, and you will always be protected.

Perfect Love is Perfect Power.
February Ninth.

THE wisely loving heart commands without exercising any authority. All things and all men obey him who obeys the Highest. He thinks, and lo! he has already accomplished! He speaks, and behold! a world hangs upon his simple utterances! He has harmonised his thoughts with the Imperishable and Unconquerable Forces, and for him weakness and uncertainty are no more. His every thought is a purpose; his every act an accomplishment; he moves with the Great Law, not setting his puny personal will against it, and he thus becomes a channel through which the Divine Power can flow in unimpeded and beneficent expression. He has thus become Power itself.

Perfect Love is Perfect Wisdom.

If you really seek Truth, you will be willing to make the effort necessary for its achievement.
February Tenth.

AT the outset, meditation must be distinguished from idle reverie. There is nothing dreamy and unpractical about it. It is a process of searching and uncompromising thought which allows nothing to remain but the simple and naked truth. Thus meditating you will no longer strive to build yourself up in your prejudices, but, forgetting self, you will remember only that you are seeking the Truth. And so you will remove, one by one, the errors which you have built around yourself in the past, and will patiently wait for the revelation of Truth which will come when your errors have been sufficiently removed.

Let the supreme object of your meditation be Truth.

As the flower opens its petals to receive the morning light, so open your soul more and more to the glorious light of Truth.

February Eleventh.

SPIRITUAL meditation and self-discipline are inseparable; you will, therefore, commence to meditate upon yourself so as to try and understand yourself, for, remember, the great object you will have in view will be the complete removal of all your errors in order that you may realise Truth. You will begin to question your motives, thoughts, and acts, comparing them with your ideal, and endeavouring to look upon them with a calm and impartial eye. In this manner you will be continually gaining more of that mental and spiritual equilibrium without which men are but helpless straws upon the ocean of life.

Soar upward on the wings of aspiration; be fearless, and believe in the loftiest possibilities.

A beginning is a cause, and, as such it must be followed by an effect.

February Twelfth.

THE nature of an initial impulse will always determine the body of its results. A beginning also presupposes an ending, a consummation, achievement, or goal. A gate leads to a path, and the path leads to some particular destination; so a beginning leads to results, and results lead to a completion.

There are right beginnings and wrong beginnings, which are followed by effects of a like nature. You can, by careful thought, avoid wrong beginnings and make right beginnings, and so escape evil results and enjoy good results. In aiming at the life of Blessedness, one of the simplest beginnings to be considered and rightly made is that which we all make every day—namely, the beginning of each day's life.

The effect will always be of the same nature as the cause.

Wisdom inheres in the common details of everyday existence.

February Thirteenth.

EVERYTHING in the universe is made of little things, and the perfection of the great is based upon the perfection up of the small. If any detail of the universe were imperfect, the whole would be imperfect. If any particle were omitted, the aggregate would cease to be. Without a grain of dust there would be no world, and the whole is perfect because the grain of dust is perfect. Neglect of the small is confusion of the great. The snowdrop is as perfect as the star; the dewdrop is as symmetrical as the planet; the microbe is not less mathematically proportioned than the man. By laying stone upon stone, plumbing and fitting each with perfect adjustment, the temple at last stands forth in all its architectural beauty.

When the parts are made perfect, the Whole will be without blemish.

To neglect small tasks, or to execute them in a perfunctory manner, is a mark of weakness and folly.

February Fourteenth.

THE great man knows the vast value that inheres in moments, words, greetings, meals, apparel, correspondence, rest, work, detached efforts, fleeting obligations, in the thousand-and-one little things which press upon him for attention— briefly, in the common details of life. He sees everything as divinely apportioned, needing only the application of dispassionate thought and action on his part to render life blessed and perfect. He neglects nothing, does not hurry, seeks to escape nothing but error and folly; attends to every duty as it is presented to him, and does not postpone and regret. By giving himself unreservedly to his nearest duty, he attains to that combined childlike simplicity and unconscious power which is greatness.

There is no way to strength and wisdom but by acting strongly and wisely in the present moment.

He who masters the small becomes the rightful possessor of the great.

February Fifteenth.

THE foolish man thinks that little faults, little indulgences, little sins, are of no consequence; he persuades himself that so long as he does not commit flagrant immoralities he is virtuous, and even holy; but he is thereby deprived of virtue and holiness, and the world knows him accordingly; it does not reverence, adore, and love him; it passes him by; he is reckoned of no account; his influence is destroyed. The efforts of such a man to make the world virtuous, his exhortations to his fellow men to abandon great vices, are empty of substance and barren of fruitage. The insignificance which he attaches to his small vices permeates his whole character, and is the measure of his manhood.

He who regards his smallest delinquencies as of the gravest nature becomes a saint.

Truth is wrapped up in infinitesimal details.

February Sixteenth.

AS the year consists of a given number of sequential moments, so a man's character and life consists of a given number of sequential thoughts and deeds, and the finished whole will bear the impress of the parts. Little kindnesses, generosities, and sacrifices make up a kind and generous character. The truly honest man is honest in the minutest details of his life. The noble man is noble in every little thing he says and does. You do not live your life in the mass; you live it in fragments, and from these the mass emerges. You can will to live each fragment nobly if you choose, and, this being done, there can be no particle of baseness in the finished whole.

Thoroughness is genius.

Truth in its very nature is ineffable and can only be lived.
February Seventeenth.

TRUTH is the one Reality in the universe, the inward Harmony, the perfect Justice, the eternal Love. Nothing can be added to it, nor taken from it. It does not depend upon any man, but all men depend upon it. You cannot perceive the beauty of Truth while you are looking out from the eyes of self. If you are vain, you will colour everything with your own vanities. If lustful, your heart and mind will be clouded with the smoke and flames of passion, and everything will appear distorted through them. If proud and opinionative, you will see nothing in the whole universe except the magnitude and importance of your own opinions. The humble Truth-lover has learned to distinguish between opinion and Truth. He who has most of Charity has most of Truth.

There is but one religion, the religion of Truth.
February Eighteenth.

YOU may easily know whether you are a child of Truth or a worshipper of self, if you will silently examine your mind, heart, and conduct. Do you harbour thoughts of suspicion, enmity, envy, lust, pride; or do you strenuously fight against these? If the former, you are chained to self, no matter what religion you may profess; if the latter, you are a candidate for Truth, even though outwardly you may profess no religion. Are you passionate, self-willed, ever seeking to gain your own ends, self-indulgent, and self-centred; or are you gentle, mild, unselfish, quit of every form of self-indulgence, and are ever ready to give up your own? If the former, self is your master; if the latter, Truth is the object of your affection.

The signs by which the Truth-lover is known are unmistakable.

That which temptation appeals to and arouses is unconquered desire.
February Nineteenth.

TEMPTATION waylays the man of aspiration until he touches the region of the divine consciousness, and beyond that border temptation cannot follow him. It is when a man begins to aspire that he begins to be tempted. Aspiration rouses up all the latent good and evil, in order that the man may be fully revealed to himself, for a man cannot overcome himself unless he fully knows himself. It can scarcely be said of the merely animal man that he is tempted, for the very presence of temptation means that there is a striving for a purer state. Animal desire and gratification is the normal condition of the man who has not yet risen into aspiration; he wishes for nothing more, nothing better, than his sensual enjoyments, and is, for the present, satisfied. Such a man cannot be tempted to fall, for he has not yet risen.

Aspiration can carry a man to heaven.

A man must know himself, if he is to know Truth.
February Twentieth.

LET the tempted one know this: that he himself is both tempter and tempted; that all his enemies are within; that the flatterers which seduce, the taunts which stab, and the flames which burn, all spring from that inner region of ignorance and error in which he has hitherto lived; and knowing this, let him be assured of complete victory over evil. When he is sorely tempted, let him not mourn, therefore, but let him rejoice in that his strength is tried and his weakness exposed. For he who truly knows and humbly acknowledges his weakness will not be slow in setting about the acquisition of strength.

He who cannot fearlessly face his lower nature cannot climb the rugged heights of renunciation.

Seek diligently the path of holiness.
February Twenty-First.

THE giving up of self is not merely the renunciation of outward things. It consists of the renunciation of the inward sin, the inward error. Not by giving up vain clothing; not by relinquishing riches; not by abstaining from certain foods; not by speaking smooth words; not by merely doing these things is the Truth found. But by giving up the spirit of vanity; by relinquishing the desire for riches; by abstaining from the lust of self-indulgence; by giving up all hatred, strife, condemnation, and self-seeking, and becoming gentle and pure at heart, by doing these things is the Truth found.

The renunciation of self is the way of Truth.

He who ceases to be passion's slave becomes a master-builder in the Temple of Destiny,
February Twenty-Second.

A MAN commences to develop power when, checking his impulses and selfish inclinations, he falls back upon the higher and calmer consciousness within him, and begins to steady himself upon a principle.

The realisation of unchanging principles in consciousness is at once the source and secret of the highest power.

When, after much searching, and suffering, and sacrificing, the light of an eternal principle dawns upon the soul, a divine calm ensues and joy unspeakable gladdens the heart.

He who has realised such a principle ceases to wander, and remains poised and self-possessed.

Only that work endures that is built upon an indestructible principle.

Men and women of real power and influence are jew.
February Twenty-Third.

IT is easy for a man, so long as he is left in the enjoyments of his possessions, to persuade himself that he believes in and adheres to the principles of Peace, Brotherhood, and Universal Love; but if, when his enjoyments are threatened, or he imagines they are threatened, he begins to clamour loudly for war, he shows that he believes in and stands upon, not Peace, Brotherhood, and Love, but strife, selfishness, and hatred.

He who does not desert his principles when threatened with the loss of every earthly thing, even to the loss of reputation and life, is the man of power, is the man whose every word endures, is the man whom the after-world honours, reveres, and worships.

There is no way to the acquirement of spiritual power except by that inward illumination and enlightenment.

All pain and sorrow is spiritual starvation, and aspiration is the cry for food.
February Twenty-Fourth.

MAN'S essential being is inward, invisible, spiritual, and as such it derives its life, its strength, from within not from without. Outward things are channels through which its energies are expended, but for renewal it must fall back on the inward silence. In so far as man seeks to drown this silence in the noisy pleasures of the senses, and endeavours to live in the conflicts of outward things, just so much does he reap the experiences of pain and sorrow, which, becoming at last intolerable, drive him back to the feet of the inward Comforter, to the shrine of the peaceful solitude within.

It is in solitude only that a man can be truly revealed to himself.

Inward harmony is spiritual power,
February Twenty-Fifth.

TAKE the principle of Divine Love, and quietly and diligently meditate upon it with the object of arriving at a thorough understanding of it. Bring its searching light to bear upon all your habits, your actions, your speech and intercourse with others, your every secret thought and desire. As you persevere in this course, the Divine Love will become more and more perfectly revealed to you, and your own shortcomings will stand out in more and more vivid contrast, spurring you on to renewed endeavour; and having once caught a glimpse of the incomparable majesty of that imperishable principle, you will never again rest in your weakness, your selfishness, your imperfection, but will pursue that Love until you have relinquished every discordant element, and have brought yourself into perfect harmony with it.

Make no stay, no resting-place, until the inmost garment of your soul is bereft of every stain.

In solitude a man gathers strength to meet the difficulties and temptations of life.
February Twenty-Sixth.

JUST as the body requires rest for the recuperation of its forces, so the spirit requires solitude for the renewal of its energies. Solitude is as indispensable to man's spiritual welfare as sleep is to his bodily well-being; and pure thought, or meditation, which is evoked in solitude, is to the spirit what activity is to the body. As the body breaks down when deprived of the needful rest and sleep, so do the spirits of men break down when deprived of the necessary silence and solitude. Man, as a spiritual being, cannot be maintained in strength, uprightness, and peace except he periodically withdraw himself from the outer world of perishable things, and reach inwardly towards the abiding and imperishable realities.

He who loves Truth, who desires and seeks wisdom, will be much alone.

Human loves are reflections of the Divine Love.
February Twenty-Seventh.

MEN, clinging to self, and to the comfortless shadows of evil, are in the habit of thinking of Divine Love as something belonging to a God who is out of reach; as something outside themselves, and that must for ever remain outside. Truly, the Love of God is ever beyond the reach of self, but when the heart and mind are emptied of self then the selfless Love, the supreme Love, the Love that is of God, or Good, becomes an inward and abiding reality.

And this inward realisation of holy Love is none other than the Love of Christ, that is so much talked about, and so little comprehended; the Love that not only saves the soul from sin, but lifts it also above the power of temptation.

Divine Love knows neither sorrow nor change.

Let a man learn to stand alone.

February Twenty-Eighth.

IF a man can find no peace within himself, where shall he find it? If he dreads to be alone with himself, what steadfastness shall he find in company? If he can find no joy in communion with his own thoughts, how shall he escape misery in his contact with others? The man who has yet found nothing within himself upon which to stand will nowhere find a place of constant rest. Without is change, and decay, and insecurity; within is all surety and blessedness. The soul is sufficient of itself. Where the need is, there is the abundant supply. Your eternal dwelling-place is within.

Be rich in yourself, be complete in yourself.

Find your centre of balance and succeed in standing alone.

February Twenty-Ninth.

UNTIL you can stand alone, looking for guidance neither to spirits nor mortals, gods nor men, but guiding yourself by the light of the truth within you, you are not unfettered and free, not altogether blessed. But do not mistake pride for self-reliance. To attempt to stand upon the crumbling foundation of pride is to be already fallen. No man depends upon others more than the proud man. His happiness is entirely in the hands of others. But the self-reliant man stands, not upon personal pride, but on an abiding law, principle, ideal, reality, within himself. Upon this he poises himself, refusing to be swept from his strong foothold either by the waves of passion within or the storms of opinion without.

Find the joy that results from well-earned freedom, the peace that flows from wise self-possession, the blessedness that inheres in native strength.

As the fountain from the hidden spring, so issues man's life from the secret recesses of his heart.

March First.

AS the heart, so is the life. The within is ceaselessly becoming the without. Nothing remains unrevealed. That which is hidden is but for a time; it ripens and comes forth at last. Seed, tree, blossom, and fruit is the fourfold order of the universe. From the state of a man s heart proceed the conditions of his life; his thoughts blossom into deeds, and his deeds bear the fruitage of character and destiny.

Life is ever unfolding from within, and revealing itself to the light, and thoughts engendered in the heart at last reveal themselves in words, actions, and things accomplished.

Mind clothes itself in garments of its own making.

There is no nobler work or higher science than that of self-perfection.

March Second.

LET man realise that life in its totality proceeds from the mind, and lo, the way of blessedness is opened to him. For he will then discover that he possesses the power to rule his mind, and to fashion it in accordance with his ideal. So will he elect to strongly and steadfastly walk those pathways of thought and action which are altogether excellent; to him life will become beautiful and sacred; and, sooner or later, he will put to flight all evil, confusion, and suffering; for it is impossible for a man to fall short of liberation, enlightenment, and peace who guards with unwearying diligence the gateway of his heart.

He who aims at the possession of a calm, wise, and seeing mind engages in the most sublime task that man can undertake.

A thought constantly repeated at last becomes a fixed habit.

March Third.

IT is in the nature of the mind to acquire knowledge by the repetition of its experiences. A thought which it is very difficult, at first, to hold and to dwell upon, at last becomes, by constantly being held in the mind, a natural and habitual condition. Just as a boy, when commencing to learn a trade, cannot even handle his tools aright, much less use them correctly, but after long repetition and practice plies them with perfect ease and consummate skill, so a state of mind at first apparently impossible of realisation is, by perseverance and practice, at last acquired and built into the character as a natural and spontaneous condition.

In this power of the mind to form and reform its habits, its conditions, is contained the basis of man's salvation, and the open door to perfect liberty by the mastery of sen.

When the heart is pure all outward things are pure.

Every sin may be overcome.
March Fourth.

A MAN'S life, in its totality, proceeds from his mind, and his mind is a combination of habits, which he can, by patient effort, modify to any extent, and over which he can gain complete ascendancy and control. Let a man realise this, and he has at once obtained possession of the key which shall open the door to his complete emancipation.

But emancipation from the ills of life (which are the ills of one s mind) is a matter of steady growth from within, and not a sudden acquisition from without. Hourly and daily must the mind be trained to think stainless thoughts, and to adopt right and dispassionate attitudes, until he has wrought out of it the Ideal of his holiest dreams.

The Higher Life is a higher living in thought, word, and deed.

Without the right performance of Duty, the higher virtues cannot be known.
March Fifth.

ALL duty should be regarded as sacred, and its faithful and unselfish performance one of the leading rules of conduct. All personal and selfish considerations should be extracted and cast away from the doing of one's duty; and when this is done, Duty ceases to be irksome, and becomes joyful. Duty is only irksome to him who craves some selfish enjoyment or benefit for himself. Let the man who is chafing under the irksome-ness of his duty look to himself, and he will find that his wearisomeness proceeds, not from the duty itself, but from his selfish desire to escape it. He who neglects duty, be it great or small, or of a public or private nature, neglects Virtue; and he who in his heart rebels against Duty rebels against Virtue.

The virtuous man concentrates his mind on the perfect doing of his own duty.

Man is the doer of his own deeds; as such he is the maker of his own character.
March Sixth.

THOSE things which befall a man are the reflections of himself; that destiny which pursued him, which he was powerless to escape by effort, or avert by prayer, was the relentless ghoul of his own wrong deeds demanding and enforcing restitution; those blessings and curses which come to him unbidden are the reverberating echoes of the sounds which he himself sent forth.

Man finds himself involved in the train of causation. His life is made up of causes and effects. It is both a sowing and a reaping. Each act of his is a cause which must be balanced by its effects. He chooses the cause (this is Free-will), he cannot choose, alter, or avert the effect (this is Fate); thus Free-will stands for the power to initiate causes, and destiny is involvement in effects.

Character is destiny.

Every form of unhappiness springs from a wrong condition of mind.
March Seventh.

ALL sin is ignorance. It is a condition of darkness and undevelopment. The wrong-thinker and the wrong-doer is in the same position in the school of life as is the ignorant pupil in the school of learning. He has yet to learn how to think and act correctly, that is, in accordance with Law. The pupil in learning is not happy so long as he does his lessons wrongly, and unhappiness cannot be escaped while sin remains unconquered.

Life is a series of lessons. Some are diligent in learning them, and they become pure, wise, and altogether happy. Others are negligent, and do not apply themselves, and they remain impure, foolish, and unhappy.

Happiness is mental harmony.

If one would find peace, he must come out of passion.
March Eighth.

SELFISHNESS, or passion, not only subsists in the gross forms of greed and glaringly ungoverned conditions of mind; it informs also every hidden thought which is subtly connected with the assumption and glorification of one s self; and it is most deceiving and subtle when it prompts one to dwell upon the selfishness of others, to accuse them of it and to talk about it. The man who continually dwells upon the selfishness in others will not thus overcome his own selfishness. Not by accusing others do we come out of selfishness, but by purifying ourselves. The way from passion to peace is not by hurling painful charges against others, but by overcoming one s self. By eagerly striving to subdue the selfishness of others, we remain passion-bound; by patiently overcoming our own selfishness we ascend into freedom.

The ascending pathway is always at hand. It is the way of self-conquest.

Aspiration—the rapture of the saints.
March Ninth.

ON the wings of aspiration man rises from earth to heaven, from ignorance to knowledge, from the under darkness to the upper light. Without it he remains a grovelling animal, earthly, sensual, unenlightened, and uninspired.

Aspiration is the longing for heavenly tilings —for righteousness, compassion, purity, love— as distinguished from desire, which is the longing for earthly things—for selfish possesions, personal dominance, low pleasures, and sensual gratifications. For one to begin to aspire means that he is dissatisfied with his low estate, and is aiming at a higher condition. It is a sure sign that he is roused out of his lethargic sleep of animality, and has become conscious of nobler attainments and a fuller life.

Aspiration makes all things possible.

The man of aspiration sees before him the pathway up to the heavenly heights.
March Tenth.

WHEN the rapture of aspiration touches the mind it at once refines it, and the dross of its impurities begins to fall away; yea, while aspiration holds the mind, no impurities can enter it, for the impure and the pure cannot at the same moment occupy the thought. But the effort of aspiration is at first spasmodic and short-lived. The mind falls back into its habitual error and must be constantly renewed.

To thirst for righteousness; to hunger for the pure life; to rise in holy rapture on the wings af angelic aspiration—this is the right road to wisdom; this is the right striving for peace; this is the right beginning of the way divine.

The lover of the pure life renews his mind daily with the invigorating glow of aspiration.

Error is sifted away. The Gold of Truth remains.
March Eleventh.

SPIRITUAL transmutation consists in an entire reversal of the ordinary self-seeking attitude of mind towards men and things, and this reversal brings about an entirely new set of experiences. Thus the desire for a certain pleasure is abandoned, cut off at its source, and not allowed to have any place in the consciousness; but the mental force which that desire represented is not annihilated, it is transferred to a higher region of thought, transmuted into a purer form of energy. The law of conservation of energy obtains universally in mind as in matter, and the force shut off in lower directions is liberated in higher realms of spiritual activity.

The clear and cloudless heights of spiritual enlightenment.

The early stage of transmutation is painful but brief, for the pain is soon transformed into pure spiritual joy.

March Twelfth.

ALONG the Saintly Way towards the divine life, the midway region of Transmutation is the Country of Sacrifice, it is the Plain of Renunciation. Old passions, old desires, old ambitions and thoughts, are cast away and abandoned, but only to reappear in some more beautiful, more permanent, more eternally satisfying form. As valuable jewels, long guarded and cherished, are thrown tearfully into the melting-pot, yet are remoulded into new and perfect adornments, so the spiritual alchemist, at first loth to part company with long-cherished thoughts and habits, at last gives them up, to discover, a little later, to his joy, that they have come back to him in the form of new faculties, rarer powers, and purer joys, spiritual jewels newly burnished, beautiful, and resplendent.

The wise man meets passion with peace, hatred with love, and returns good for evil.

The present is the synthesis of the entire past; the net result of all that a man has ever thought and done is contained within hint.

March Thirteenth.

IT is this knowledge of the Perfect Law working through and above all tilings; of the Perfect Justice operating in and adjusting all human affairs, that enables the good man to love his enemies, and to rise above all hatred, resentment, and complaining; for he knows that only his own can come to him, and that, though he be surrounded by persecutors, his enemies are but the blind instruments of a faultless retribution; and so he blames them not, but calmly receives his accounts, and patiently pays his moral debts. But this is not all; he does not merely pay his debts; he takes care not to contract any further debts. He watches himself and makes his deeds faultless.

Characteristics are fixed habits of mind, the results of deeds.

Heaven and hell are in this world.

March Fourteenth.

NOTHING comes unbidden; where the shadow is, there also is the substance. That which comes to the individual is the product of his own deeds. As cheerful industry leads to greater industry and increasing prosperity, and labour shirked or undertaken discontentedly leads to a lesser degree of labour and decreasing prosperity, so with all the varied conditions of life as we see them—they are the effects of deeds, destinies wrought by the thoughts and deeds of each particular individual. So also with the vast variety of characters—they are the ripening and ripened growth of the sowing of deeds, a sowing not confined solely to this visible life, but going backward through that infinite life which traverses the portals of innumerable births and deaths, and which also will extend into the illimitable future, reaping its own harvests, eating the sweet and bitter fruits of its own deeds.

Life is a great school for the development of character.

Purification of the heart by repetitive thought on pure things.
March Fifteenth.

MAN is a thought-being, and his life and character are determined by the thoughts in which he habitually dwells. By practice, association, and habit, thoughts tend to repeat themselves with greater and greater ease and frequency, and so fix the character in a given direction by producing that automatic action which is called "habit." By daily dwelling upon pure thoughts, the man of meditation forms the habit of pure and enlightened thinking which leads to pure and enlightened actions, and well-performed actions. By the ceaseless repetition of pure thoughts, he at last becomes one with those thoughts, and is a purified being, manifesting his attainment in pure actions.

Attainment of divine knowledge by embodying such purity in practical life.

He who will control himself will put an end to all his sufferings.
March Sixteenth.

BLESSED is that day, and not to be forgotten, when a man discovers that he himself is his own undoer and his own saviour. That within himself is the cause of all his suffering and lack of knowledge, and that also within is the source of all peace, enlightenment, and Godliness. Selfish thoughts, impure desires, and acts not shaped by Truth are the baneful seeds from which all suffering springs; while selfless thoughts, pure aspirations, and the sweet acts of Truth are the seeds from which all blessedness grows.

He who will deny himself will find the holy place where calmness lives.

He who will purify himself will destroy all his ignorance.
March Seventeenth.

HE who governs his tongue is greater than a successful disputant in the arena of intellectualism; he who controls well his mind is more powerful than the king of many nations; and he who holds himself in entire subjection is more than gods and angels. When a man who is enslaved by self realises that he must work out his own salvation, in that moment he will rise up in the dignity of his divine manhood and say, "Henceforward I will be a master in Israel, and not a slave in the House of Bondage."

Not until a man realises this, and commences to patiently purify his inner life, can he find the way which leads to lasting peace.

A life of perfect peace and blessedness by means of self-government and self-enlightenment.

Impatience is a handmaid of impulse, and never helped any man.
March Eighteenth.

YOU will be greatly helped if you devote at least one hour every day to quiet meditation on lofty moral subjects and their application to everyday life. In this way you will cultivate a calm, quiet strength, and win develop right perception and correct judgment. Do not be anxious to hurry matters. Do your duty to the very uttermost; live a disciplined and self-denying life; conquer impulse, and guide your actions by moral and spiritual Principles, as distinguished from your feelings, firmly believing that your object will be, in its own time, completely accomplished.

Still go on becoming, and as you grow more perfect you will make fewer mistakes and will suffer less.

The diadem of the King of Truth is a righteous life, his sceptre is the sceptre of peace, and his throne is in the hearts of mankind.
March Nineteenth.

IN every heart there are two kings, but one is a usurper and tyrant; he is named self, and his thoughts and deeds are those of lust, hatred, passion, and strife; the other, the rightful monarch, is named Truth, and his thoughts and deeds are those of purity and love, meekness and peace. Brother, sister, to what monarch dost thou bow? What king hast thou crowned in thy heart? Well is it with thy soul if Thou canst say: "I bow down to the Monarch of Truth; in my inmost heart I have crowned the King of Peace." Blessed indeed and immortal shall he be who shall find in the inward and heavenly places the King of Righteousness, and shall bow his heart to Him.

Power resides in blamelessness of heart. All earthly things are symbols.

It is by the eradication of the inward errors and impurities alone that a knowledge of Truth can be gained. There is no other way to wisdom and peace.
March Twentieth.

THE peace which passeth understanding is a peace which no event or circumstance can shake or mar, because it is not merely a passing calm between two storms, but is an abiding peace that is born of knowledge. Men have not this peace, because they do not understand, because they do not know, and they do not understand and know because they are blinded and rendered ignorant by their own errors and impurities; and whilst they are unwilling to give these up, they cannot but remain entirely ignorant of impersonal Principles.

Whilst a man loves his lusts he cannot love wisdom.

If we could suffer, even partly, through others, our sufferings would be unjust.
March Twenty-First.

ARE our sufferings and troubles entirely the result of our own ignorance and wrong-doing, or are they partly or wholly brought about by others, and by outward conditions?

Our sufferings are just, and are entirely the result of our own ignorance, error, and wrongdoing.

"Ye suffer from yourselves, none else compels." If this were not so, if a man could commit an evil deed and escape, the consequences of that deed being visited upon an innocent person, then there would be no Law of Justice, and without such a Law the universe could not, even for a single moment, exist. All would be chaos. Upon the surface, men appear to suffer through others, but it is only an appearance an appearance which a deeper knowledge dispels.

Man is not the result of outward conditions; outward conditions are the result of man.

In the knowledge of truth there is freedom.
March Twenty-Second.

MEN suffer because they love self, and do not love righteousness, and loving self they love their delusions, and it is by these that they are bound. There is one supreme liberty of which no man can be deprived by any but himself—the liberty to love and to practise righteousness.

This includes all other liberties. It belongs to the whipped and chained slave equally as to the king, and he who will enter into tins liberty will cast from him every chain. By this the slave will walk out from the presence of his oppressor, who will be powerless to stay him. By this the king will cease to be defiled by his surrounding luxuries, and will be a king indeed.

No outward oppressor can burden the righteous heart.

Joy is to the sinless!
March Twenty-Third.

THE wise man knows. For him anxiety, fear, disappointment, and unrest have ceased, and under whatever condition or circumstance he may be placed his calmness will not be broken, and he will bend and adjust everything with capacity and wisdom. Nothing will cause him grief. When friends yield up the body of flesh, he knows that they still are, and does not sorrow over the shell they have discarded. None can injure him, for he has identified himself with that which is unaffected by change.

The knowledge which brings peace, then, is the knowledge of unchangeable Principles arrived at by the practice of pure goodness, righteousness, becoming one with which a man becomes immortal, unchangeable, indestructible.

Peace is to the pure.

Love, meekness, gentleness, self-accusation, forgiveness, patience, compassion, reproof—these are the works of the Spirit.
March Twenty-Fourth.

THE flesh flatters; the Spirit reproves. The flesh blindly gratifies; the Spirit wisely disciplines.

The flesh loves secrecy; the Spirit is open and clear.

The flesh remembers the injury of a friend; the Spirit forgives the bitterest enemy.

The flesh is noisy and rude; the Spirit is silent and gracious.

The flesh is subject to moods; the Spirit is always calm.

The flesh incites to impatience and anger; the Spirit controls with patience and serenity.

The flesh is thoughtless; the Spirit is thoughtful.

Hatred, pride, harshness, accusing others, revenge, anger, cruelty, and flattery—these are the works of the flesh.

You can only help others in so far as you have uplifted and purified yourself.
March Twenty-Fifth.

A TRUTH is first perceived, and afterwards realised. The perception may be instantaneous, the realisation is almost invariably a process of gradual unfoldment. You will have to learn to love, regarding yourself as a child; and as you make progress in learning, the Divine will unfold within you. You can only learn to love by constantly meditating upon Love as a divine principle, and by adjusting, day by day, all your thought, and words, and acts to it. Watch yourself closely, and when you think, or say, or do anything which is not born of pure unselfish love, resolve that you will henceforth guard yourself in that direction. By so doing you win every day grow purer, tenderer, holier, and soon you will find it easy to love, and will realise the Divine within you.

When love is perfected and revealed in the heart, Christ is known.

Follow faithfully where the inward light leads you.
March Twenty-Sixth.

IT is well to become conscious of your shortcomings, for, having realised them, and feeling the necessity of overcoming them, you will, sooner or later, rise above them into the pure atmosphere of duty and unselfish love. You should not picture dark things in the future, but if you think of the future at all, think of it as bright. Above all, do your duty each day, and do it cheerfully and unselfishly, and then each day will bring its own measure of joy and peace, and the future will hold much happiness for you. The best way to overcome your faults is to perform all your duties faithfully, without thinking of any gain to yourself, and to do all you can to make others happy; speaking kindly to all, doing kind things when you can, and not retaliating when others do or say unkind things.

Put your whole heart into the present, living it, minute by minute, hour by hour, and day by day, self-governed and pure.

The righteous man is invincible. No enemy can possibly overcome him.
March Twenty-Seventh.

THE righteous man, having nothing to hide, committing no acts which require stealth, and harbouring no thoughts and desires which he would not like others to know, is fearless and unashamed. His step is firm, his body upright, and his speech direct, and without ambiguity. He looks everybody in the face. How can he fear any, who wrongs none? How can he be ashamed before any, who deceives none? And ceasing from all wrong, he can never be wronged; ceasing from all deceit, he can never be deceived. It is impossible for evil to overcome good, so the righteous man can never be brought low by the unrighteous.

He cannot be afflicted by weariness and unrest whose heart is at peace with all.

It is better to love than to accuse and denounce.
March Twenty-Eighth.

THERE is that outburst of passion which is called "righteous indignation," and it appears to be righteous, but looked at from a higher conception of conduct it is seen to be not righteous. There is a certain stamp of nobility about indignation at wrong or injustice, and it is certainly far higher and nobler than indifference, but there is a loftier nobility still, by which it is seen that indignation is never necessary, and where love and gentleness take its place, they overcome the wrong much more effectually. A person that is apparently wronged requires our pity, but the one who wrongs requires still more our compassion, for he is ignorantly laying up for himself a store of suffering: he must reap the wrong he is sowing. When divine compassion is perceived in its fullness and beauty, indignation and all forms of passion cease to exercise any influence over us.

If a man would do a noble thing, and does not do it he is not exalted thereby, but debased.
March Twenty-Ninth.

THE term Goodness does not mean sickly sentiment, but inward virtue, the direct result of which is strength and power; therefore, the good man is not weak, the weak man is not good.

We should not judge the souls of others in the spirit of condemnation; but we can judge of our own life and conduct by results. There is nothing more certain than this, the evil doer speedily proves that his evil produces misery; the good man demonstrates that his goodness results in happiness.

It is a fact that one may "flourish like a green bay tree" and yet be unrighteous, but we should also remember that the bay tree at last perishes, or is cut down, and such is the fate of the unrighteous.

An exalted being apart from an exalted life is inconceivable and cannot be.

We know nothing higher than Goodness.

March Thirtieth.

THE Teachers of mankind are few. A thousand years may pass by without the advent of such a one; but when the true Teacher does appear, the distinguishing feature by which he is known is his life. His conduct is different from other men, and his teaching is never derived from any man or book, but from his own life. The Teacher first lives, and then teaches others how they may likewise live. The proof and witness of his teaching is in himself, his life. Out of millions of preachers, one only is ultimately accepted by mankind as the true Teacher, and the one who is thus accepted and exalted is he who lives. The supreme aim of all religions is to teach men how to live.

Love is far beyond the reach of all selfish argument and can only be lived.

March Thirty-First.

JESUS gave to the world a code of rules, by the observance of which all men could become sons of God, could live the Perfect Life. These rules or precepts are so simple, direct, and unmistakable that it is impossible to misunderstand them. So plain and unequivocal are they that even an unlettered child could grasp their meaning without difficulty. All of them are directly related to human conduct, and can be applied only by the individual in his own life. To carry out the spirit of these rules in one's daily conduct constitutes the whole duty of life, and lifts the individual into the full consciousness of his divine origin and nature, of his oneness with God, the Supreme Good.

Men everywhere, in their inmost hearts, know that Goodness is divine.

A man has no character, no soul, no life, apart from his thoughts and deeds.

April First.

EACH man is responsible for the thoughts which he thinks and the acts which he does, for his state of mind, and the life which he lives. No power, no event, no circumstance, can compel a man to evil and unhappiness. He himself is his own compeller. He thinks and acts by his own volition. No being, however wise and great—not even the Supreme—can make him good and happy. He himself must choose the good, and thereby find the happy.

This life of triumph is not for those who are satisfied with any lower conditions; it is for those who thirst for it and are willing to achieve it; who are as eager for righteousness as the miser is for gold. It is always at hand, and is offered to all, and blessed are they who accept and embrace it; they will enter the world of Truth; they will find the Perfect Peace.

There is a larger, higher, nobler, diviner life than that of sinning and suffering.

Man is; and as he thinks, so he is.
April Second.
MAN'S life is actual; his thoughts are actual; his deeds are actual. To occupy ourselves with the investigation of things that are, is the way af wisdom. Man, considered as above, beyond, and separate from, mind and thought, is speculative and not actual, and to occupy ourselves with the study of things that are not, is the way of folly.

Man cannot be separated from his mind; his life cannot be separated from his thoughts. Mind, thought, and life are as inseparable as light, radiance, and colour. The facts are all-sufficient, and contain within themselves the ground-work of all knowledge concerning them.

To live is to think and act, and to think and act is to Change.

Man as mind is subject to change. He is not something "made" and finally completed, but has within him the capacity for progress.
April Third.
THE purification of the heart, the thinking of right thoughts, and the doing of good deeds—what are they but calls to a higher, nobler mode of thought energising forces urging men to effort in the choosing of thoughts which shall lift them into realms of greater power, greater good, greater bliss?

Aspiration, meditation, devotion—these are the chief means which men in all ages employ to reach up to higher modes of thought, wider airs of peace, vaster realms of knowledge, for as he thinketh in his heart, so is he; he is saved from himself—from his own folly and suffering by creating within, new habits of thought; by becoming a new thinker, a new man.

Man's being is modified by every thought he thinks. Every experience affects his character.

Only the choosing of wise thoughts, and, necessarily the doing of wise deeds, leads to wisdom.
April Fourth.
THE multitudes, unenlightened concerning their spiritual nature, are the slaves of thought, but the sage is the master of thought. They follow blindly; he chooses intelligently. They obey the impulse of the moment, thinking of their immediate pleasure and happiness; he commands and subdues impulse, resting upon that which is permanently right. They, obeying blind impulse,

violate the law of righteousness; he, conquering impulse, obeys the law of righteousness. The sage stands face to face with the facts of life. He knows the nature of thought. He understands and obeys the law of his being.

Thought determines character, conditions, knowledge.

Law cannot be partial It is an unvarying mode of action, disobeying which, we are hurt; obeying, we are made happy.

April Fifth.

IT is not less kind that we should suffer the penalty of our wrong-doing than that we should enjoy the blessedness of our right-doing. If we could escape the effects of our ignorance and sin, all security would be gone, and there would be no refuge, for we could then be equally deprived of the result of our wisdom and goodness. Such a scheme would be one of caprice and cruelty, whereas law is a method of justice and kindness.

Indeed, the supreme law is the principle of eternal kindness, faultless in working, and infinite in application. It is none other than that

"Eternal Love, for ever full, for ever flowing free," of which the Christian sings; and the "Boundless Compassion" of Buddhistic precept and poetry.

Every pain we suffer brings us nearer to the knowledge of the Divine Wisdom.

Seers of the Cosmos do not mourn over the scheme of things.

April Sixth.

BUDDHA always referred to the moral law of the universe as the Good Law, and indeed it is not rightly perceived if it is thought of as anything but good, for in it there can be no grain of evil, no element of unkindness. It is no iron-hearted monster crushing the weak and destroying the ignorant, but a soothing love and brooding compassion shielding the tenderest from harm, and protecting the strongest from a too destructive use of their strength. It destroys an evil, it preserves an good. It enfolds the tiniest seedling in its care, and it destroys the most colossal wrong with a breath. To perceive it, is the beatific vision; to know it, is the beatific bliss; and they who perceive and know it are at peace; they are glad for ever more.

The wise man bends his will and subjects his desire to the Divine Order.

Rise above the allurements of sin, and enter the Divine Consciousness, the Transcendent Life.

April Seventh.

THERE comes a time in the process of transmutation when, with the decrease of evil and the accumulation of good, there dawns in the mind a new vision, a new consciousness, a new man. And when this is reached, the saint has become a sage; he has passed from the human life to the divine life. He is "born again" and there begins for him a new round of experiences; he wields a new power; a new universe opens out before his spiritual gaze. This is the stage of Transcendence; this I call the Transcendent Life. When Transcendence is attained, then the limited personality is outgrown, and the divine life is known; evil is transcended, and Good is all-in~all.

As passion is the keynote of the self-life, so serenity is the keynote of the transcendent life.

When Perfect Good is realised and known, then calm vision is acquired.

April Eighth.

THE transcendent life is ruled, not by passions, but by principles. It is founded, not upon fleeting impulses, but upon abiding laws. In its clear atmosphere, the orderly sequence of al things is revealed, so that there is seen to be no more room for sorrow, anxiety, or regret. While men are involved in the passions of self, they load themselves with cares, and trouble over many things; and more than all else do they trouble over their own little, burdened, pain-stricken personality, being anxious for its fleeting pleasures, for its protection and preservation, and for its eternal safety and continuance. Now in the life that is wise and good all this is transcended. Personal interests are replaced by universal purposes, and all cares, troubles, and anxieties concerning the pleasure and fate of the personality are dispelled like the feverish dreams of a night.

Universal Good is seen.

Evil is an experience, and not a power

April Ninth.

IF it (evil) were an independent power in the universe, it could not be transcended by any being. But though not real as a power, it is real as a condition, an experience, for all experience is of the nature of reality. It is a state of ignorance, of undevelopment, and as such it recedes and disappears before the light of knowledge, as the intellectual ignorance of the child vanishes before the gradually accumulating learning, or as darkness dissolves before the rising light.

The painful experiences of evil pass away as the new experiences of good enter into and possess the field of consciousness.

The trancendent man is he who is above and beyond the dominion of self; he has trancended evil.

Whatsoever happens to the good man cannot cause him perplexity or sorrow, for he knows its cause and issue.

April Tenth.

IN looking back on the self-life which he has transcended, the divinely enlightened man sees that all the afflictions of that life were his schoolmasters teaching him, and leading him upward, and that in the measure that he penetrated their meaning, and lifted himself above them, they departed from him. Their mission to teach him having ended, they left him triumphant master of the field; for the lower cannot teach the higher; ignorance cannot instruct wisdom; evil cannot enlighten good; nor can the pupil set lessons for the master. That which is transcended cannot reach up to that which trancends. Evil can only teach in its own sphere, where it is regarded as a master; in the sphere of good it has no place, no authority.

The strong traveller on the highroad of truth knows no such thing as resignation to evil; he knows only obedience to good.

He is bravo who conquers another: but he who conquers himself is supremely noble.

April Eleventh.

BY the way of self-conquest is the Perfect Peace achieved. Man cannot understand it, cannot approach it, until he sees the supreme necessity of turning away from the fierce fighting of things without, and entering upon the noble warfare against evils within. He is already on the Saintly Way who has realised that the enemy of the world is within, and not without; that his own ungoverned thoughts are the source of confusion and strife; that his own unchastened desires are the violaters of his peace, and of the peace of the world.

If a man has conquered lust and anger, hatred and pride, selfishness and greed, he has conquered the world.

He who is victorious over another may in turn be defeated; but he who overcomes himself will never be subdued.

Force and strife work upon the passions and fears, but love and peace reach and reform the heart.

April Twelfth.

HE who is overcome by force is not thereby overcome in his heart: he may be a greater enemy than before; but he who is overcome by the spirit of peace is thereby changed at heart. He that was an enemy has become a friend.

The pure-hearted and wise have peace in their hearts; it enters into their actions; they apply it in their lives. It is more powerful than strife; it conquers where force would fail. Its wings shield the righteous. Under its protection, the harmless are not harmed. It affords a secure shelter from the heat of selfish struggle. It is a refuge for the defeated, a tent for the lost, and a temple for the pure.

When, divine good is practised, life is bliss. Bliss is the normal condition of the good man.

He who has realised the Love that is divine has become a new man.

April Thirteenth.

AND this Love, this Wisdom, this Peace, this tranquil state of mind and heart, may be attained to, may be realised, by all who are willing and ready to and who are prepared to humbly enter into a comprehension of all that the giving up of self involves. There is no arbitrary power in the universe, and the strongest chains of fate by which men are bound are self-forged. Men are chained to that which causes suffering because they desire to be so, because they love their chains, because they think their little dark prison of self is sweet and beautiful, and they are afraid that if they desert that prison they will lose all that is real and worth having.

"Ye suffer from yourselves, none else compels, None other holds ye that ye live and die."

To the divinely wise, knowledge and Love are one and inseparable.

The world does not understand the Love that is selfless because it is engrossed in the pursuit of its own pleasures.

April Fourteenth.

AS the shadow follows the form, and as smoke comes after fire, so effect follows cause, and suffering and bliss follow the thoughts and deeds of men. There is no effect in the world around us but has its hidden or revealed cause, and that cause is in accordance with absolute justice. Men reap a harvest of suffering because in the near or distant past they have sown the seeds of evil; they reap a harvest of bliss also as a result of their own sowing of the seeds of good. Let a man meditate upon this, let him strive to understand it, and he will then begin to sow only seeds of good, and will burn up the tares and weeds which he has formerly grown in the garden of his heart.

It is toward the complete realisation of this divine Love that the whole world is moving.

He who purifies his own heart is the world's greatest benefactor.
April Fifteenth.

THE world is, and will be for many years to come, shut out from that Golden Age which is the realisation of selfless Love. You, if you are willing, may enter it now, by rising above your selfish self; if you will pass from prejudice, hatred, and condemnation to gentle and forgiving love.

Where hatred, dislike, and condemnation are, selfless Love does not abide. It resides only in the heart that has ceased from all condemnation. He who knows that Love is at the heart of all things, and has realised the all-sufficing power of that Love, has no room in his heart for condemnation.

Let men and women take this course, and lo! the Golden Age is at hand.

Only the pure in heart see God.
April Sixteenth.

HE whose heart is centred in the supreme Love does not brand and classify men; does not seek to convert men to his own views, nor to convince them of the superiority of his methods. Knowing the Law of Love, he lives it, and maintains the same calm attitude of mind and sweetness of heart towards all. The debased and the virtuous, the foolish and the wise, the learned and the unlearned, the selfish and the unselfish, receive alike the benediction of his tranquil thought.

You can only attain to this supreme knowledge, this divine Love, by unremitting endeavour in self-discipline, and by gaining victory after victory over yourself.

Enter into the New Birth, and the Love that does not die will be awakened within you, and you will be at peace.

Where there is pure spiritual knowledge, Love is perfected and fully realised.
April Seventeenth.

TRAIN your mind in strong, impartial, and gentle thought; train your heart in purity and compassion; train your tongue to silence and to true and stainless speech; so shall you enter the way of holiness and peace, and shall ultimately realise the immortal Love. So living, without seeking to convert, you will convince; without arguing, you will teach; not cherishing ambition, the wise will find you out; and without striving to gain men's opinions, you will subdue their hearts. For Love is all-conquering, all-powerful; and the thoughts, and deeds, and words of Love can never perish.

This is the realisation of selfless Love.

Rejoice! for the morning has dawned: The Truth has awakened us.

April Eighteenth.

WE have opened our eyes, and the dark night of terror is no more. Long have we slept in matter and sensation; long did we struggle in the painful nightmare of evil; but now we are awake in Spirit and Truth: We have found the Good, and the struggle with evil is ended.

We slept, yet knew not that we slept. We suffered, yet knew not that we suffered. We were troubled in our dreaming, yet none could awake us, for all were dreaming like ourselves. Yet there came a pause in our dreaming; our sleep was stayed. Truth spoke to us, and we heard; and lo! we opened our eyes, and saw. We slumbered, and saw not; we slept, and knew not; but now we are awake and see. Yea, we know we are awake because we have seen Holiness, and we love sin no more.

How beautiful is Truth! How glorious is the realm of reality! How ineffable is the bliss of Holiness!

Abandon error for Truth, and illusion for Reality.

April Nineteenth.

TO sin is to dream, and. to love sin is to love darkness. They who love darkness are involved in the darkness; they have not yet seen the light. He who has seen the light does not choose to walk in darkness. To see the Truth is to love it, and, in comparison, error has no beauty. The dreamer is now in pleasure, now in pain; this hour in confidence, the next in fear. He is without stability, and has no abiding refuge. When the monsters of remorse and retribution pursue him, whither can he fly? There is no place of safety unless he awake. Let the dreamer struggle with his dream; let him strive to realise the illusory nature of all self-seeking desire, and lo! he will open his spiritual eyes upon the world of Light and Truth. He will be happy, sane, and peaceful, seeing things as they are.

Truth is the Light of the universe, the day of the mind.

The Knowledge of Truth is an abiding consolation.

April Twentieth.

WHEN all else fails, Truth does not fail. When the heart is desolate and the world affords no shelter, Truth provides a peaceful refuge and a quiet rest. The cares of life are many, and its path is beset with difficulties; but Truth is greater than care, and is superior to all difficulties. Truth lightens our burdens; it lights up our pathway with the radiance of joy. Loved ones pass away, friends fail, and possessions disappear. Where then is the voice of comfort? Where is the whisper of consolation? Truth is the comforter of the comfortless, and the consoler of them that are deserted. Truth does not pass away, nor fail, nor disappear. Truth bestows the consolation of abiding peace. Be alert, and listen, that ye may hear the call of Truth, even the voice of the Great Awakener.

Truth removes the sting from affliction, and disperses the clouds of trouble.

He who dings to his delusions, loving self and sin cannot find the Truth.

April Twenty-First.

TRUTH brings joy out of sorrow, and peace out of perturbation; it points the selfish to the Way of Good, and sinners to the Path of Holiness. Its spirit is the doing of Righteousness. To the earnest and faithful it brings consolation; upon the obedient it bestows the crown of peace. I take refuge in Truth: Yea, in the Spirit of Good, in the knowledge of Good, and in the doing of Good I abide. And I am reassured and comforted. It is to me as though malice were not, and hatred had vanished away. Lust is confined to the nethermost darkness, it hath no way in Truth s transcendent Light. Pride is broken up and dissolved, and vanity is melted away as a mist. I have set my face towards the Perfect Good, and my feet in the Blameless Way; and because of this I am consoled.

I am strengthened and comforted, having found refuge in Truth.

A pure heart and a blameless life avail. They are filled with joy and peace.

April Twenty-Second.

OUR good deeds remain with us, they save and protect us. Evil deeds are error. Our evil deeds follow us, they overthrow us in the hour of temptation. The evil doer is not protected from sorrow; but the good doer is shielded from all harm. The fool says unto his evil deed, "Remain thou hidden, be thou unexposed"—but his evil is already published, and his sorrow is sure. If we are in evil, what shall protect us? What keep us from misery and confusion? Nor man nor woman, nor wealth nor power, nor heaven nor earth, shall keep us from confusion. From the results of evil there is no escape; no refuge and no protection. If we are in Good, what shall overtake us? What bring us to misery and confusion? Nor man nor woman, nor poverty nor sickness, nor heaven nor earth, shall bring us to confusion.

There is a straight way and a quiet rest.

Be glad and not sorrowful, all ye who love Truth! For your sorrows shall pass away, like the mists of the morning.

April Twenty-Third.

DISCIPLE: Teacher of teachers, instruct Thou me.

Master: Ask, and I will answer. Disciple: I have read much, but am ignorant still; I have studied the doctrines of the schools, but have not become wise thereby; I know the scriptures by heart, but peace is hidden from me. Point out to me, O Master! the way of knowledge. Reveal to me the highway of divine wisdom; lead Thou Thy child into the path of peace.

Master: The way of knowledge, O Disciple! is by searching the heart; the highway of wisdom is by the practice of righteousness; and by a sinless life is found the way of peace.

Behold where Love Eternal rests concealed! (The deathless Love that seemed so far away!) E'en in the lowly heart; it stands revealed To him who lives the sinless life to-day.

Great is the conquest which thou hast entered upon, even the mighty conquest of thyself; be faithful and thou shalt overcome.

April Twenty-Fourth.

DISCIPLE: Lead me, O Master! for my darkness is very great! Will the darkness lift, O Master? Will trial end in victory, and will there be an end to my many sorrows?

Master: When thy heart is pure the darkness will disappear. When thy mind is freed from passion, thou wilt reach the end of trial, and when the thought of self-preservation is yielded up, there will be no more cause for sorrow. Thou art now upon the way of discipline and purification; all my disciples must walk that way. Before thou canst enter the white light of knowledge, before thou canst behold the full glory of Truth, all thy impurities must be purged away, thy delusions all dispelled, and thy mind fortified with endurance. Relax not thy faith in Truth; forget not that Truth is eternally supreme; remember that I, the Lord of Truth, am watching over thee.

Be faithful, and endure, and I will teach thee all things.

Blessed is he who obeys the Truth, he shall not remain comfortless.

April Twenty-Fifth.

DISCIPLE: What are the greater and the lesser powers?

Master: Hear me again, O Disciple! Walking faithfully the path of discipline and purification, not abandoning it, but submitting to its austerities, thou wilt acquire the three lesser powers of discipleship; thou wilt also receive the three greater powers. And the greater and the lesser powers will render thee invincible. Self-control, Self-reliance, and Watchfulness—these are the three lesser powers. Steadfastness, Patience, Gentleness—these are the three greater powers. When thy mmd is well-controlled, and in thy keeping; when thou reliest upon no external aid, but upon Truth alone; and when thou art ceaselessly watchful over thy thoughts and actions—then thou wilt approach the Supreme Light.

Thy darkness will pass away for ever, and joy and light will wait upon thy footsteps.

Be strenuous in effort, patient in endurance, strong in resolution.

April Twenty-Sixth.

BY these four things is the heart defiled— the craving for pleasure, the clinging to temporal things, the love of self, the lust for personal continuance; from these four defilements spring all sins and sorrows. Wash thou thy heart; put away sensual cravings; detach thy mind from the wish for possessions; abandon self-defence and sell-importance. Thus putting away all cravings, thou wilt attain to satisfaction; detaching thy mind from the love of perishable things, thou wilt acquire wisdom; abandoning the thought of self, thou wilt come to peace. He who is pure is free from desire; he does not crave for sensual excitements; he sets no value on perishable things; he is the same in riches and poverty, in success or failure, in victory or defeat, in life or death. His happiness remains, his rest is sure.

Hold fast to love, and let it shape thy doing.

Instruct me in the doing which is according to the Eternal, so that I may be watchful, and fail not.

April Twenty-Seventh.

THE unrighteous man is swayed by his feelings; likes and dislikes are his masters; prejudices and partialities blind him; desiring and suffering, craving and sorrowing, self-control he knows not, and great is his unrest. The righteous man is master of his moods; likes and dislikes he has abandoned as childish things; prejudice and partiality he has put away. Desiring nothing, he does not suffer; not craving enjoyment, sorrow does not overtake him; perfect in self-control, great peace abides with him.

Do not condemn, resent, or retaliate; do not argue, or become a partisan. Maintain thy calmness with all sides; be just, and speak the truth. Act in gentleness, compassion, and charity. Be infinitely patient. Hold fast to love, and let it shape thy doing. Have goodwill to all without distinction. Think equally of all, and be disturbed by none.

Be thoughtful and wise, strong and kindhearted.

Be watchful, that no thought of self creep in again and stain thee.
April Twenty-Eighth.
THINK of thyself as abolished. In all thy doing think of the good of others and of the world, and not of pleasure or reward to thyself. Thou art no longer separate and divided from men, thou art one with all. No longer strive against others for thyself, but sympathise with all. Regard no man as thine enemy, for thou art the friend of all men. Be at peace with all. Pour out compassion on all living things, and let boundless charity adorn thy words and deeds. Such is the glad way of Truth; such is the doing which is according to the Eternal. ruled with joy is the right-doer; he acts from principles which do not change and pass away. He is one with the Eternal, and has passed beyond unrest. The peace of the righteous man is perfect; it is not disturbed by change and impermanence. Freed from passion, he is equal-minded, calm, and does not sorrow; he sees things as they are, and is no more confused.

Open thine eyes to the Eternal Light.

Knowledge is for him who seeks; wisdom crowneth him who strives; Peace in sinless silence speaks: All things perish, Truth survives.
April Twenty-Ninth.
INCREASE thy strength and self-reliance; make The spectres of thy mind obey thy will; See thou command thyself, nor let no mood, No subtle passion nor no swift desire Hurl thee to baseness; but, shouldst thou be

hurled, Rise, and regain thy manhood, taking gain Of lowliness and wisdom from thy fall. Strive ever for the mastery of thy mind, And glean some good from every circumstance That shall confront thee; make thy store of

strength Richer for ills encountered and o'ercome. Submit to naught but nobleness; rejoice Like a strong athlete straining for the prize, When thy full strength is tried.

Follow where Virtue leads High and still higher; Listen where Pureness pleads, Quench not her fire. Lo! he shall see Reality, Who cometh upward, cleansed from all desire.

Deliverance shall him entrance who strives with sifts and sorrows, tears and pains, Till he attains.

April Thirtieth.

BE not the slave

Of lusts and cravings and indulgences, Of disappointments, miseries, and Fears, doubts, and lamentations, but control Thyself with calmness: master that in thee Which masters others, and which heretofore Has mastered thee: let not thy passions rule, But rule thy passions; subjugate thyself Till passion is transmuted into peace, And wisdom crown thee; so shalt thou attain And, by attaining, know.

Look thou within. Lo! In the midst of change Abides the Changeless; at the heart of strife The Perfect Peace reposes. At the root Of all the restless striving of the world Is passion. Whoso follows passion findeth pain, But whoso conquers passion findeth peace.

I am ignorant, yet strive to know; nor will I cease to strive till I attain.

Comfort ye! The heights of Blessed Vision ye shall reach.

May First.

EOLAUS: I know that sorrow follows passion; know That grief and emptiness, and heartaches wait Upon all earthly joys; so am I sad; Yet Truth must be, and being, can be found; And though I am in sorrow, this I know— I shall be glad when I have found the Truth. Prophet: There is no gladness like the joy of

Truth. The pure in heart swim in a sea of bliss That evermore nor sorrow knows, nor pain; For who can see the Cosmos and be sad? To know is to be happy; they Who have attained Perfection; these are they Who live, and know, and realise the Truth.

He findeth Truth who findeth self-control.

Not in any of the three worlds can the soul find lasting satisfaction, apart from the realisation of righteousness.

May Second.

EVERY soul, consciously or unconsciously, hungers for righteousness, and every soul seeks to gratify that hunger in its own particular way, and in accordance with its own particular state of knowledge. The hunger is one, and the righteousness is one, but the pathways by which righteousness is sought are many. They who seek consciously are blessed, and shall shortly find that final and permanent satisfaction of soul which righteousness alone can give, for they have come into a knowledge of the true path. They who seek unconsciously, although for a time they may bathe in a sea of pleasure, are not blessed, for they are carving out for themselves pathways of suffering, over which they must walk with torn and wounded feet, and the soul will cry out for its lost heritage— the eternal heritage of the righteous.

Blessed are they who earnestly and intelligently seek.

Glorious, radiant, free, detached from the tyranny of self!
May Third.

THE journey to the Kingdom may be a long and tedious one, or it maybe short and rapid. It may occupy a minute, or it may take a thousand ages. Everything depends on the faith and belief of the searcher. The majority cannot "enter in because of their unbelief"; for how can men realise righteousness when they do not believe in it, nor in the possibility of its accomplishment? Neither is it necessary to leave the outer world, and one s duties therein. Nay, it can only be found through the unselfish performance of one's duty. But all who believe, and aspire to achieve, will sooner or later arrive at victory, if, amid all their worldly duties, they faint not, nor lose sight of the Ideal Goodness, and continue, with unshaken resolve, to press on to Perfection.

The outward life harmonises itself with the inward music.

The regulation and purification of conduct.
May Fourth.

THE whole journey from the Kingdom of Strife to the Kingdom of Love resolves itself into a process which may be summed up in the following words:—The regulation and purification of conduct. Such a process must, if assiduously pursued, necessarily lead to perfection. It will also be seen that as the man obtains the mastery over certain forces within himself, he arrives at a knowledge of all the laws which operate in the realm of all these forces, and by watching the ceaseless working of cause and effect within himself, until he understands it, he then understands it in its universal adjustments in the body of humanity.

The process is also one of simplification of the mind, a sifting away of all but the essential gold in character.

He lives no longer for himself, he lives for others: and so living, he enjoys the highest bliss, the deepest peace.

Apart from the earnest striving lo live out the teachings of Jesus there can be no true life.

May Fifth.

A GOOD man is the flower of humanity, and to daily grow purer, nobler, more Godlike, by overcoming some selfish tendency, is to be continually drawing nearer to the Divine Heart. "He that would be My disciple, let him deny himself daily," is a statement which none can misunderstand or misapply, howsoever he may ignore it. Nowhere in the universe is there any substitute for Goodness; and until a man has this, he has nothing worthy or enduring. To the possession of Goodness there is only one way, and that is, to give up all and everything that is opposed to Goodness. Every selfish desire must be eradicated; every impure thought must be yielded up; every clinging to opinion must be sacrificed; and it is in the doing of this that constitutes the following of Christ.

That which is above all creeds, beliefs, and opinions is a loving and self-sacrificing heart.

To dwell in love always and towards all is to live the true life, is to have Life itself.

May Sixth.

JESUS so lived, and all men may so live, if they will humbly and faithfully carry out His precepts. So long as they refuse to do this, clinging to their desires, passions, and opinions, they cannot be ranked as His disciples; they are the disciples of self. " Verily, verily, I say unto you: whosoever committeth sin is the servant of sin," is the searching declaration of Jesus. Let men cease to delude themselves with the belief that they can retain their bad tempers, their lusts, their harsh words and judgments, their personal hatreds, their petty contentions and darling opinions, and yet have Christ. All that divides man from man, and man from Goodness, is not of Christ, for Christ is Love.

Sin and Christ cannot dwell together, and he who accepts the Christ-life of pure Goodness ceases from sin.

When Christ is disputed about, Christ is lost.

May Seventh.

IT is no less selfish and sinful to cling to opinion than to cling to impure desire. knowing this, the good man gives up himself unreservedly to the Spirit of Love, and dwells in Love towards all, contending with none, condemning none, hating none, but loving all, seeing behind their opinions, their creeds, and their sins, into their striving, suffering, and sorrowing hearts. "He that loveth his life shall lose it." Eternal life belongs to him who win obediently relinquish his petty, narrowing, sin-loving, strife-producing personal self, for only by so doing can he enter into the large, beautiful, free, and glorious life of abounding Love. Herein is the Path of Life; for the Straight Gate is the Gate of Goodness.

The narrow way is the Way of Renunciation, or self- sacrifice.

A man can learn nothing unless he regards himself as a learner.

May Eighth.

HOW am I acting towards others?

" What am I doing for others?"

"How am I thinking of others?"

Are my thoughts of, and acts towards others, prompted by unselfish love, as I would theirs should be to me; or are they the outcome of personal dislike, of petty revenge, or of narrow bigotry and condemnation? as a man, in the sacred silence of his soul, asks himself these searching questions, applying all his thoughts and acts to the spirit of the primary precept of the Christ, his understanding will become illuminated, so that he will unerringly see where he has hitherto failed; and he will see what he has got to do in rectifying his heart and conduct, and the way in which it is to be done.

Evil is not worth resisting. The practice of the good is supremely excellent.

Personal antipathies, however natural they may be to the animal man, can have no place in the divine life.

May Ninth.

WHILST a man is engaged in resisting evil, he is not only not practising the good, he is actually involved in the like passion and prejudice which he condemns in another; and as a direct result of his attitude of mind, he himself is resisted by others as evil. Resist a man, a party, a religion, a government, as evil, and you yourself will be resisted as evil. He who considers it as a great vil that he should be persecuted and condemned, let him cease to persecute d condemn. Let him turn away from all that he has hitherto regarded as l, and begin to look for the good. So deep and far-reaching is this precept the practice of it will fake a man far up the heights of spiritual knowledge ttainment.

He who will keep the precepts of Jesus will conquer himself, and will become divinely illuminated.

Humanity is essentially divine.
May Tenth.
SO long has man dwelt in the habitations of sin that he has at last come to regard himself as native to it, and as being cut off from the Divine Source, which he believes to be outside and away from him. Man is primarily a spiritual being, and as such, is of the nature and substance of the Eternal Spirit, the Unchangeable Reality, which men call God. Goodness, not sin, is his rightful condition; perfection, not imperfection, is his heritage, and this a man may enter into and realise now if he will grant the condition, which is the denial or abandonment of self, that is, of his feverish desires, his proud will, his egotism and self-seeking—all that which St. Paul calls the "natural man."

Jesus, in His divine goodness, knew the human heart, and He knew that it was good.

He who would find how good at heart men are, let hint throw away all his ideas and suspicions about the "evil" in others, and find and practise the good within himself.
May Eleventh.
MAN has within him the divine power by which he can rise to the highest heights of spiritual achievement; by which he can shake off sin and shame and sorrow, and do the will of the Father, the Supreme Good; by which he can conquer all the powers of darkness within, and stand radiant and free; by which he can subdue the world, and scale the lofty pinnacles of God. This can man, by choice, by resolve, and by his divine strength, accomplish; but he can only accomplish it in and by obedience; he must choose meekness and lowliness of heart; he must abandon strife for peace; passion for purity; hatred for love; self-seeking for self-sacrifice, and must overcome evil with good.

This is the holy way of Truth; this is the safe and abiding salvation; this is the yoke and burden of the Christ.

The Gospel of Jesus is a Gospel of living and doing.
May Twelfth.
THAT Jesus was meek, and lowly, and loving, and compassionate, and pure is very beautiful, but it is not sufficient; it is necessary that you also should be meek, and lowly, and loving, and compassionate, and pure. That

Jesus subordinated His own will to the will of the Father, it is inspiring to know, but it is not sufficient; it is necessary that you, too, should likewise subordinate your will to that of the overruling Good. The grace and beauty and goodness that were in Jesus can be of no value to you, cannot be understood by you, unless they are also in you, and they can never be in you until you practice them, for, apart from doing, the qualities which constitute Goodness do not, as far as you are concerned, exist.

Pure Goodness is religion, and outside it there is no religion.

They are the doers of the Father's will who shape their conduct to the Divine precepts.

May Thirteenth.

TO us and to all there is no sufficiency, no blessedness, no peace to be derived from the goodness of another, not even the goodness of God; not until the goodness is done by us, not until it is, by constant effort, incorporated into our being, can we know and possess its blessedness and peace. Therefore, thou who adorest Jesus for His divine qualities, practise those qualities thyself, and thou too shalt be divine.

The teaching of Jesus brings men back to the simple truth that righteousness, or right-doing, is entirely a matter of individual conduct, and not a mystical something apart from a man's thoughts and actions, and that each must be righteous for himself; each must be a doer of the word, and it is a man's own doing that brings him peace and gladness of heart, not the doing of another.

It is only the doer of forgiveness who tastes the sweets of forgiveness.

The Christ is the Spirit of Love.

May Fourteenth.

WHEN Jesus said, "Without Me ye can I do nothing," He spoke not of His perishable form, but of the Universal Spirit of Love, of which His conduct was a perfect manifestation; and this utterance of His is the statement of a simple truth; for the works of men are vain and worthless when they are done for personal ends, and he himself remains a perishable being, immersed in darkness and fearing death, so long as he lives in his personal gratifications. The animal in man can never respond to and know the divine; only the divine can respond to the divine. The spirit of hatred in man can never vibrate in unison with the Spirit of Love; Love only can apprehend Love, and become linked with it. Man is divine; man is of the substance of Love; this he may realise if he will relinquish the impure, personal elements which he has hitherto been blindly following, and will fly to the impersonal Realities of the Christ Spirit.

In this Principle of Love, all knowledge, Intelligence, and Wisdom are contained.

Love is not complete until it is lived by man.
May Fifteenth.

EVERY precept of Jesus demands the unconditional sacrifice of some selfish, personal element, before it can be carried out. Man cannot know the Real whilst he clings to the unreal; he cannot do the work of Truth whilst he clings to error. Whilst a man cherishes lust, hatred, pride, vanity, sell-indulgence, covetousness, he can do nothing, for the works of all these sinful elements are unreal and perishable. Only when he takes refuge in the Spirit of Love within, and becomes patient, gentle, pure, pitiful, and forgiving, does he the works of Righteousness, and bears the fruits of Life. The vine is not a vine without its branches, and even then it is not complete until those branches bear fruit.

Daily practising love towards all in heart and mmd and deed, harbouring no injurious or impure thoughts, he discovers the imperishable Principles of his being.

Man's only refuge from sin is sinless Love.

Before a man can know Love as the abiding Reality within him, he must utterly abandon all those human tendencies which frustrate us perfect manifestation.
May Sixteenth.

A MAN can only consciously ally himself to the Vine of Love by deserting all stife, and hatred, and condemnation, and impurity, and pride, and self-seeking, and by thinking and doing loving deeds. By so doing he awakens within him the divine nature which he has heretofore been crucifying and denying. Every time a man gives way to anger, impatience, greed, pride, vanity, or any form of personal selfishness, he denies the Christ, he shuts himself out from Love. And thus only is Christ denied, and not by refusing to adopt a formulated creed. Christ is only known to him who by constant striving has converted himself from a sinful to a pure being, who by noble, moral effort has succeeded in relinquishing that perishable self, which is the source of all suffering and sorrow and unrest, and has become rational, gentle, peaceful, loving, and pure.

Such glorious realisation is the crown of evolution, the supreme aim of existence.

As self is the root cause of all strife and suffering, so Love is the root cause of all peace and bliss.

May Seventeenth.

THOSE who are at rest in the Kingdom do not look for happiness in any outward possession. They see that all such possessions are mere transient effects that come when they are required, and, after their purpose is served, pass away. They never think of these tilings (money, clothing, food, etc.) except as mere accessories and effects of the true Life. They are, therefore, freed from all anxiety and trouble, and, resting in Love, they are the embodiment of Happiness. Standing upon the imperishable Principles of Purity, Compassion, Wisdom, and Love, they are immortal, and know they are immortal; they are one with God, the Supreme Good, and know they are one with God. Seeing the realities of things, they can find no room anywhere for condemnation.

All men are essentially divine, though unaware of their divine nature.

All so-called evil is seen to be rooted in ignorance.

May Eighteenth.

LET it not be supposed that the children of the Kingdom live in ease and indolence (these two sins are the first that have to be eradicated when the search for the Kingdom is entered upon); they live in a peaceful activity; in fact, they only truly live, for the life of self, with its train of worries, griefs, and fears, is not real life. They perform all their duties with the most scrupulous diligence, apart from thoughts of self, and employ all their means, as well as powers and faculties, which are greatly intensified, in building up the Kingdom of Righteousness in the hearts of others, and in the world around them. This is their work, first by example, then by precept. They sorrow no more, but live in perpetual gladness, for, though they see the suffering in the world, they also see the final Bliss and the Eternal Refuge.

Whosoever is ready may come now.

Heaven is not a speculative thing beyond the tomb but a real, ever-present Heaven in the heart.

May Nineteenth.

THE only salvation recognised and taught by Jesus is salvation from sin, and the effects of sin, here and now; and this must be effected by utterly abandoning sin, which, having done, the Kingdom of God is realised in the heart as a state of perfect knowledge, perfect blessedness, perfect peace.

"Except a man be born again, he cannot see the Kingdom of God." A man must become a new creature, and how can he become new except by utterly abandoning the old? That man's last state is worse than his first who imagines that, though still continuing to cling to his old temper, his old opinionativeness, his old vanity, his old selfishness, he is constituted a new creature in some mysterious and unexplainable way by the adoption of some particular theology or religious formula.

Heaven is where Love rules, and where peace is never absent.

To the faithful, humble, and true will be revealed the sublime Vision of the Perfect One.

May Twentieth.

GOOD news indeed is that message of Jesus which reveals to man His divine possibilities; which says in substance to sin-stricken humanity, "Take up thy bed and walk; which tells man that he need no longer remain the creature of darkness and ignorance and sin, if he will but believe in Goodness, and will watch and strive and conquer until he has actualised in his life the Goodness that is sinless. And in thus believing and overcoming, man has not only the guide of that Perfect Rule which Jesus has embodied in His precepts, he has also the inward Guide, the Spirit of Truth in his own heart, "The Light that lighteth every man that cometh into the world," which, as he follows it, will infallibly witness to the divine origin of those precepts.

Realise the perfect Goodness of the Eternal Christ.

The Kingdom of Heaven is perfect trust, perfect knowledge, perfect peace.

May Twenty-First.

THE children of the Kingdom are known by their life. They manliest the fruits of the Spirit—"love, joy, peace, long-suffering, kindness, goodness, faithfulness, meekness, temperance, self-control" —under all circumstances and vicissitudes. They are entirely free from anger, fear, suspicion, jealousy, caprice, anxiety, and grief. Living in the Righteousness of God, they manifest qualities which are the very reverse of those which obtain in the world, and which are regarded by the world as foolish. They demand no rights; they do not defend themselves; do not retaliate; do good to those who attempt to injure them; manifest the same gentle spirit towards those who oppose and attack them, as towards those who agree with them; do not pass judgment on others; condemn no man and no system, and live at peace with all.

That Kingdom is in the heart of every man and woman.

Find the Kingdom by daily effort and patient work.

May Twenty-Second.

THE Temple of Righteousness is built, and its four walls are the four Principles—Purity, Wisdom, Compassion, Love. Peace is its roof, its floor is Steadfastness, its entrance door is Selfless Duty, its atmosphere is Inspiration, and its music is the Joy of the perfect. It cannot be shaken, and, being eternal and indestructible, there is no more need to seek protection in taking thought for the things of the morrow. And the Kingdom of Heaven being established in the heart, the obtaining of the material necessities of life is no more considered, for, having found the Highest, all these things are added as effect to cause, the struggle for existence has ceased, and the spiritual, mental, and material needs are daily supplied from the Universal Abundance.

Pay the price . . . the unconditional abandonment of self.

All things are possible now, and only now.

May Twenty-Third.

NOW is the reality in which time is contained. It is more and greater than time; it is an ever-present reality. It knows neither past nor future, and is eternally potent and substantial. livery minute, every day, every year is a dream as soon as it has passed, and exists only as an imperfect and unsubstantial picture in the memory, if it be not entirely obliterated.

Past and future are dreams; now is a reality. All things are now; all power, all possibility, all action is now. Not to act and accomplish now is not to act and accomplish at all. To live in thoughts of what you might have done, or in dreams of what you mean to do, this is folly; but to put away regret, to anchor anticipation, and to do and to work now, this is wisdom.

Man has all power now.

Cease to tread every byway that tempts thy soul into the shadow-land.

May Twenty-Fourth.

MAN has all power now; but not knowing this, he says, "I will be perfect next year, or, in so many years, or in so many lives." The dwellers in the Kingdom of God, who live only in the now, say, I am perfect now, and refraining from all sin now, and ceaselessly guarding all the portals of the mind, not looking to the past nor to the future, nor turning to the left or right, they remain eternally holy and blessed. "Now is the accepted time, now is the day of salvation." Say to yourself, "I will live in my Ideal now; I will be my Ideal now; and all that tempts me away from my Ideal I will not listen to;

I will listen only to the voice of my Ideal." Thus resolving, and thus doing, you shall not depart from the Highest, and shall eternally manifest the Truth.

Manifest thy native and divine strength now.

Be resolute. Be of single purpose. Renew your resolution daily.
May Twenty-Fifth.

IN the hour of temptation do not depart from the right path. Avoid excitement. When passions are aroused, restrain and subdue them. When the mind would wander, bring it back to rest on higher things. Do not think—"I can get Truth from the Teacher, or from the books." You can acquire Truth only by practice. The teacher and the books can do no more than give instructions; and you must apply them. Those only who practise faithfully the rules and lessons given, and rely entirely upon their own efforts, will become enlightened. The Truth must be earned. Do not be led away by phenomenal appearances, or seek communications with spirits, or the dead; but attain to virtue, wisdom, and knowledge of the Supreme Law by the practice of Truth. Trust the Teacher; trust the Law; trust the path of Righteousness.

Put away all wavering and doubt, and practise the lessons of wisdom with unlimited faith.

Avoid exaggerations. The Truth is sufficient.
May Twenty-Sixth.

SPEAK only words which are truthful and sincere. Do not deceive either by word, look, or gesture. Avoid slander as you would a deadly snake, lest you be caught in its toils. He who speaks evil of another cannot find the way of peace. Put away all dissipations of idle gossip. Do not talk about the private affairs of others, or discuss the ways of Society, or criticise the eminent. Do not recriminate, or accuse others of offences, but meet all offences with blameless conduct. Do not condemn those who are not walking in the righteous path, but protect them with compassion, walking the path yourself. Quench the flame of anger with the pure water of Truth. Be modest in your words, and do not utter, or participate in, coarse, frivolous, or unseemly jests. Gravity and reverence are marks of purity and wisdom.

Do not dispute about Truth, but live it.

Abstinence, sobriety, and self-control are good.
May Twenty-Seventh.

DO your duty with the utmost faithfulness, putting away an thought of reward. Let no thought of pleasure or self entice you from your duty. Do not interfere with the duties of others. Be upright in all things. Under the most severe trial, though your happiness and life should seem to be at stake, do not swerve from the right. The man of unconquerable integrity is invincible; he cannot be confounded, and he escapes from the painful mazes of doubt and bewilderment. If one should abuse or accuse, or speak ill of you, remain silent and self-controlled, striving to understand that the wrong-doer cannot injure you unless you retaliate, and allow yourself to be carried away by the same wrong condition of mind. Strive, also, to meet the evil-doer with compassion, seeing how he is injuring himself.

The pure-minded cannot think, "I have been injured by another." They know no enemy but self.

Let your charity increase and extend till self is swallowed up in kindness.
May Twenty-Eighth.
BEAR no ill-will. Subdue anger and overcome hatred. Think of all, and act towards all, with the same unalterable kindness and compassion. Do not, under the severest trial, give way to bitterness, or words of resentment; but meet anger with calmness, mockery with patience, and hatred with love. Do not be a partisan, but be a peacemaker. Do not increase division between man and man, or promote strife by taking sides with one party against another, but give equal justice, equal love, equal goodwill to all. Do not disparage other teachers, other religions, or other schools of thought. Do not set up barriers between rich and poor, employer and employed, governor and governed, master and servant, but be equal-minded towards all, perceiving their several duties. By constantly controlling the mind, subduing bitterness and resentment, and striving to acquire a steadfast kindness, the spirit of goodwill will at last be born.

Be strong, energetic, steadfast.

Be right-minded, intelligent, and clear-seeing.
May Twenty-Ninth.
BRING reason to bear on all things. Test all things. Be eager to know and understand. Be logical in thought. Be consistent in word and action. Bring the searchlight of knowledge to bear on your condition of mind, in order to simplify it and remove its errors. Question yourself with searching scrutiny. Let go of belief, hearsay, and speculation, and lay hold on knowledge. He who stands upon knowledge acquired by practice is filled with a sublime yet lowly confidence, and is able to speak the word of Truth with power. Master the task of discrimination. Learn to distinguish between good and evil; to

perceive the facts of life, and understand them in their relation one to another. Awake the mind to see the orderly sequence of cause and effect in all things, both mental and material. Thus will be revealed the worthlessness of pleasure-seeking and sin, and the glory and gladness of a life of sublime virtue and spotless purity.

Truth is. There is no chaos.

Train your mind to grasp the Great Law of Causation which is unfailing justice.
May Thirtieth.

THEN you will see, not with fleshly eyes, but with the pure and single eye of Truth. You will then understand your nature perceiving how, as a mental being, you have evolved through countless ages of experience, how you have risen, through an unbroken line of lives, from low to high, and from high to higher still—how the ever-changing tendencies of the mind have been built up by thought and action—how your deeds have made you what you are. Thus, understanding your own nature, you will understand the nature of all beings, and will dwell always in compassion. You will understand the Great Law, not only universally and in the abstract, but also in its particular application to individuals. Then self will be ended. It will be dispersed like a cloud, and Truth will be all in all.

Find no room for hatred, no room for self, no room for sorrow.

Be self-reliant, but let thy self-reliance be saintly and not selfish.
May Thirty-First.

FOLLY and wisdom, weakness and strength, are within a man, and not in any external thing, neither do they spring from any external cause. A man cannot be strong for another, he can only be strong for himself; he cannot overcome for another, he can only overcome for himself. You may learn of another, but you must accomplish for yourself. Put away all external props, and rely upon the Truth within you. A creed will not bear a man up in the hour of temptation; he must possess the inward Knowledge which slays temptation. A speculative philosophy will prove a shadowy tiling in the time of calamity; a man must have the inward Wisdom which puts an end to grief. The Unfailing Wisdom is found only by constant practice in pure thinking and well-doing; by harmonising one s mind and heart to those things which are beautiful, lovable, and true.

Goodness is the aim of all religions.

The incentive to self-sacrificing labour does not reside in any theory about the universe, but in the spirit of love and compassion.

June First.

THE spirit of love does not decrease when a man realises that perfect justice obtains in the spiritual government of the world; on the other hand, it is increased and intensified, for he knows that men suiter because they do not understand, because they err in ignorance. "The comfortably conditioned" are frequently involved in greater suffering than the poor, and, like others, are garnering their own mixed harvest of happiness and suffering. This teaching of Absolute Justice is not more encouraging for the rich than for the poor, for while it tells the rich, who are selfish and oppressive, or who misuse their wealth, that they must reap the results of all their actions, it also tells the suffering and oppressed that, as they are now reaping what they have formerly sown, they may, and surely will, by sowing the good seeds of purity, love, and peace, shortly also reap a harvest of good, and so rise above their present woes.

The painful consequences of all self-seeking must be met and passed through.

Man is the maker of happiness and misery.

June Second.

FIXED attitudes of mind determine courses of conduct, and from courses of conduct come those reactions caned happinesses and unhappinesses. This being so, it follows that, to alter the reactive condition, one must alter the active thought. To exchange misery for happiness it is necessary to reverse the fixed attitude of mind and habitual course of conduct which is the cause of misery, and the reverse effect will appear in the mind and life. A man has no power to be happy while thinking and acting selfishly; he cannot be unhappy while thinking and acting unselfishly. Wheresoever the cause is, there the effect will appear. Man cannot abrogate effects, but he can alter causes. He can purify his nature; he can remould his character. There is great power in self-conquest; there is great joy in transforming oneself.

Each man is circumscribed by his own thoughts.

Men live in spheres low or high according to the nature of their thoughts.

June Third.

CONSIDER the man whose mind is suspicious, covetous, envious. How small and mean and drear everything appears to him. Having no grandeur in himself, he sees no grandeur anywhere, being ignoble himself, he is incapable of seeing nobility in any being; selfish as he himself is, he sees in the most exalted acts of unselfishness only motives that are mean and base.

Consider again the man whose mind is unsuspecting, generous, magnanimous. How wondrous and beautiful is his world. He sees men as true, and to him they are true. In his presence the meanest forget their nature, and for the moment become like himself, getting a glimpse, albeit confused, in that temporary upliftment of a higher order of things, of an immeasurably nobler and happier life.

Refrain from harbouring thoughts that are dark and hateful, and cherish thoughts that are bright and beautiful.

The small-minded man and the large-hearted man live in two different worlds though they be neighbours.

June Fourth.

THE kingdom of heaven is not taken by I violence, but he who conforms to its principles receives the password. The ruffian moves in a society of ruffians; the saint is one of an elect brotherhood whose communion is divine music. All men are mirrors reflecting according to their own surface. All men, looking at the world of men and things, are looking into a mirror which gives back their own reflection.

Each man moves in the limited or expansive circle of his own thoughts, and all outside that circle is non-existent to him. He only knows that which he has become. The narrower the boundary, the more convinced is the man that there is no further limit, no other circle. The lesser cannot contain the greater, and he has no means of apprehending the larger minds; such knowledge comes only by growth.

Men, like schoolboys, find themselves in standards or classes to which their ignorance or knowledge entitles them.

The world of things is the other half of the world of thoughts.

June Fifth.

THE inner informs the outer. The greater embraces the lesser. Matter is the counterpart of mind. Events are streams of thoughts. Circumstances are combinations of thought, and the outer conditions and actions of others in which each man is involved, are intimately related to his own mental needs and development. Man is a part of his surroundings. He is not separate from his fellows, but is bound closely to them by the peculiar intimacy and interaction of deeds, and by those fundamental laws of thought which are the roots of human society.

One cannot alter external things to suit his passing whims and wishes, but he can set aside his whims and wishes; he can so alter his attitude of mind towards externals, that they will assume a different aspect. He cannot mould the actions of others towards him, but he can rightly fashion his actions towards them.

Things follow thoughts. Alter your thoughts, and things will receive a new adjustment.

The perfecting of one's own deeds is man's highest duty and most sublime accomplishment.

June Sixth.

THE cause of your bondage as of your deliverance is within. The injury that comes to you through others is the rebound of your own deed, the reflex of your own mental attitude. They are the instruments, you are the cause. Destiny is ripened fruits. The fruit of life, both bitter and sweet, is received by each man in just measure. The righteous man is free. None can injure him; none can destroy him; none can rob him of his peace. His attitude towards men, born of understanding, disarms their power to wound him. Any injury which they may try to inflict rebounds upon themselves to their own hurt, leaving him unharmed and untouched. The good that goes from him is his perennial fount of happiness, his eternal source of strength. Its root is serenity, its flower is joy.

External things and deeds are powerless to injure you.

The man is the all-important factor.

June Seventh.

A MAN imagines lie could do great things if he were not hampered by circumstances—by want of money, want of time, want of influence, and want of freedom from family ties. In reality the man is not hindered by these things at all. He, in his mind, ascribes to them a power which they do not possess, and he submits, not to them, but to his opinions about them, that is, to a weak element in his nature. The real "want" that hampers him is the want of the right attitude of mind. When he regards his circumstances as spurs to his resources, when he sees that his so-called drawbacks are the very steps up which he is to mount successfully to his achievement, then his necessity gives birth to invention, and the "hindrances" are transformed into aids.

He who complains of his circumstances has not yet become a man.

Nothing can prevent us from accomplishing the aims of our life.
June Eighth.

MAN'S power subsists in discrimination and choice Man does not create one jot of the universal conditions or laws; they are the essential principles of things, and are neither made nor unmade. He discovers, not makes, them. Ignorance of them is at the root of the world s pain. To defy them is folly and bondage. Who is the freer man, the thief who denes the laws of his country, or the honest citizen who obeys them? Who, again, is the freer man, the fool who thinks he can live as he likes, or the wise man who chooses to do only that which is right?

Man is, in the nature of things, a being of habit, and this he cannot alter; but he can alter his habits. He cannot alter the law of his nature, but he can adapt his nature to the law.

He is the good man whose habits of thought and action are good.

He becomes the master of the lower by enlisting in the service of the higher.
June Ninth.

MAN repeats the same thoughts, the same actions, the same experiences over and over again, until they are incorporated with his being, until they are built into his character as part of himself. Evolution is mental accumulation. Man to-day is the result of millions of repetitious thoughts and acts. He is not ready-made, he becomes, and is still becoming. His character is pre-determined by his own choice. The thought, the act, which he chooses, that, by habit, he becomes.

Thus each man is an accumulation of thoughts and deeds. The characteristics which he manifests instinctively and without effort are lines of thought and action become, by long repetition, automatic; for it is the nature of habit to become, at last, unconscious, to repeat, as it were, itself without any apparent choice or effort on the part of its possessor; and in due time it takes such complete possession of the individual as to appear to render his will powerless to counteract it.

Habit is repetition. Faculty is fixed habit.

By thoughts man binds himself.
June Tenth.

IT is true that man is the instrument of mental forces—or to be more accurate, he is those forces—but they are not blind, and he can direct them into new channels. In a word, he can take himself in hand and reconstruct his habits; for though it is also true that he is born with a given character, that character is the product of numberless lives during which it has been slowly built up by choice and effort, and in this life it will be considerably modified by new experiences.

No matter how apparently helpless a man has become under the tyranny of a bad habit, or a bad characteristic—and they are essentially the same—he can, so long as sanity remains, break away from it and become free.

A changed attitude of mind changes the character, the habits, the life.

The body is the image of the mind.
June Eleventh.

ONE who sutlers in body will not necessarily at once be cured when he begins to fashion his mind on moral and harmonious principles; indeed, for a time, while the body is bringing to a crisis, and throwing off the effects of former inharmonies, the morbid condition may appear to be intensified. As a man does not gain perfect peace immediately he enters upon the path of righteousness, but must, except in rare instances, pass through a painful period of adjustment, neither does he, with the same rare exception, at once acquire perfect health. Time is required for bodily as well as mental readjustment, and even if health is not reached, it will be approached. If the mind be made robust, the bodily condition will take a secondary and subordinate place, and will cease to have that primary importance which so many give to it.

Mental harmony, or moral wholeness, makes for bodily health.

Reach out into a comprehension of the Infinite.
June Twelfth.

WHILST vainly imagining that the I pleasures of earth are real and satisfying pain and sorrow continually remind man of their unreal and unsatisfying nature. Ever striving to believe that complete satisfaction is to be found in material things, he is conscious of an inward and persistent revolt against this belief, which revolt is at once a refutation of his essential mortality, and an inherent and imperishable proof that only in the immortal, the eternal, the infinite, can he find abiding satisfaction and unbroken peace.

Man is essentially and spiritually divine and eternal, and, immersed in mortality and troubled unrest, he is striving to enter into a consciousness of his real nature.

The common ground of faith—the root and spring of all religion—the heart of Love!

The restful Reality of the Eternal Heart.
June Thirteenth.

THE spirit of man is inseparable from I the Infinite, and can be satisfied with nothing short of the Infinite, and the burden of pain will continue to weigh upon man's heart, and the shadows of sorrow to darken his pathway, until, ceasing from wanderings in the dream-world of matter, he comes back to his home in the reality of the Eternal.

As the smallest drop of water detached from the ocean contains all the qualities of the ocean, so man, detached in consciousness from the Infinite, contains within himself its likeness; and as the drop of water must, by the law of nature, ultimately find its way back to the ocean and lose itself in its silent depths, so must man, by the unfailing law of his nature, at last return to his source, and lose himself in the heart of the Infinite.

To become one with the Infinite is the goal of man.

Enter into perfect harmony with the Eternal Law, which is Wisdom, Love, and Peace.
June Fourteenth.

THIS divine state is, and must ever be, incomprehensible to the merely personal. Personality, separateness,
selfishness, are one and the same, and are the antithesis of wisdom and divinity. By the unqualified surrender of the personality, separateness and selfishness cease, and man enters into the possession of his divine heritage of immortality and infinity.

Such surrender of the personality is regarded by the worldly and selfish mind as the most grievous of all calamities, the most irreparable loss, yet it is the one supreme and incomparable blessing, the only real and lasting gain. The mind unenlightened upon the inner laws of being and upon the nature and destiny of its own life clings to transient appearances, things which have in them no enduring substantiality, and so clinging, perishes, for the time being, amid the shattered wreckage of its own illusions.

Love is universal, supreme, all-sufficing. This is the realisation of selfless love.

When a man s soul is clouded with selfishness in any or every form, he loses the power of spiritual discrimination, and confuses the temporal with the eternal.
June Fifteenth.

MEN cling to and gratify the flesh as though it were going to last for ever, and though they try to forget the nearness and inevitably of its dissolution, the dread of death and of the loss of all that they cling to clouds their happiest hours, and the chilling shadow of their own selfishness follows them like a remorseless

And with the accumulation of temporal comforts and luxuries, the divinity within men is drugged, and they sink deeper and deeper into materiality, into the perishable life of the senses; and where there is sufficient intellect, theories concerning the immortality of the flesh come to be regarded as infallible truths.

The perishable in the universe can never become permanent; the permanent can never pass away.

Man cannot immortalise the flesh.
June Sixteenth.

ALL nature in its myriad forms of life is changeable, impermanent, unenduring. Only the informing Principle of nature endures. Nature is many, and is marked by separation. The informing Principle is one, and is marked by unity. By overcoming the senses and the selfishness within, which is the overcoming of nature, man emerges from the chrysalis of the personal and illusory, and wings himself into the glorious light of the impersonal, the region of Truth, out of which all perishable forms come.

Let men, therefore, practise self-denial; let them conquer their animal inclinations; let them refuse to be enslaved by luxury and pleasure; let them practise virtue, and grow daily into higher and ever higher virtue, until at last they grow into the Divine.

Only by realising the God state of consciousness does man enter into immortality.

This only is true service to forget oneself in love towards all.
June Seventeenth.

WHOEVER fights ceaselessly against his own selfishness, and strives to supplant it with all-embracing love, is a saint, whether he live in a cottage or in the midst of riches and influence; or whether he preaches or remains obscure.

To the worldling, who is beginning to aspire towards higher things, the saint, such as a sweet St. Francis of Assisi, or a conquering St. Anthony, is a glorious and inspiring spectacle; to the saint, an equally enrapturing sight is that of the sage, sitting serene and holy, the conqueror of sin and sorrow, no more tormented by regret and remorse, and whom even temptation can never reach; and yet even the sage is drawn on by a still more glorious vision, that of the Saviour actively manifesting His knowledge in selfless works, and rendering His divinity more potent for good by sinking Himself in the throbbing, sorrowing heart of mankind.

Only the work that is impersonal can live.

Where duties, howsoever humble, are done without self-interest, and with joyful sacrifice, there is true service and enduring work.

June Eighteenth.

IT is given to the world to learn one great and divine lesson——the lesson of absolute unselfishness. The saints, sages, and saviours of all time are they who have submitted themselves to this task, and have learned and lived it. All the scriptures of the world are framed to teach this one lesson, all the great teachers reiterate it. It is too simple for the world which, scorning it, stumbles along in the complex ways of selfishness.

To search for this righteousness is to walk the Way of Truth and Peace, and he who enters this Way will soon perceive that Immortality which is independent of birth and death, and will realise that in the divine economy of the universe the humblest effort is not lost. The world will not have finished its long journey until every soul has entered into the blissful realisation of its own divinity.

A pure heart is the end of all religion and the beginning of divinity.

In the external universe there is ceaseless turmoil, change, and unrest; at the heart of all things there is undisturbed repose; in this deep silence dwelleth the Eternal.

June Nineteenth.

AS there are depths in the ocean which the fiercest storm cannot reach, so there are silent, holy depths in the heart of man which the storms of sin and sorrow can never disturb. To reach this silence and to live consciously in it is peace.

Discord is rife in the outward world, but unbroken harmony holds sway at the heart of the universe. The human soul reaches blindly toward the harmony of the sinless state, and to reach this state and to live consciously in it is peace. Come away, for a while, from external things, from the pleasure of the senses, from the arguments of the intellect, from the noise and the excitements of the world, and withdraw yourself into the inmost chamber of your heart, and there, free from the sacrilegious intrusion of all selfish desires, you will find a holy calm, a blissful repose; the faultless eye of Truth will open within you, and you will see things as they really are.

Become as little children.

Hatred severs human lives, fosters persecution, and hurls nations into ruthless war.

June Twentieth.

MEN cry peace! peace! where there is no peace, but, on the contrary, discord, disquietude, and strife. Apart from that wisdom which is inseparable from self-renunciation, there can be no real and abiding peace.

The peace which results from social comfort, passing gratification, or worldly victory is transitory in its nature, and is burnt up in the heat of fiery trial. Only the Peace of Heaven endures through all trial, and only the selfless heart can know the Peace of Heaven.

Holiness alone is undying peace. Self-control leads to it, and the ever-increasing Light of Wisdom guides the pilgrim on his way. It is partaken of in a measure as soon as the path of virtue is entered upon, but it is only realised in its fullness when self disappears in the consummation of a stainless life.

This inward peace, this silence, this harmony, this love is the Kingdom of Heaven.

Realise the Light that never fades.

June Twenty-First.

IF, O reader! you would realise the Joy that never ends, and the tranquillity that cannot be disturbed; if you would leave behind for ever your sins, your sorrow, your anxieties, and perplexities; if, I say, you would partake of this salvation, this supremely glorious Life, then conquer yourself. Bring every thought, every impulse, every desire into perfect obedience to the divine power resident within you. There is no other way to peace but this; and if you refuse to walk it, your much praying and your strict adherence to ritual will be fruitless and unavailing, and neither gods nor angels can help you. Only to him that overcometh is given the white stone of the regenerate life, on which is written the New and Ineffable Name.

The holy place within you is your real and eternal self: it is the divine within you.

Spiritual Principles can only be acquired after long discipline in the pursuit and practice of Virtue.
June Twenty-Second.

HE schoolmaster never attempts to teach his pupils the abstract principles of mathematics at the commencement; he knows that by such a method teaching would be vain, and learning impossible. He first places before them a very simple sum, and, having explained it, leaves them to do it. When, after repeated failures and ever-renewed effort, they have succeeded in doing it correctly, a more difficult task is set them, and then another and another; and not until the pupils have, through many years of diligent application, mastered all the lessons in arithmetic does he attempt to unfold to them the underlying mathematical principles.

Thus practice ever precedes knowledge even in the ordinary things of the world, and in spiritual things, in the living of the higher life, this law is rigid in its exactions.

Truth can only be arrived at by daily and hourly doing the lessons of Virtue.
June Twenty-Third.

IN a properly governed household the child is first taught to be obedient, and to conduct itself properly under all circumstances. The child is not even told why it must do this, but is commanded to do it, and only after it has so far succeeded in doing what is right and proper is it told why it should do it. No father would attempt to teach his child the principles of ethics before exacting from it the practice of filial duty and social virtue.

Virtue can only be known by doing, and the knowledge of Truth can only be arrived at by perfecting oneself in the practice of Virtue; and to be complete in the practice and acquisition of Virtue is to be complete in the knowledge of Truth.

Undaunted by failure, and made stronger by difficulties.

Learn the lessons of Virtue, and thus build up in the strength of knowledge, destroying ignorance and the ills of life.
June Twenty-Fourth.

WHERE Love is, God is, and where Goodness lives There Christ abides; and he who daily strives

'Gainst self and selfishness, shaping his mind For Truth and Purity, shall surely find The Master's presence in his inmost heart. God shall be one with him (and not apart) Who overcomes himself, and makes his life Godlike and holy; banishing all strife Far from him; letting hate and anger die, And greed and pride and fleshly lusts that lie To God and Goodness: great shall be his peace, Happy and everlasting his release From pain and sorrow who doth conquer sin. To the pure heart comes God and dwells therein: He only who the Path of Good hath trod Hath found the Life that's "hid with Christ in God."

"Make pure thy heart, and thou wilt make thy life Rich, sweet, and beautiful, unmarred by strife."

Stimulate the mind to watchfulness and reflection.
June Twenty-Fifth.

IT will be seen that the first step in the discipline of the mind is the over-coming of indolence. This is the easiest step, and until it is perfectly accomplished the other steps cannot be taken. The clinging to indolence constitutes a complete barrier to the Path of Truth. Indolence consists in giving the body more ease and sleep than it requires, in procrastinating, and in shirking and neglecting those things which should receive immediate attention. This condition of laziness must be overcome by rousing up the body at an early hour, giving it just the amount of sleep it requires for complete recuperation, and by doing, promptly and vigorously, every task and duty, no matter how small, as it comes along.

The heart must be purified of sensual and gustatory lust.

A listless mind could not achieve any kind of success.
June Twenty-Sixth.

SUCCESS is rooted in a subtle mental brooding along a given line. It subsists in an individual characteristic, or combination of characteristics, and not in a particular circumstance, or set of circumstances. The circumstances appear, it is true, and form part of the success, but these would be useless without the mind that can penetrate and utilise them.

At the root of every success there is some form of well-husbanded and well-directed energy. There has been some persistent brooding of the mind upon a project. Success is like a flower: it may appear more or less suddenly, but it is the finished product of a long series of efforts, of preparatory stages. Men see the success, but the preparation for it, the innumerable mental processes that led up to it, are hidden from them.

Without exertion nothing can be accomplished.

In order to achieve the higher forms of success, a man must give up anxiety, hurry, and fussiness.

June Twenty-Seventh.

PRESSING forward persistently along a given way is sure to lead to a destination that is definitely associated with that way. Frequent going aside, or turning back, will render effort fruitless; no destination will he reached; success will remain afar off.

Effort, and the more effort, and then effort again, is the keynote of success. As the simple old saying has it:

"If at first you don't succeed, Try again." All the precepts of successful business men are precepts of doing; all the precepts of the wise teachers are precepts of doing. To cease to do is to cease to be of any use in the economy of life. Doing means effort, exertion.

Transmute the energy that wears and breaks down into that deeper and less obtrusive kind that preserves and builds up.

The silent, calm people will manifest a more enduring form of success than those who are noisy and restless.

June Twenty-Eighth.

WHEN a man exchanges coppers for silver, and silver for gold, he does not thereby give up the use of money; he exchanges a heavy mass for one that is lighter and smaller but more valuable. So when a man exchanges hurry for deliberation, and deliberation for calmness, he does not give up effort, he merely exchanges a diffusive and more or less ineffective energy for a more highly concentrated, effective, and valuable form.

Yet even the crudest forms of effort are necessary at first, for without them to begin with the higher forms could not be acquired. The child must crawl before it can walk; it must babble before it can talk; it must talk before it can compose. Man begins in weakness and ends in strength, but from beginning to end he advances by the efforts he makes, by the exertion he puts forth.

The root of success is in character.

The law which punishes us is the law which preserves us.

June Twenty-Ninth.

WHEN in their ignorance men would destroy themselves, its everlasting arms are thrown about them in loving, albeit sometimes painful, protection. Every pain we suffer brings us nearer to the knowledge of the Divine Wisdom. Every blessedness we enjoy speaks to us of the perfection of the Great Law, and of the fullness of bliss that shall be man's when he has come to his heritage of divine knowledge. We progress by learning, and we learn, up to a certain point, by suffering. When the heart is mellowed by love, the law of love is perceived in all its wonderful kindness; when wisdom is acquired, peace is assured.

We cannot alter the law of things, which is of sublime perfection, but we can alter ourselves so as to comprehend more and more of that perfection, and make its grandeur ours.

To wish to bring down the perfect to the imperfect is the crown of folly, but to strive to bring the imperfect up to the perfect is the height of wisdom.

Seers of the Cosmos do not mourn over the scheme of things.

June Thirtieth.

SEERS of the Cosmos see the universe as a perfect whole, and not as an imperfect jumble of parts. The Great Teachers are men of abiding joy and heavenly peace.

The blind captive of unholy desire may cry:

"Ah! Love, could you and I with Him conspire To grasp this sorry scheme of things entire, Would we not shatter it to bits, and then Remould it nearer to the heart's desire?"

This is the wish of the voluptuary, the wish to enjoy unlawful pleasures to any extent, and not reap any painful consequences. It is such men who regard the universe as a "sorry scheme of things." They want the universe to bend to their will and desire; want lawlessness, not law; but the wise man bends his will and subjects his desires to the Divine Order, and he sees the universe as the glorious perfection of an infinitude of parts.

To perceive it, is the beatific vision; to know it, is the beatific bliss.

Wisdom is the aim of every philosophy.

July First.

IN whatever condition a man finds himself, he can always find the True; and he can find it only by so utilising his present condition as to become strong and wise. The effeminate hankering after rewards, and the craven fear of punishment, let them be put away for ever, and let a man joyfully bend himself to the faithful performance of all his duties, forgetting himself and his worthless pleasures, and living strong and pure and self-contained; so shall he surely find the Unfailing Wisdom, the God-like Patience and Strength. "The situation that has not its Duty, its Ideal, was never yet occupied by man." All that is beautiful and blessed is in thyself, not in thy neighbour's wealth. Thou art poor? Thou art poor indeed if thou art not stronger than thy poverty!

Thou hast suffered calamities? Tell me, wilt thou cure calamity by adding anxiety to it? There is no evil but will vanish if thou wilt wisely meet it.

Canst thou mend a broken vase by weeping over it?

The might of meekness!
July Second.

THE man who conquers another by force is strong; the man who conquers himself by Meekness is mighty. He who conquers another by force will himself likewise be conquered; he who conquers himself by Meekness will never be overthrown, for the human cannot overcome the divine. The meek man is triumphant in defeat. Socrates lives the more by being put to death; in the crucified Jesus the risen Christ is revealed; and Stephen, in receiving his stoning, defies the hurting power of stones. That which is real cannot be destroyed, but only that which is unreal. When a man finds that within him which is real, which is constant, abiding, changeless, and eternal, he enters into that Reality, and becomes meek. All the powers of darkness will come against him, but they will do him no hurt, and will at last depart from him.

Meekness is a divine quality, and as such is all powerful.

Nothing is hidden from him who overcomes himself.
July Third.

INTO the cause of causes shalt thou penetrate, and lifting, one after another, every veil of illusion, shalt reach at last the inmost Heart of Being. Thus becoming one with Life, thou shalt know all life, and, seeing into causes, and knowing realities, thou shalt be no more anxious about thyself, and others, and the world, but shalt see that all things that are, are engines of the Great Law. Canopied with gentleness, thou shalt bless where others curse; love where others hate; forgive where others condemn; yield where others strive; give up where others grasp; lose where others gain. And in their strength they shall be weak; and in thy weakness thou shalt be strong; yea, thou shalt mightily prevail. "Therefore, when Heaven would save a man, it enfolds him with gentleness."

He that hath not unbroken gentleness hath not Truth.

How can he fear any who wrongs none?
July Fourth.

THE righteous man is invincible. No enemy can possibly overcome or con-found him; and he needs no other protection than that of his own integrity and holiness. As it is impossible for evil to overcome Good, so the righteous man can never be brought low by the unrighteous. Slander, envy, hatred, malice can never reach him, nor cause him any suffering, and those who try to injure him only succeed ultimately in bringing ignominy upon themselves.

The righteous man having nothing to hide, committing no acts which require stealth, and harbouring no thoughts and desires which he would not like others to know, is fearless and unashamed. His step is firm, his body upright, and his speech direct and without ambiguity. He looks everybody in the face. How can he be ashamed before any who deceives none?

Ceasing from all wrong you can never be wronged; ceasing from all deceit you can never be deceived.

The universe is preserved because Love is at the Heart of it.
July Fifth.

THE Children of Light who abide in the Kingdom of Heaven see the universe, and all that it contains, as the manifestation of one Law—the Law of Love. They see Love as the moulding, sustaining, protecting, and perfecting Power immanent in all things animate and inanimate. To them Love is not merely and only a rule of life, it is the Law of life, it is Life itself. Knowing this, they order their whole life in accordance with Love, not regarding their own personality. By thus practising obedience to the Highest, to divine Love, they become conscious partakers of the power of Love, and so arrive at perfect Freedom as Masters of Destiny. Love is Perfect Harmony, pure bliss, and contains, therefore, no element of suffering. Let a man think no thought and do no act that is not in accordance with pure Love, and suffering shall no more trouble him.

Love is the only preserving power.

To know Love is to know that there is no harmful power in the whole universe.
July Sixth.

IF a man would know Love, and partake of its undying bliss, he must practise it in his heart; he must become Love. He who always acts from the spirit of Love is never deserted, is never left in a dilemma or difficulty, for Love (impersonal Love) is both Knowledge and Power. He who has learned how to Love has learned how to master every difficulty, how to transmute every failure into success, how to clothe every event and condition in garments of blessedness and beauty.

The way to Love is by self-mastery, and, travelling that way, a man builds himself up in Knowledge as he proceeds. Arriving at Love, he enters into full possession of body and mind, by right of the divine Power which he has earned. "Perfect Love casteth out fear."

Perfect Love is perfect Harmlessness. And he who has destroyed in himself all thoughts of harm, and all desire to harm, receives the universal protection.

By self-enlightenment is Perfect Freedom found,
July Seventh.

THERE is no bondage in the Heavenly Life. There is Perfect Freedom. This is its great glory. This Supreme Freedom is gained only by obedience. He who obeys the Highest co-operates with the Highest, and so masters every force within himself and every condition without. A man may choose the lower and neglect the Higher, but the Higher is never overcome by the lower: herein lies the revelation of Freedom. Let a man choose the Higher and abandon the lower; he shall then establish himself as an overcomer, and shall realise Perfect Freedom.

To give the reins to inclination is the only slavery; to conquer oneself is the only freedom. The slave to self loves his chains, and will not have one of them broken for fear he would be depriving himself of some cherished delight. He thus defeats and enslaves himself.

The Land of Perfect Freedom lies through the Gate of Knowledge.

Man will be free when he is freed from self.
July Eighth.

ALL outward oppression is but the shadow and effect of the real oppression within. For ages the oppressed have cried for liberty, and a thousand man-made statutes have failed to give it to them. They can give it only to themselves; they shall find it only in obedience to the Divine Statutes which are inscribed upon their hearts. Let them resort to the inward Freedom, and the shadow of oppression shall no more darken the earth. Let men cease to oppress themselves, and no man shall oppress his brother. Men legislate for an outward freedom, yet continue to render such freedom impossible of achievement by fostering an inward condition of enslavement. They thus pursue a shadow without, and ignore the substance within. All outward forms of bondage and oppression will cease to be when man ceases to be the willing bond-slave of passion, error, and ignorance.

Freedom is to the free!

The True, the Beautiful, the Great is always childlike, and is perennially fresh and young.
July Ninth.

THE great man is always the good man; he is always simple. He draws from, nay, lives in, the inexhaustible fountain of divine Goodness within; he inhabits the Heavenly Places; communes with the vanished great ones; lives with the Invisible: he is inspired, and breathes the airs of Heaven. He who would be great, let him learn to be good. He will therefore become great by not seeking greatness. Aiming at greatness, a man arrives at nothingness; aiming at nothingness he arrives at greatness. The desire to be great is an indication of littleness, of personal vanity and obtrusiveness. The willingness to disappear from gaze, the utter absence of self-aggrandisement, is the witness of greatness. Littleness seeks and loves authority. Greatness is never authoritative, and it thereby becomes the authority to which the after ages appeal.

Be thy simple self, thy better self, the impersonal self, and lo! thou art great!

The greatness that is flawless, rounded, and complete is above and beyond all art.
July Tenth.

WOULDST thou preach the living Word? Thou shalt forgo thyself, and become that Word. Thou shalt know one thing—that the human heart is good, is divine; thou shalt live one thing—Love. Thou shalt love all, seeing no evil, believing no evil; then, though thou speak but little, thy every act shall be a power, thy every word a precept. By thy pure thought, thy selfless deed, though it appear hidden, thou shalt preach, down the ages, to untold multitudes of aspiring souls.

To him who chooses Goodness, sacrificing all, is given that which includes all. He becomes the possessor of the Best, communes with the Highest, and enters the company of the Great.

The greatness that is flawless, rounded, and complete is above and beyond all art. It is Perfect Goodness in manifestation: therefore the greatest souls are always Teachers.

Every natural law has its spiritual counterpart.
July Eleventh.

THOUGHTS arc seeds, which, falling in the soil of the mind, germinate and develop until they reach the completed stage, blossoming into deeds good or bad, brilliant or stupid, according to their nature, and ending as seeds of thought to be again sown in other minds. A teacher is a sower of seed, a spiritual agriculturist, while he who teaches himself is the wise farmer of his own mental plot. The growth of a thought is as the growth of a plant. The seed must be sown seasonably, and time is required for its full development into the plant of knowledge and the flower of wisdom.

The seen is the mirror of the unseen.

Energy to be productive must not only be directed towards good ends, it must be carefully controlled and conserved.

July Twelfth.

THE advice of one of the Great Teachers to his disciples, "Keep wide awake," tersely expresses the necessity for tireless energy if one's purpose is to be accomplished, and is equally good advice to the salesman as to the saint. "Eternal vigilance is the price of liberty," and liberty is the reaching of one's fixed ends. It was the same Teacher who said: "If anything is to be done, let a man do it at once; let him attack it vigorously! "The wisdom of this advice is seen when it is remembered that action is creative, that increase and development follow upon legitimate use. To get more energy we must use to the full that which we already possess. Only to him that puts his hand vigorously to some task do power and freedom come.

Noise and hurry are so much energy running to waste.

It is a great delusion that noise means power.

July Thirteenth.

WHERE calmness is, there is the greatest power. Calmness is the sure indication of a strong, well-trained, patiently disciplined mind. The calm man knows his business, be sure of it. His words are few, but they tell. His schemes are well planned, and they work true, like a well-balanced machine. He sees a long way ahead, and makes straight for his object. The enemy, Difficulty, he converts into a friend, and makes profitable use of him, for he has studied well how to "agree with his adversary while he is in the way with him." Like a wise general, he has anticipated all emergencies. Indeed, he is the man who is prepared beforehand. In his meditations, in the counsels of his judgment, he has conferred with causes, and has caught the bent of all contingencies. He is never taken by surprise; is never in a hurry; is safe in the keeping of his own steadfastness; and is sure of his ground.

Working steam is not heard. It is the escaping steam which makes a great noise.

Energy is the first pillar in the temple of prosperity.
July fourteenth.

CALMNESS, as distinguished from the dead placidity of languor, is the acme of concentrated energy. There is a focused mentality behind it. In agitation and excitement the mentality is dispersed. It is irresponsible, and is without force or weight. The fussy, peevish, irritable man has no influence. He repels, not attracts. He wonders why his "easy-going" neighbour succeeds, and is sought after, while he, who is always hurrying, worrying, and troubling (he miscalls it striving), fails, and is avoided. His neighbour, being a calmer man, not more easygoing but more deliberate, gets through more work, does it more skilfully, and is more self-possessed and manly. This is the reason of his success and influence. His energy is controlled and used, while the other man's energy is dispersed and abused.

No energy means no capacity.

The spendthrift can never become rich, but, if he begin with riches, must soon become poor.
July Fifteenth.

THE poor man who is to become rich must begin at the bottom, and must not wish, or try, to appear affluent by attempting something far beyond his means. There is always plenty of room and scope at the bottom, and it is a safe place from which to begin, as there is nothing below, and everything above. Many a young business man comes at once to grief by swagger and display, which he foolishly imagines are necessary to success, but which, deceiving no one but himself, lead quickly to ruin. A modest and true beginning, in any sphere, will better ensure success than an exaggerated advertisement of one's standing and importance.

The thrifty and prudent are on the way to riches.

Vanity leading to excessive luxury in clothing is a vice which should be studiously avoided by virtuous people.
July Sixteenth.

AN obtrusive display in clothing and jewellery bespeaks a vulgar and empty mind. Modest and cultured people are modest and becoming in their dress, and their spare money is wisely used in further enhancing their culture and virtue. Education and progress are of more importance to them than needless, vain apparel; and literature, art, and science are encouraged thereby. A true refinement is in the mind and behaviour, and a mind adorned with virtue and intelligence cannot add to its attractiveness (though it may detract from it) by an ostentatious display of the body.

Simplicity in dress, as in other things, is the best.

Money wasted can be restored; health wasted can be restored; but time wasted can never be restored.

July Seventeenth.

THE man who gets up early in order to think and plan, that he may weigh and consider and forecast, will always manifest greater skill and success in his particular pursuit than the man who lies in bed till the last moment, and only gets up in time to begin breakfast. An hour spent in this way before breakfast will prove of the greatest value in making one's efforts fruitful. It is a means of calming and clarifying the mind, and of focusing one's energies so as to render them more powerful and effective. The best and most abiding success is that which is made before eight o'clock in the morning. He who is at his business at six o'clock will always—all other conditions being equal—be a long way ahead of the man who is in bed at eight.

The day is not lengthened for any man.

Wisdom is the highest form of skill.

July Eighteenth.

THERE is one right way of doing everything, even the smallest, and a thousand wrong ways. Skill consists in finding the one right way, and adhering to it. The inefficient bungle confusedly about among the thousand wrong ways, and do not adopt the right one when it is pointed out to them. They do this in some cases because they think, in their ignorance, that they know best, thereby placing themselves in a position where it becomes impossible to learn, even though it be only to learn how to clean a window or sweep a floor. Thoughtlessness and inefficiency are all too common. There is plenty of room in the world for thoughtful and efficient people. Employers of labour know how difficult it is to get the best workmanship. The good workman, whether with tools or brains, whether with speech or thought, will always find a place for the exercise of his skill.

Skill is gained by thoughtfulness and attention.

There is no striking a cheap bargain with prosperity.

July Nineteenth.

AS the bubble cannot endure, so the fraud cannot prosper. He makes a feverish spurt in the acquirement of money, and then collapses. Nothing is ever gained, ever can be gained, by fraud. It is but wrested for a time, to be again returned with heavy interest. But fraud is not confined to the unscrupulous swindler. All who are getting, or trying to get, money without giving an equivalent are practising fraud, whether they know it or not. Men who are anxiously scheming how to get money without working for it are frauds, and mentally they are closely allied to the thief and swindler under whose influence they come, sooner or later, and who deprives them of their capital.

Prosperity must be purchased, not only with intelligent labour, but with moral force.

Sterling integrity tells wherever it is, and stamps its hall-mark on all transactions.
July Twentieth.

TO be complete and strong, integrity must embrace the whole man, and extend to all the details of his life; and it must be so thorough and permanent as to withstand all temptations to swerve into compromise. To fail in one point is to fail in all, and to admit, under stress, a compromise with falsehood, howsoever necessary and insignificant it may appear, is to throw down the shield of integrity, and to stand exposed to the onslaughts of evil.

The man who works as carefully and conscientiously when his employer is away as when his eye is on him, will not long remain in an inferior position. Such integrity in duty, in performing the details of his work, will quickly lead him into the fertile regions of prosperity.

The man of integrity is in line with the fixed law of things. He is like a strong tree whose roots are fed by perennial springs, and which no tempest can lay low.

Ignorant men imagine that dishonesty is a short cut to prosperity.
July Twenty-First.

HONESTY is the surest way to success. The clay at last comes when the dishonest man repents in sorrow and suffering; but no man ever needs to repent of having been honest. Even when the honest man fails—as he does sometimes through lacking other of those pillars, such as energy, economy, or system—his failure is not the grievous thing that it is to the dishonest mem, for he can always rejoice in the fact that he has never defrauded a fellow-being. Even in his darkest hour he finds repose in a clear conscience.

The dishonest man is morally short-sighted.

Strong men have strong purposes, and strong purposes lead to strong achievements.

July Twenty-Second.

INVINCIBILITY is a glorious protector, but it only envelops the man whose integrity is perfectly pure and unassailable. Never to violate, even in the most insignificant particular, is to be invincible against all the assaults of innuendo, slander, and misrepresentation. The man who has failed in one point is vulnerable, and the shaft of evil, like the arrow in the heel of Achilles, will lay him low. Pure and perfect integrity is proof against all attack and injury, enabling its possessor to meet all opposition and persecution with dauntless courage and sublime equanimity. No amount of talent, intellect, or business acumen can give a man that power of mind and peace of heart which come from an enlightened acceptance and observance of lofty moral principles.

Moral force is the greatest power.

The test of a man is in his immediate acts, and not in his ultra sentiments.

July Twenty-Third.

SYMPATHY should not be confounded with that maudlin and superficial sentiment which, like a pretty flower without root, presently perishes and leaves behind neither seed nor fruit. To fall into hysterical weeping when parting with a friend, or on hearing of some suffering abroad, is not sympathy. Neither are bursts of violent indignation against the cruelties and injustices of others any indication of a sympathetic mind. If one is cruel at home—if he badgers his wife, or beats his children, or abuses his servants, or stabs his neighbours with shafts of sarcasm— what hypocrisy is in his profession of love for suffering people who are outside the immediate range of his influence! What shallow sentiment informs his bursts of indignation against the injustices and hard-heartedness in the world around him!

Sympathy is a deep, inexpressible tenderness which is shown in a consistently self-forgetful, gentle character.

Lack of sympathy arises in egotism; sympathy arises in love.

July Twenty-Fourth.

SYMPATHY leads us to the hearts of all men, so that we become spiritually united to them, and when they suffer we feel the pain; when they are glad, we rejoice with them; when they are despised and persecuted, we spiritually descend with them into the depths, and take into our hearts their humiliation and distress; and he who has this binding, uniting spirit of sympathy can never be cynical and condemnatory, can never pass thoughtless and cruel judgments upon his fellows, because in his tenderness of heart he is ever with them in their pain.

But to have reached this ripened sympathy, it must needs be that he has loved much, suffered much, and sounded the dark depths of sorrow. It springs from acquaintance with the profoundest experiences, so that a man has had conceit, thoughtlessness, and selfishness burnt out of his heart.

Sympathy, in its real and profound sense, is oneness with others in their strivings and sufferings.

Gentleness is the hall-mark of spiritual culture.
July Twenty-Fifth.
LET a man beware of greed, of meanness, of envy, of jealousy, of suspicion, for these things, if harboured, will rob him of all that is best in life, aye, even all that is best in material things, as well as all that is best in character and happiness. Let him be liberal of heart and generous of hand, magnanimous and trusting, not only giving cheerfully and often of his substance, but allowing his friends and fellow-men freedom of thought and action—let him be thus, and honour, plenty, and prosperity will come knocking at his door for admittance as his friends and guests.

Gentleness is akin to divinity.

A gentle man—one whose good behaviour is prompted by thoughtfulness and kindliness—is always loved, whatever may be his origin.
July Twenty-Sixth.
THE man who has perfected himself in gentleness never quarrels. He never returns the hard word; he leaves it alone, or meets it with a gentle word, which is far more powerful than wrath. Gentleness is wedded to wisdom, and the wise man has overcome all anger in himself, and so understands how to overcome it in others. The gentle man is saved from most of the disturbances and turmoils with which uncontrolled men afflict themselves. While they are wearing themselves out with wasteful and needless strain, he is quiet and composed, and such quietness and composure are strong to win in the battle of life.

Argument analyses the outer skin, but sympathy reaches to the heart.

Spurious things have no value, whether they be bric-a-brac or men.
July Twenty-Seventh.

IT is all-important that we be real; that we harbour no wish to appear other than what we are; that we simulate no virtue, assume no excellency, adopt no disguise. The hypocrite thinks he can hoodwink the world and the eternal law of the world. There is but one person that he hoodwinks, and that is himself, and for that the law of the world inflicts its righteous penalty. There is an old theory that the excessively wicked are annihilated. I think to be a pretender is to come as near to annihilation as a man can get, for there is a sense in which a man is gone, and in his place there is but a mirage of shams.

The sound-hearted man becomes an exemplar: he is, more than a man; he is a reality, a force, a moulding principle.

Evil is an experience, and not a power.
July Twenty-Eighth.

THE painful experiences of evil pass away as the new experiences of good enter into and possess the field of consciousness. And what are the new experiences of good? They are many and beautiful—such as the joyful knowledge of freedom from sin; the absence of remorse; deliverance from all the torments of temptation; ineffable joy in conditions and circumstances which formerly caused deep affliction; imperviousness to hurt by the actions of others; great patience and sweetness of character; serenity of mind under all circumstances; emancipation from doubt, fear, and anxiety; freedom from all dislike, envy, and enmity.

Evil is a state of ignorance, of undevelopment, and as such it recedes and disappears before the light of knowledge.

When divine good is practised, life is bliss.
July Twenty-Ninth.

TO have transcendent virtue is to enjoy transcendent felicity. The beatific blessedness which Jesus holds out is promised to those having the beatific virtues—to the merciful, the pure in heart, the peacemakers, and so on. The higher virtue does not merely and only lead to happiness, it is happiness. It is impossible for a man of transcendent virtue to be unhappy. The cause of unhappiness must be sought and found in the self-loving elements, and not in the self-sacrificing qualities. A man may have virtue and be unhappy, but not so if he have divine virtue. Human virtue is mingled with self, and therefore with sorrow; but from divine virtue every taint of self has been purged away, and with it every vestige of misery.

Truth lies upward and beyond.

Where passion is, peace is not; where peace is, passion is not.
July Thirtieth.
EN pray for peace, yet cling to passion; they foster strife, yet pray for heavenly rest. This is ignorance, profound spiritual ignorance; it is not to know the first letter in the alphabet of things divine. Hatred and love, strife and peace, cannot dwell together in the same heart. Where one is admitted as a welcome guest, the other will be turned away as an unwelcome stranger. He who despises another will be despised by others; he who opposes his fellow-men will himself be resisted. He should not be surprised, and mourn, that men are divided. He should know that he is propagating strife. He should understand his lack of peace.

By the way of self-conquest is the Perfect Peace achieved.

If men only understood That the wrong act of a brother Should not call from them another.
July Thirty-First.
IF men only understood

That their wrong can never smother

The wrong doing of another;

That by hatred hate increases, And by Good all evil ceases, They would cleanse their hearts and actions, Banish thence all vile detractions— If they only understood.

If men only understood That the heart that sins must sorrow, That the hateful mind to-morrow Reaps its barren harvest, weeping, Starving, resting not, nor sleeping, Tenderness would fill their being, They would see with Pity's seeing—

If they only understood.

If men only understood How Love conquers . . .. They would ever Live in Love, in hatred never— If they only understood.

Let a man abandon self, let him overcome the world, let him deny the personal; by this pathway only can he enter into the heart of the Infinite.
August First.
"GOODWILL gives insight," and only he who has so conquered his personality that he has but one attitude of mind, that of goodwill, is possessed of divine insight, and is capable of distinguishing the true from the false. The supremely good man is, therefore, the wise man, the divine man, the

enlightened seer, the knower of the Eternal. Where you find unbroken gentleness, enduring patience, sublime lowliness, graciousness of speech, self-control, self-forgetfulness, and deep and abounding sympathy, look there for the highest wisdom, seek the company of such a one, for he has realised the Divine, he lives with the Eternal, he has become one with the Infinite. Those who are spiritually awakened have alone comprehended the Universal Reality where all appearances are dispersed and dreaming and delusion are destroyed.

To centre one's life in the Great Law of Love is to enter into rest, harmony, peace.

To enter into a realisation of the Infinite and Eternal is to rise superior to time.
August Second.
TO refrain from all participation in evil
and discord , to cease from all resistance to evil, and from the omission of that which is good, and to fall back upon unswerving obedience to the holy calm within, is to enter into the inmost heart of things, is to attain to a living, conscious experience of that eternal and infinite principle which must ever remain a hidden mystery to the merely perceptive intellect. Until this principle is realised, the soul is not established in peace, and he who so realises is truly wise, not wise with the wisdom of the learned, but with the simplicity of a blameless heart and of a divine manhood.

There is one Great Law which exacts unconditional obedience, one unifying principle which is the basis of all diversity, one eternal Truth wherein all the problems of earth pass away like shadows.

To realise this Law, this Unity, this Truth, is to enter into the Infinite, is to become one with the Eternal.

Become established in Immortality, Heaven, and the Spirit, which make up the Empire of Light.
August Third.
ENTERING into the Infinite is not a mere theory or sentiment. It is a vital experience which is the result of assiduous practice in inward purification. When the body is no longer to be, even remotely, the real man; when all appetites and desires are thoroughly subdued and purified; when the emotions are rested and calm; and when the oscillation of the intellect ceases and perfect poise is secured, then, and not till then, does consciousness become one with the Infinite; not till then is childlike wisdom and profound peace secured.

Men grow weary and grey over the dark problems of life, and finally pass away and leave them unsolved because they cannot see their way out of the darkness of the personality, being too much engrossed in its limitations.

Seeking to save his personal life, man forfeits the greater impersonal Life of Truth; clinging to the perishable, he is shut out from a knowledge of the Eternal.

Self and error are synonymous.
August Fourth.

ERROR is involved in the darkness of unfathomable complexity, but eternal simplicity is the glory of Truth.

Love of self shuts men out from Truth, and seeking their own personal happiness they lose the deeper, purer, and more abiding bliss. Says Carlyle, "There is in man a higher than happiness. He can do without happiness, and instead thereof find blessedness. . . . Love not pleasure, love God. This is the Everlasting Yea, wherein all contradiction is solved; wherein whoso walks and works, it is well with him."

He who has yielded up that self, that personality that most men love, and to which they cling with such fierce tenacity has left behind him all perplexity, and has entered into a simplicity so profoundly simple as to be looked upon by the world, involved as it is in a network of error, as foolishness.

At rest in the Infinite.

The region of Reality. Unchanging principle.
August Fifth.

WHEN a man has yielded up his lusts, his errors, his opinions and prejudices, he has entered into possession of the knowledge of God, having slain the selfish desire for heaven, and along with it the ignorant fear of hell; having relinquished even the love of life itself, he has gained supreme bliss and Life Eternal, the Life which bridges life and death, and knows its own immortality. Having yielded up all without reservation, he has gained all, and rests in peace on the bosom of the Infinite.

Only he who has become so free from self as to be equally content to be annihilated as to live, or to live as to be annihilated, is fit to enter into the Infinite. Only he who, ceasing to trust his perishable self, has learned to trust in boundless measure the Great Law, the Supreme Good, is prepared to partake of undying bliss.

By the surrender of self all difficulties are overcome.

There is no more regret, nor disappointment, nor remorse, where all selfishness has ceased.

August Sixth.

THE spirit of Love which is manifested as a perfect and rounded life is the crown of being and the supreme end of knowledge upon this earth. How does a man act under trial and temptation? Many men boast of being in possession of Truth who are continually swayed by grief, disappointment, and passion, and who sink under the first little trial that comes along. Truth is nothing if not unchangeable, and in so far as a man takes his stand upon Truth does he become steadfast in virtue, does he rise superior to his passions and emotions and changeable personality.

Men formulate perishable dogmas, and call them Truth. Truth cannot be formulated; it is ineffable, and ever beyond the reach of intellect. It can only be experienced by practice; it can only be manifested in a stainless heart and a perfect life.

He who is patient, calm, and forgiving under all circumstances manifests the Truth.

Practise heart-virtue, and search humbly and diligently for the Truth.

August Seventh.

TRUTH will never be proved by wordy arguments and learned treatises, for if men do not perceive the Truth in infinite patience, undying forgiveness, and all-embracing compassion, no words can ever prove it to them.

It is an easy matter for the passionate to be calm and patient when they are in the midst of calmness, or when they are alone. It is equally easy for the uncharitable to be gentle and kind when they are dealt kindly with, but he who retains his patience and calmness under all trial, who remains sublimely meek and gentle under the most trying circumstances, he, and he alone, is possessed of the spotless Truth. And this is so because such lofty virtues belong to the Divine, and can only be manifested by one who has attained to the highest wisdom, who has relinquished his passionate and self-seeking nature, who has realised the supreme and unchangeable Law, and has brought himself into harmony with it.

There is one great all-embracing Law which is the foundation of the universe, the Law of Love.

To become possessed of a knowledge of the Law of Love, to enter into conscious harmony with it, is to become immortal, invincible, indestructible.

August Eighth.

IT is because of the effort of the soul to realise this Law that men come again and again to live, to suffer, and to die; and when realised, suffering ceases, personality is dispersed, and the fleshly life and death are destroyed, for consciousness becomes one with the Eternal.

The Law is absolutely impersonal, and its highest manifested expression is that of Service. When the purified heart has realised Truth, it is then called upon to make the last, the greatest, and holiest sacrifice, the sacrifice of the well-earned enjoyment of Truth. It is by virtue of this sacrifice that the divinely-emancipated soul comes to dwell amongst the lowliest and least, and to be esteemed the servant of all mankind.

The Spirit of Love is alone singled out as worthy to receive the unstinted worship of posterity.

Truth cannot be limited.

August Ninth.

THE glory alike of the saint, the sage, and the saviour is this—that he has realised the most profound lowliness, the most sublime unselfishness; having given up all, even his own personality, all his works are holy and enduring, for they are freed from every taint of self. He gives, yet never thinks of receiving; he works, yet without regretting the past or anticipating the future, and never looks for reward

When the farmer has tilled and dressed his land and put in the seed, he knows that he has done all that he can possibly do, and that now he must trust to the elements, and wait patiently for the course of time to bring about the harvest, and that no amount of expectancy on his part will affect the result, liven so, he who has realised the Truth goes forth as a sower of the seeds of goodness, purity, love, and peace, without expectancy, and never looking for results, knowing that there is the Great Over-ruling Law which brings about its own harvest in due time, and which is alike the source of preservation and destruction.

Every holy man became such by unremitting perseverance in self-sacrifice.

He who enters upon the holy way begins by restraining his passions.

August Tenth.

WHAT the saints, sages, and saviours have accomplished, you likewise may accomplish if you will only tread the way which they trod and pointed out, the way of self-sacrifice, of self-denying service. Truth is very simple. It says, "Give up self," "Come unto Me" (away from all that defiles) "and I will give you rest." All the mountains of commentary that have been piled upon it cannot hide it from the heart that is earnestly seeking for righteousness. It does not require learning; it can be known in spite of learning. Disguised under many forms by erring, self-seeking men, the beautiful simplicity and clear transparency of Truth remains unaltered and undimmed, and the unselfish heart enters into and partakes of its shining radiance. Not by weaving complex theories, not by building up speculative philosophies, is Truth realised; but by weaving the web of inward purity, by building up the Temple of a stainless life, is Truth realised.

Saint ship is the beginning of holiness.

Only when you identify yourself with the Divine can you be said to be "clothed and in your right mind."

August Eleventh.

THE divine within is the abode of peace, the temple of wisdom, the dwelling-place of immortality. Apart from this inward resting-place, this Mount of Vision, there can be no true peace, no knowledge of the Divine, and if you can remain there for one minute, one hour, or one day, it is possible for you to remain there always.

All your sins and sorrows, your fears and anxieties, are your own, and you can cling to them or you can give them up. Of your own accord you cling to your unrest; of your own accord you can come to abiding peace. No one else can give up sin for you; you must give it up yourself. The greatest Teacher can do no more than walk the way of Truth for himself, and point it out to you; you yourself must walk it for yourself. You can obtain freedom and peace alone by your own efforts, by yielding up that which binds the soul, and which is destructive of peace.

Give up all self-seeking; give up self, and lo! the Peace of God is yours.

Come out of the storms of sin and anguish.

August Twelfth.

O THOU who wouldst teach men of

Truth! Hast thou passed through the desert of doubt? Art thou purged by the fires of sorrow?

Hath truth The fiends of opinion cast out. Of thy human heart? Is thy soul so fair That no false thought can ever harbour there?

O thou who Wouldst teach men of Love!

Hast thou passed through the place of despair? Hast thou wept through the dark night of grief? does it move

(Now freed from its sorrow and care) Thy human heart to pitying gentleness, Looking on wrong, and hate, and ceaseless stress?

O thou who Wouldst teach men of Peace!

Hast thou crossed the wide ocean of strife? Hast thou found on the Shores of the Silence release

From all the wild unrest of life? From thy human heart hath all striving gone, Leaving but Truth, and Love, and Peace alone?

Enter the inward resting-place.

Make yourself pure and lovable, and you will be loved by all.

August Thirteenth.

THINK of your servants with kindness, consider their happiness and comfort, and never demand of them that extremity of service which you yourself would not care to perform were you in their place. Rare and beautiful is that humility of soul by which a servant entirely forgets himself in his master's good; but far rarer, and more beautiful with a divine beauty, is that nobility of soul by which a man, forgetting his own happiness, seeks the happiness of those who are under his authority, and who depend upon him for their bodily sustenance. And such a man's happiness is increased tenfold, nor does he need to complain of those whom he employs. Said a well-known and extensive employer of labour, who never needs to dismiss an employee: "I have always had the happiest relations with my workpeople. If you ask me how it is to be accounted for, I can only say that it has been my aim from the first to do to them as I would wish to be done by."

Be friendly towards others, and friends will soon flock round you.

To dwell continually in good thoughts is to throw around oneself a psychic atmosphere of sweetness and power which leaves its impress upon all who come in contact with it.

August Fourteenth.

AS the rising sun puts to rout the helpless shadows, so are all the impotent forces of evil put to flight by the searching rays of positive thought which shine forth from a heart made strong in purity and faith.

Where there is sterling faith and uncompromising purity there is health, there is success, there is power. In such a one, disease, failure, and disaster can find no lodgment, for there is nothing on which they can feed.

Even physical conditions are largely determined by mental states, and to this truth the scientific world is rapidly being drawn. The old, materialistic belief that a man is what his body makes him is rapidly passing away, and is being replaced by the inspiring belief that man is superior to his body, and that his body is what he makes it by the power of thought.

There is no evil in the universe but has its root and origin in the mind.

Renounce.
August Fifteenth.

IF you are given to anger, worry, jealousy, greed, or any other inharmonious state of mind, and expect perfect physical health, you are expecting the impossible, for you are continually sowing the seeds of disease in your mind. Such conditions of mind are carefully shunned by the wise man, for he knows them to be far more dangerous than a bad drain or an infected house. If you would be free from all physical aches and pains, and would enjoy perfect physical harmony, then put your mind in order, and harmonise your thoughts. Think joyful thoughts; think loving thoughts; let the elixir of goodwill course through your veins, and you will need no other medicine. Put away your jealousies, your suspicions, your worries, your hatreds, your selfish indulgences, and you will put away your dyspepsia, your biliousness, your nervousness and aching joints.

If you would secure health, you must learn to work without friction.

Order your thoughts and you will order your life.
August Sixteenth.

POUR the oil of tranquillity upon the turbulent waters of the passions and prejudices, and the tempests of misfortune, however they may threaten, will be powerless to wreck the barque of your soul, as it threads its way across the ocean of life. And if that barque be piloted by a cheerful and never-failing faith, its course will be doubly sure, and many perils will pass it by which would otherwise attack it. By the power of faith every enduring work is accomplished. Faith in the Supreme; faith in the over-ruling Law; faith in your work, and in your power to accomplish that work—here is the rock upon which you must build if you would achieve, if you would stand and not fall.

Follow, under all circumstances, the highest promptings within you.

Let your heart grow large and loving and unselfish, and great and lasting will be your influence and success.

August Seventeenth.

CULTIVATE a pure and unselfish spirit, and combine with purity and faith singleness of purpose, and you are evolving from the elements enduring success of greatness and power.

If your present position is distasteful to you, and your heart is not in your work, nevertheless perform your duties with scrupulous diligence; and whilst resting your mind in the idea that the better position and greater opportunities are waiting for you, ever keep an active mental outlook for budding possibilities, so that when the critical moment arrives, and the new channel presents itself, you will step into it with your mind fully prepared for the undertaking, and with that intelligence and foresight which is born of mental discipline.

Whatever your task may be, concentrate your whole mind upon it, throw into it all the energy of which you are capable. The faultless completion of small tasks leads inevitably to larger tasks.

Learn by constant practice how to husband your resources, and to concentrate them, at any moment, upon a given point.

Passion is not power; it is the abuse of power, the dispersion of power.

August Eighteenth.

WHEN that young man, whom I knew, passing through continual reverses and misfortunes, was mocked by his friends and told to desist from further effort, and he replied, "The time is not far distant when you will marvel at my good fortune and success," he showed that he was possessed of that silent and irresistible power which has taken him over innumerable difficulties, and crowned his life with success.

If you have not this power, you may acquire it by practice, and the beginning of power is likewise the beginning of wisdom. You must commence by overcoming those purposeless trivialities to which you have hitherto been a willing victim. Boisterous and uncontrolled laughter, slander and idle talk, and joking merely to raise a laugh—all these things must be put on one side as so much waste of valuable energy.

Be of single aim; have a legitimate and useful purpose, and devote yourself unreservedly to it.

Happiness is that inward state of perfect satisfaction which is joy and peace.
August Nineteenth.

THE satisfaction which results from gratified desire is brief and illusionary, and is always followed by an increased demand for gratification. Desire is insatiable as the ocean, and clamours louder and louder as its demands are attended to. It claims ever-increasing service from its deluded devotees, until at last they are struck down with physical or mental anguish, and are hurled into the purifying fires of suffering. Desire is the region of hell, and all torments are centred there. The giving up of desire is the realisation of heaven, and all delights await the pilgrim there.

"I sent my soul through the invisible, Some letter of that after life to spell, And by and by my soul returned to me, And whispered, 'I myself am heaven and hell.'"

Heaven and hell are inward states.

To seek selfishly is only to lose happiness
August Twentieth.

SINK into self and all its gratifications, and you sink into hell; rise above self into that state of consciousness which is the utter denial and forgetfulness of self, and you enter heaven. Self is blind, without judgment, not possessed of true knowledge, and always leads to suffering. Correct perception, unbiased judgment, and true knowledge belong only to the divine state, and only in so far as you realise this divine consciousness can you know what real happiness is. So long as you persist in selfishly seeking for your own happiness, so long will happiness elude you, and you will be sowing the seeds of wretchedness. In so far as you succeed in losing yourself in the service of others, in that measure will happiness come to you, and you will reap a harvest of bliss.

Abiding happiness will come to you when, ceasing to selfishly cling, you are willing to give up.

Whatsoever you constantly meditate upon you will not only come to understand, but will grow more and more into its likeness.
August Twenty-First.

SPIRITUAL meditation is the pathway to Divinity. It is the mystic ladder which reaches from earth to heaven, from error to Truth, from pain to peace. Every saint has climbed it; every sinner must sooner or later come to it, and every weary pilgrim that turns his back upon self and the world, and sets his face resolutely towards the Father's Home, must plant his feet upon its golden rounds. Without its aid you cannot grow into the divine state, the divine likeness, the divine peace, and the fadeless glories and unpolluting joys of Truth will remain hidden from you.

If you constantly dwell upon that which is selfish and debasing, you will ultimately become selfish and debased.

If you would enter into possession of profound and abiding peace, come now and enter the path of meditation.

August Twenty-Second.

SELECT some portion of the day in which to meditate, and keep that period sacred to your purpose. The best time is the very early morning when the spirit of repose is upon everything. All natural conditions will then be in your favour; the passions, after the long bodily fast of the night, will be subdued, the excitements and worries of the previous day will have died away, and the mind, strong and yet restful, will be receptive to spiritual instruction. Indeed, one of the first efforts you will be called upon to make will be to shake off lethargy and indulgence, and if you refuse you will be unable to advance, for the demands of the spirit are imperative.

The sluggard and the self-indulgent can have no knowledge of Truth.

The direct outcome of your meditations will be a calm, spiritual strength.

August Twenty-Third.

IF you are given to hatred or anger, you will meditate upon gentleness and forgiveness, so as to become acutely alive to a sense of your harsh and foolish conduct. You will then begin to dwell in thoughts of love, of gentleness, of abounding forgiveness; and as you overcome the lower by the higher, there will gradually, silently steal into your heart a knowledge of the divine Law of Love with an understanding of its bearing upon all the intricacies of life and conduct. And in applying this knowledge to your every thought, word, and act, you will grow more and more gentle, more and more loving, more and more divine. And thus with every error, every selfish desire, every human weakness; by the power of meditation is it overcome; and as each sin, each error, is thrust out, a fuller and clearer measure of the Light of Truth illumines the pilgrim soul.

Great is the overcoming power of holy thought.

Meditation will enrich the soul with saving remembrance in the hour of strife, of sorrow, or of temptation.

August Twenty-Fourth.

AS, by the power of meditation, you grow in wisdom, you will relinquish, more and more, your selfish desires which are fickle, impermanent, and productive of sorrow and pain; and will take your stand, with increasing steadfastness and trust, upon unchangeable principles, and will realise heavenly rest.

The use of meditation is the requirement of a knowledge of eternal principles, and the power which results from meditation is the ability to rest upon and trust those principles, and so become one with the Eternal. The end of meditation is, therefore, direct knowledge of Truth, God, and the realisation of divine and profound peace.

Strive to rise, by the power of meditation, above all selfish clinging to partial gods or party creeds; above dead formalities and lifeless ignorance.

Remember that you are to grow into Truth by steady perseverance.

Believe that a life of perfect holiness is possible.

August Twenty-Fifth.

SO believing, so aspiring, so meditating, divinely sweet and beautiful will be your spiritual experiences, and glorious the revelations that will enrapture your inward vision. As you realise the divine Love, the divine Justice, the Perfect Law of Good, or God, great will be your bliss and deep your peace. Old things will pass away, and all things will become new. The veil of the material universe, so dense and impenetrable to the eye of error, so thin and gauzy to the eye of Truth, will be lifted and the spiritual universe will be revealed. Time will cease, and you will live only in Eternity. Change and mortality will no more cause you anxiety and sorrow, for you will become established in the unchangeable, and will dwell in the very heart of immortality.

He who believes climbs rapidly the heavenly hills.

Where self is, Truth is not; where Truth is, self is not.

August Twenty-Sixth.

UPON the battlefield of the human soul two masters are ever contending for the crown of supremacy, for the kingship and dominion of the heart; the master of self, called also the "Prince of this world," and the master of Truth, called also the Father God. The master self is that rebellious one whose weapons are passion, pride, avarice, vanity, self-will, implements of darkness;

the master Truth is that meek and lowly one whose weapons are gentleness, patience, purity, sacrifice, humility, love, instruments of Light.

In every soul the battle is waged, and as a soldier cannot engage at once in two opposing armies, so every heart is enlisted either in the ranks of self or of Truth. There is no half-and-half course. Jesus, the manifested Christ, declared that "No man can serve two masters; for either he will hate the one and love the other; or else he will hold to the one and despise the other. Ye cannot serve God and Mammon."

You cannot perceive the beauty of Truth while you are looking out through the eyes of self .

The lovers of Truth worship Truth with the sacrifice of self.
August Twenty-Seventh.

DO you seek to know and to realise Truth? Then you must be prepared to sacrifice, to renounce to the uttermost, for Truth in all its glory can only be perceived and known when the last vestige of self has disappeared.

The eternal Christ declared that he who would be His disciple must "deny himself daily." Are you willing to deny yourself, to give up your lusts, your prejudices, your opinions? If so, you may enter the narrow way of Truth, and find that peace from which the world is shut out. The absolute denial, the utter extinction of self is the perfect state of Truth, and all religions and philosophies are but so many aids to this supreme attainment.

As you let self die, you will be reborn in Truth.

Every holy man is a saviour of mankind.
August Twenty-Eighth.

WHEN men, lost in the devious ways of error and self, have forgotten the "heavenly birth." the state of holiness and Truth, they set up artificial standards by which to judge one another, and make acceptance of, and adherence to, their own particular theology the test of Truth; and so men are divided one against another, and there is ceaseless enmity and strife, and unending sorrow and suffering.

Reader, do you seek to realise the birth into Truth? There is only one way: Let self die. All those lusts, appetites, desires, opinions, limited conceptions, and prejudices to which you have hitherto so tenaciously clung, let them fall from you. Let them no longer hold you in bondage, and Truth will be yours. Cease to look upon your own religion as superior to all others, and strive humbly to learn the supreme lesson of charity.

To be in the world and yet not of the world is the highest perfection.

The cause of all power, as of all weakness, is within.

August Twenty-Ninth.

A THOROUGH understanding of this Great Law which permeates the universe leads to the acquirement of that state of mind known as obedience. To know that justice, harmony, and love are supreme in the universe is likewise to know that all adverse and painful conditions are the result of our own disobedience to that Law. Such knowledge leads to strength and power, and it is upon such knowledge alone that a true life and an enduring success and happiness can be built. To be patient under all circumstances, and to accept all circumstances as necessary factors in your training, is to rise superior to all painful conditions, and to overcome them with an overcoming which is sure, and which leaves no fear of their return, for by the power of obedience to law they are utterly slain.

There is no progress apart from unfoldment within.

There is no sure foothold in prosperity or peace except by orderly advancement in knowledge.

August Thirtieth.

PERHAPS the chains of poverty hang heavily upon yon, and you are friendless and alone, and you long with an intense longing that your load may be lightened; but the load continues, and you seem to be enveloped in an ever-increasing darkness. Perhaps you complain, you bewail your lot, you blame your birth, your parents, your employer, or the unjust Powers who have bestowed upon you so undeservedly poverty and hardship, and upon another affluence and ease. Cease your complaining and fretting; none of these things which you blame are the cause of your poverty; the cause is within yourself, and where the cause is, there is the remedy.

There is no room for a complainer in a universe of law, and worry is soul-suicide.

What your thoughts are, that is your real self.

August Thirty-First.

THE world around, both animate and inanimate, wears the aspect with which your thoughts clothe it. "All that we are is the result of what we have thought; it is founded on our thoughts; it is made up of our thoughts." Thus said Buddha, and it therefore follows that if a man is happy, it is because he dwells in happy thoughts; if miserable, because he dwells in despondent and debilitating thoughts. Whether one be fearful or fearless, foolish or wise, troubled or serene, within that soul lies the cause of its own state or states, and never without. And now I seem to hear a chorus of voices exclaim, "But do you realty mean to say that outward circumstances do not affect our minds?" I do not say that, but I say this, and know it to be an infallible truth, that circumstances can only affect you in so far as you allow them to do so. You are swayed by circumstances because you have not a right understanding of the nature, use, and power of thought.

To make a useful and happy life dependent upon health is to put matter before mind, is to subordinate spirit to body.

September First.

MEN of robust minds do not dwell upon their bodily condition if it be in any way disordered—they ignore it, and work on, live on, as though it were not. This ignoring of the body not only keeps the mind sane and strong, but it is the best resource for curing the body. If we cannot have a perfectly sound body, we can have a healthy mind, and a healthy mind is the best route to a sound body.

A sickly mind is more deplorable than a disordered body, and it leads to sickness of body. The mental invalid is in a far more pitiable condition than the bodily invalid. There are invalids (every physician knows them) who only need to lift themselves into a strong, unselfish, happy frame of mind to discover that their body is whole and capable.

Moral principles are the soundest foundations for health, as well as for happiness.

Men are not made unhappy by poverty, but by the thirst for riches.

September Second.

WHERE there is a cause its effect will appear; and were affluence the cause of immorality, and poverty the cause of degradation, then every rich man would become immoral, and every poor man would come to degradation.

An evil-doer will commit evil under any circumstances, whether he be rich or poor, or midway between the two conditions. A right-doer will do right howsoever he be placed. Extreme circumstances may help to bring out the evil which is already there awaiting its opportunity, but they cannot cause the evil, cannot create it.

Poverty is more often in the mind than in the purse. So long as a man thirsts for more money he will regard himself as poor, and in that sense he is poor, for covetousness is poverty of mind.

A miser may be a millionaire, but he is as poor as when he was penniless.

A man is great in knowledge, great in himself, and great in his influence in the world, in the measure that he is great in self-control.
September Third.
WONDERFUL as are the forces in nature, they are vastly inferior to that combination of intelligent forces which comprise the mind of man, and which dominate and direct the blind mechanical forces of nature. Therefore, it follows that to understand, control, and direct the inner forces of passion, desire, will, and intellect, is to be in possession of the destinies of men and nations.

He who understands and dominates the forces of external nature is the natural scientist; but he who understands and dominates the internal forces of the mind is the divine scientist; and the laws which operate in gaining a knowledge of external appearances operate also in gaining a knowledge of internal verities.

The end of knowledge is use, service, the increase of the comfort and happiness of the world.

All things, whether visible or invisible, are subservient to, and fall within the scope of, the infinite and eternal law and causation.
September Fourth.
PERFECT justice upholds the universe; perfect justice regulates human life and conduct. All the varying conditions of life, as they obtain in the world to-day, are the results of this law reacting on human conduct. Man can (and does) choose what causes he shall set in operation, but he cannot change the nature of effects; he can decide what thoughts he shall think, and what deeds he shall do, but he has no power over the results of those thoughts and deeds; these are regulated by the over-ruling law.

Man has all power to act, but his power ends with the act committed. The result of the act cannot be altered, annulled, or escaped; it is irrevocable.

Evil thoughts and deeds produce conditions of suffering; good thoughts and deeds determine conditions of blessedness.

Man's power is limited to, and his blessedness or misery is determined by, his own conduct.
September Fifth.
LIFE may be likened to a sum in arithmetic. It is bewilderingly difficult and complex to the pupil who has not yet grasped the key to its correct solution, but once this is perceived and laid hold of it becomes as astonishingly simple as it was formerly profoundly perplexing. Some idea of this relative simplicity

and complexity of life may be grasped by fully recognising and realising the fact that, while there are scores, and perhaps hundreds, of ways in which a sum may be done wrong, there is only one way by which it can be done right, and that when the right way is found the pupil knows it to be right; his perplexity vanishes, and he knows that he has mastered the problem.

In life there can be no falsifying of results; the eye of the Great Law reveals and exposes.

Selfish thoughts and bad deeds will not produce a useful and beautiful life.
September Sixth.

LIFE is like a piece of cloth, and the threads of which it is composed are individual lives. The threads, while being independent, are not confounded one with the other. Each follows its own course. Each individual suffers and enjoys the consequences of his own deeds, and not the deeds of another. The course of each is simple and definite; the whole forming a complicated, yet harmonious, combination of sequences. There are action and reaction, deed and consequence, cause and effect, and the counterbalancing reaction, consequence, and effect is always in exact ratio with the initiatory impulse.

Each man makes or mars his own life.

Man is responsible only for his own deeds; he is the custodian of his own actions.
September Seventh.

THE "problem of evil" subsists in a man's own evil deeds, and it is solved when those deeds are purified. Says Rousseau:

"Man, seek no longer the origin of evil; thou thyself art its origin."

Effect can never be divorced from cause; it can never be of a different nature from cause. Emerson says:

"Justice is not postponed; a perfect equity adjusts the balance in all parts of life."

And there is a profound sense in which cause and effect are simultaneous, and form one perfect whole. Thus, upon the instant that a man thinks, say, a cruel deed, that same instant he has injured his own mind; he is not the same man he was the previous instant; he is a little viler and a little more unhappy; and a number of successive thoughts and deeds would produce a cruel and wretched man.

An immediate nobility and happiness attend the thinking of a kind thought, or doing a kind deed.

Without strength of mind, nothing worthy of accomplishment can be done.
September Eighth.

THE cultivation of that steadfastness and stability of character which is commonly called "will-power" is one of the foremost duties of man, for its possession is essentially necessary both to his temporal and external well-being. Fixedness of purpose is at the root of all successful efforts, whether in things worldly or spiritual, and without it man cannot be otherwise than wretched, and dependent upon others for that support which should be found within himself.

The true path of will-cultivation is only to be found in the common everyday life of the individual, and so obvious and simple is it that the majority, looking for something complicated and mysterious, pass it by unnoticed.

The direct and only way to greater strength is to assail and conquer weaknesses.

In the training of the will the first step is the breaking away from bad habits.
September Ninth.

HE who has succeeded in grasping this simple, preliminary truth will perceive that the whole science of will-cultivation is embodied in the following seven rules:

1. Break off bad habits.
2. Form good habits.
3. Give scrupulous attention to the duty of the present moment.
4. Do vigorously, and at once, whatever has to be done.
5. Live by rule.
6. Control the tongue.
7. Control the mind.

Anyone who earnestly meditates upon, and diligently practises, the above rules will not fail to develop that purity of purpose and power of will which will enable him to successfully cope with every difficulty, and pass triumphantly through every emergency.

By submitting to a bad habit one forfeits the right to rule over himself.
September Tenth.

HE who thus avoids self-discipline, and looks about for some "occult secrets" for gaining will-power at the expenditure of little or no effort on his part, is deluding himself, and is weakening the willpower which he already possesses.

The strength of will which is gained by success in overcoming bad habits enables one to initiate good habits; for, while the conquering of a bad habit requires merely strength of purpose, the forming of a new one necessitates the intelligent direction of purpose. To do this, a man must be mentally active and energetic, and must keep a constant watch upon himself.

Thoroughness is a step in the development of the will which cannot be passed over. Slipshod work is an indication of weakness.

Perfection should be aimed at, even in the smallest task.

September Eleventh.

BY not dividing the mind, but giving the whole attention to each separate task as it presents itself, singleness of purpose and intense concentration of mind are gradually gained—two mental powers which give weight and worth of character, and bring repose and joy to their possessor.

Doing vigorously, and at once, whatever has to be done is equally important. Idleness and a strong will cannot go together, and procrastination is a total barrier to the acquisition of purposeful action. Nothing should be "put off" until another time, not even for a few minutes. That which ought to be done now should be done now. This seems a little thing, but it is of far-reaching importance. It leads to strength, success, and peace.

Live according to principle, and not according to passion.

Thoroughness consists in doing little things as though they were the greatest things in the world.

September Twelfth.

THAT the little things of lite are of primary importance is a truth not generally understood, and the thought that little things can be neglected, thrown aside, or slurred over is at the root of that lack of thoroughness which is so common, and which results in imperfect work and unhappy lives.

When one understands that the great things of the world and of life consist of a combination of small things, and that without this aggregation of small things the great things would be non-existent, then he begins to pay careful attention to those things which he formerly regarded as insignificant.

He who acquires the quality of thoroughness becomes a man of usefulness and influence.

The cause of the common lack of thoroughness lies in the thirst for pleasure.
September Thirteenth.

EVERY employer of labour knows how difficult it is to find men and women who will put thought and energy into their work, and do it completely and satisfactorily. Bad workmanship abounds. Skill and excellence are acquired by few. Thoughtlessness, carelessness, and laziness are such common vices that it should cease to appear strange that, in spite of "social reform," the ranks of the unemployed should continue to swell, for those who scamp their work to-day will, another day, in the hour of deep necessity, look and ask for work in vain.

The law of "the survival of the fittest" is not based on cruelty, it is based on justice; it is one aspect of that divine equity which everywhere prevails. Vice is "beaten with many stripes"; if it were not so, how could virtue be developed? The thoughtless and lazy cannot take precedence of, or stand equally with, the thoughtful and industrious.

The mind that is occupied with pleasure cannot also be concentrated upon the perfect performance of duty.

He who lacks thoroughness in his worldly duties will also lack the same in spiritual things.
September Fourteenth.

THOROUGHNESS is completeness, perfection; it means doing a thing so well that there is nothing left to be desired; it means doing one's work, if not better than anyone else can do it, at least not worse than the best that others do. It means the exercise of much thought, the putting forth of great energy, the persistent application of the mind to its task, the cultivation of patience, perseverance, and a high sense of duty. An ancient teacher said, "If anything has to be done, let a man do it, let him attack it vigorously "; and another teacher said, "Whatsoever thy hand findeth to do, do it with thy might."

It is better to be a whole-souled worldling than a halfhearted religionist.

He who has not learned how to be gentle, loving, and happy has learned very little.
September Fifteenth.

DESPONDENCY, irritability, anxiety, complaining, condemning, and grumbling—all these are thought-cankers, mind-diseases; they are the indications of a wrong mental condition, and those who suffer therefrom would do well to remedy their thinking and conduct. It is true there is much sin and misery in the world, so that all our love and compassion are needed, but our misery is not needed—there is already too much of that. No, it is our cheerfulness and our happiness that are needed, for there is too little of that. We can give nothing better to the world than beauty of life and character; without this, all other things are vain; this is pre-eminently excellent; it is enduring, real, and not to be overthrown, and it includes all joy and blessedness.

A man's surroundings are never against him; they are there to aid him.

You can transform everything around you if you will transform yourself
September Sixteenth.

UNBROKEN sweetness of conduct in the face of all outward antagonism is the infallible indication of a self-conquered soul, the witness of wisdom, and the proof of the possession of Truth.

A sweet and happy soul is the ripened fruit of wisdom, and it sheds abroad the invisible aroma of its influence, gladdening the hearts of others, and purifying the world.

If you would have others true, be true; if you would have the world emancipated from misery and sin, emancipate yourself; if you would have your home and your surroundings happy, be happy.

And this you will naturally and spontaneously do as you realise the good in yourself.

Commence to live free from all wrong and evil. Peace of mind and true reform lie this way.

Immortality is here and now, and is not a speculative something beyond the grave.
September Seventeenth.

IMMORTALITY does not belong to time, and will never be found in time: it belongs to Eternity; and just as time is here and now, so is Eternity here and now, and a man may find that Eternity and establish himself in it, if he will overcome the self that derives its life from the unsatisfying and perishable things of time.

Whilst a man remains immersed in sensation, desire, and the passing events of his day-by-day existence, and regards those sensations, desires, and passing events as of the essence of himself, he can have no knowledge of immortality. The thing which such a man desires, and which he mistakes for immortality, is persistence; that is, a continuous succession of sensations and events of time.

Persistence is the antithesis of immortality.

The death of the body can never bestow upon a man immortality.
September Eighteenth.

SPIRITS are not different from men, and live their little feverish life of broken consciousness, and are still immersed in change and mortality. The mortal man, he who thirsts for the persistence of his pleasure-loving personality, is still mortal after death, and only lives another life with a beginning and an end, without memory of the past or knowledge of the future.

The immortal man is he who has detached himself from the things of time by having ascended into that state of consciousness which is fixed and unvariable, and is not affected by passing events and sensations. He is as one who has awakened out of his dream, and he knows that his dream was not an enduring reality, but a passing illusion. He is a man with knowledge, the knowledge of both states—that of persistence, and that of immortality.

The immortal man is in full possession of himself.

The mortal man lives in the time or world state of consciousness which begins and ends.
September Nineteenth.

THE immortal man remains poised and steadfast under all changes, and the death of his body will not in any way interrupt the eternal consciousness in which he abides. Of such a one it is said, "He shall not taste of death," because he has stepped out of the stream of mortality, and established himself in the abode of Truth. Bodies, personalities, nations, and worlds pass away, but Truth remains, and its glory is undimmed by time. The immortal man, then, is he who has conquered himself; who no longer identifies himself with the self-seeking forces of the personality, but who has trained himself to direct those forces with the hand of a master, and so has brought them into harmony with the causal energy and source of all things.

The immortal man lives in the cosmic or heaven state of consciousness, in which there is neither beginning nor end, but an eternal now.

The overcoming of self is the annihilation of all the sorrow-producing elements.
September Twentieth.

THE doctrine of the overcoming or annihilation of self is simplicity itself; indeed, so simple, practical, and close at hand is it that a child of five, whose mind has not yet become clouded with theories, theological schemes, and speculative philosophies, would be far more likely to comprehend it than many older people who have lost their hold upon simple and beautiful truths by the adoption of complicated theories.

The annihilation of self consists in weeding out and destroying all those elements in the soul which lead to division, strife, suffering, disease, and sorrow. It does not mean the destruction of any good and beautiful and peace-producing quality.

The overcoming of self is the cultivation of all the divine qualities.

He who would overcome his enemy the tempter must discover his stronghold and place of concealment, and must also find out the unguarded gates in his own fortress where the enemy effects so easy an entrance.

September Twenty-First.

TEMPTATION, with all its attendant torments, can be overcome here and now, but it can only be overcome with knowledge. It is a condition of darkness, or of semi-darkness. The fully enlightened soul is proof against all temptation. When a man fully understands the source, nature, and meaning of temptation, in that hour he will conquer it, and will rest from his long travail; but whilst he remains in ignorance, attention to religious observances and much praying and reading of Scripture will fail to bring him peace.

This is the holy warfare of the saints.

All temptation comes from within.

September Twenty-Second.

MEN fail to conquer, and the fight is indefinitely prolonged, because they labour, almost universally, under two delusions; first, that all temptations come from without; and second, that they are tempted because of their goodness. Whilst a man is held in bondage by these delusions, he will make no progress; when he has shaken them off, he will pass on rapidly from victory to victory, and will taste of spiritual joy and rest.

The source and cause of all temptation is in the inward desire; that being purified and eliminated, outward objects and extraneous powers are utterly powerless to move the soul to sin or to temptation. The outward object is merely the occasion of the temptation, never the cause; this is in the desire of the one tempted.

A man is tempted because there are certain desires or states of mind which he has come to regard as unholy.

The good in a man is never tempted. Goodness destroys temptation.
September Twenty-Third.

IT is the evil in a man that is aroused and tempted. The measure of a man's temptations is the exact register of his own unholiness. As a man purifies his heart, temptation ceases, for when a certain unlawful desire has been taken out of the heart the object which formerly appealed to it can no longer do so, but becomes dead and powerless, for there is nothing left in the heart that can respond to it. The honest man cannot be tempted to steal, let the occasion be ever so opportune; the man of purified appetites cannot be tempted to gluttony and drunkenness; he whose mind is calm m the strength of inward virtue can never be tempted to anger, and the wiles and charms of the wanton fall upon the purified heart as empty, meaningless shadows.

Temptation shows a man just where he is.

The Great Law is good—the man of integrity is superior to fear, and failure, and poverty, and shame, and disgrace.
September Twenty-Fourth.

THE man who, fearing the loss of present pleasures or material comforts, denies the truth within him can be injured, and robbed, and degraded, and trampled upon, because he has first injured, robbed, and degraded, and trampled upon his own nobler self; but the man of steadfast virtue, of unblemished integrity, cannot be subject to such conditions, because he has denied the craven self within him and has taken refuge in Truth. It is not the scourge and the chains which make a man a slave, but the fact that he is a slave.

Slander, accusation, and malice cannot affect the righteous man, nor call from him any bitter response, nor does he need to go about to defend himself and prove his innocence. Innocence and integrity alone are a sufficient answer to all that hatred may attempt.

The man of integrity turns all evil things to good account.
September Twenty-Fifth.

LET the man of integrity rejoice and be glad when he is severely tried; let him be thankful that he has been given an opportunity of proving his loyalty to the noble principles which he has espoused; and let him think, " Now is the hour of holy opportunity! Now is the day of triumph lor Truth! Though I lose the whole world, I will not desert the right!" So thinking, he will return good for evil, and will think compassionately of the wrong-doer.

The slanderer, the backbiter, and the wrongdoer may seem to succeed for a time, but the Law of Justice prevails; the man of integrity may seem to fail for a time, but he is invincible, and in none of the worlds, visible or invisible, can there be a forged weapon that shall prevail against him.

The man of integrity can never be subdued by the forces of darkness, having subdued all those forces within himself.

Without discrimination a man is mentally blind.
September Twenty-Sixth.

A MAN'S mind and life should be free from confusion. He should be prepared to meet every mental, material, and spiritual difficulty, and should not be intricately caught (as many are) in the meshes of doubt, indecision, and uncertainty when troubles and so-called misfortunes come along. He should be fortified against every emergency that can come against him; but such mental preparedness and strength cannot be attained in any degree without discrimination, and discrimination can only be developed by bringing into play and constantly exercising the analytical faculty.

Mind, like muscle, is developed by use.

Confusion, suffering, and spiritual darkness follow the thoughtless.
September Twenty-Seventh.

THE man who is afraid to think searchingly upon his opinions, and to reason critically upon his position, will have to develop moral courage before he can acquire discrimination.

A man must be true to himself, fearless with himself, before he can perceive the pure principles of Truth, before he can receive the all-revealing Light of Truth.

The more Truth is inquired of, the brighter it shines; it cannot suffer under examination and analysis.

The more error is questioned, the darker it grows; it cannot survive the entrance of pure and searching thought.

To "prove all things" is to find the good and to throw away the evil.

He who reasons and meditates learns to discriminate; he who discriminates discovers the eternally True.

Harmony, blessedness, and the Light of Truth attend upon the thoughtful.

Belief is an attitude of mind determining the whole course of one's life.

September Twenty-Eighth.

BELIEF is the basis of all action, and, this being so, the belief which dominates the heart or mind is shown in the life. Every man acts, thinks, lives in exact accordance with the belief which is rooted in his innermost being, and such is the mathematical nature of the laws which govern mind that it is absolutely impossible for anyone to believe in two opposing conditions at the same time. For instance, it is impossible to believe in justice and injustice, hatred and love, peace and strife, self and truth. Every man believes in one or the other of these opposites, never in both, and the daily conduct of every man indicates the nature of his belief.

Belief and conduct are inseparable, for the one determines the other.

Justice reigns, and all that is called injustice is fleeting and illusory.
September Twenty-Ninth.

THE man who is continually getting enraged over the injustice of his fellow men, who talks about himself being badly treated, or who mourns over the lack of justice in the world around him, shows by his conduct, his attitude of mind, that he believes in injustice. However he may protest to the contrary, in his inmost heart he believes that confusion and chaos are dominant in the universe, the result being that he dwells in misery and unrest, and his conduct is faulty.

Again, he who believes in love, in its stability and power, practises it under all circumstances, never deviates from it, and bestows it alike upon enemies as upon friends.

The man who believes in justice remains calm through all trials and difficulties.

Every thought, every act, every habit, is the direct outcome of belief.
September Thirtieth.

MEN are saved from error by belief in the supremacy of Truth. They are saved from sin by belief in Holiness or Perfection. They are saved from evil by belief in Good, for every belief is manifested in the life. It is not necessary to inquire as to a man's theological belief, for that is of little or no account, for what can it avail a man to believe that Jesus died for him, or that Jesus is God, or that he is "justified by faith," if he continues to live in his lower, sinful nature? All that is necessary to ask is this: "How does a man live?" "How does he conduct himself under trying circumstances?" The answer to these questions will show whether a man believes in the power of evil or in the power of Good.

When our belief in a thing ceases, we can no longer cling to or practise it.

A man cannot cling to anything unless he believes in it; belief always precedes action, therefore a man's deeds and life are the fruits of his belief.

October First.

HE who believes in all those things that are good will love them, and live in them , he who believes in those things that are impure and selfish will love them, and cling to them. The tree is known by its fruits.

A man's beliefs about God, Jesus, and the Bible are one thing , his life, as bound up in his actions, is another , therefore a man's theological belief is of no consequence , but the thoughts which he harbours, his attitude of mind towards others, and his actions—these, and these only, determine and demonstrate whether the belief of a man's heart is fixed in the false or the true.

There are only two beliefs which vitally affect the life, and they are: belief in good and belief in evil.

As the fruit to the tree and the water to the spring, so is action to thought.

October Second.

THE sudden falling, when greatly tempted, into some grievous sin by one who was believed, and who believed himself, to stand firm, is seen neither to be a sudden nor a causeless thing when the hidden processes of thought which led up to it are revealed. The falling was merely the end, the outworking, the finished result of what commenced in the mind probably years before. The man had allowed a wrong thought to enter his mind; and a second and a third time he had welcomed it, and allowed it to nestle in his heart. Gradually he became accustomed to it, and cherished and fondled, and tended it; and so it grew until at last it attained such strength and force that it attracted to itself the opportunity which enabled it to burst forth and ripen into act.

All sin and temptation are the natural outcome of the thoughts of the individual.

Guard well your thoughts, reader, for what you really are in your secret thoughts to-day you will become in actual deed.

October Third.

THERE is nothing hidden that shall not be revealed, and every thought that is harboured in the mind must, by virtue of the impelling force which is inherent in the universe, at last blossom into act good or bad, according to its nature. The divine Teacher and the sensualist are both the product of their own thoughts, and have become what they are as the result of the seeds of thought which they have implanted, or allowed to fall, into the garden of the heart, and have afterwards watered, tended, and cultivated.

Let no man think he can overcome sin and temptation by wrestling with opportunity; he can only overcome them by purifying his thoughts.

A man can only attract that to him which is in harmony with his nature.

As a being of thought, your dominant mental attitude will determine your condition in life.

October Fourth.

YOU are the thinker of your thoughts, and as such you are the maker of your self and condition. Thought is causal and creative, and appears in your character and life in the form of results. There are no accidents in your life. Both its harmonies and antagonisms are the responsive echoes of your thoughts. A man thinks, and his life appears.

If your dominant mental attitude is peaceable and lovable, bliss and blessedness will follow you; if it be resistant and hateful, trouble and distress will cloud your pathway. Out of ill-will will come grief and disaster; out of good-will, healing and reparation.

The boundary lines of your thoughts are self-erected fences.

Pain, grief, sorrow, and misery are the fruits of which passion is the flower.

October Fifth.

WHERE the passion-bound soul sees only injustice, the good man, he who has conquered passion, sees cause and effect, sees the Supreme Justice. It is impossible for such a man to regard himself as treated unjustly, because he has ceased to see injustice. He knows that no one can injure or cheat him, having ceased to injure or cheat himself. However passionately or ignorantly men may act towards him, it cannot possibly cause him any pain, for he knows that whatever comes to him (it may be abuse and persecution) can only come as the effect of what he himself has formerly sent out. He therefore regards all things as good, rejoices m all things, loves his enemies, blesses them that curse him, regarding them as the blind but beneficent instruments by which he is enabled to pay his moral debts to the Great Law.

The Supreme Justice and the Supreme Love are one.

The history of a nation is the building of its deeds.
October Sixth.

AS a body is built of cells, and a house of bricks, so a man's mind is built of thoughts. The various characters of men are none other than compounds of thoughts of varying combinations. Herein we see the deep truth of the saying, "As a man thinketh in his heart, so is he. Individual characteristics are fixed processes of thought; that is, they are fixed in the sense that they have become an integral part of the character, that they can be only altered or removed by a protracted effort of the will, and by much self-discipline. Character is built in the same way as a tree or a house is built—namely, by the ceaseless addition of new material, and that material is thought. By the aid of millions of bricks a city is built; by the aid of millions of thoughts a character, a mind, is built.

Every man is a mind-builder.
October Seventh.

PURE thoughts, wisely chosen and well placed, are so many durable bricks which will never crumble away, and from which a finished and beautiful building, and one which affords comfort and shelter for its possessor, can be rapidly erected. Bracing thoughts of strength, of confidence, of duty; inspiring thoughts of a large, free, unfettered, and unselfish life, are useful bricks with which a substantial mind-temple can be raised; and the building of such a temple necessitates that old and useless habits of thought be broken down and destroyed.

" Build thee more stately mansions, O my soul, As the swift seasons roll."

Each man is the builder of himself.

Working in harmony with the fundamental laws of the universe.
October Eighth.

IF a man is to build up a successful strong, and exemplary life—a life that will stoutly resist the fiercest storms of adversity and temptation—it must be framed on a few, simple, undeviating moral principles.

Four of these principles are: Justice, Rectitude, Sincerity, and Kindness. These four ethical truths are to the making of a life what the four lines of a square are to the building of a house. If a man ignores them and thinks to obtain success and happiness by injustice, trickery, and selfishness, he is in the position of a builder who imagines he can build a strong and durable habitation while ignoring the relative arrangement of mathematical lines, and he will, in the end, obtain only disappointment and failure.

Build like a true workman.

It is a common error to suppose that little things can be passed by, and that the greater things are more important.

October Ninth.

HE who adopts the four ethical principles as the law and base of his life, who raises the edifice of character upon them, who in his thoughts and words and actions does not wander from them, whose every duty and every passing transaction is performed in strict accordance with their exactions, such a man, laying down the hidden foundations of integrity of heart securely and strongly, cannot fail to raise up a structure which shall bring him honour; and he is building a temple in which he can repose in peace and blessedness —even the strong and beautiful Temple of his life.

He who would have a life secure and blessed must carry the practice of the moral principles into every detail of it.

When aspiration is united to concentration, the result is meditation.

October Tenth.

WHEN a man intensely desires to reach and realise a higher, purer, and more radiant life than the merely worldly and pleasure-loving life, he engages in aspiration; and when he earnestly concentrates his thoughts upon the finding of that life, he practises meditation.

Without intense aspiration there can be no meditation. Lethargy and indifference are fatal to its practice. The more intense the nature of the man, the more readily will he find meditation and the more successfully will he practise it. A fiery nature will most rapidly scale the heights of Truth in meditation, when its aspirations have become sufficiently awakened.

Meditation is necessary to spiritual success.

When a man aspires to know and realise the Truth, he gives attention to conduct, to self-purification.

October Eleventh.

BY concentration a man can scale the highest heights of genius, but he cannot scale the heavenly heights of Truth; to accomplish this he must meditate. By concentration a man may acquire the wonderful comprehension and vast power of a Caesar; by meditation he may reach the divine wisdom and perfect peace of a Buddha. The perfection of concentration is power; the perfection of meditation is wisdom. By concentration men acquire skill in the doing of the things of life—in science, art, trade, etc.—but by meditation they acquire skill in life itself; in right living, enlightenment, wisdom, etc. Saints, sages, saviours—wise men and divine teachers— are the finished products of holy meditation.

Love Truth so fully and intensely as to become wholly absorbed in it.

The object of meditation is divine enlightenment, Man is a thought-being, and his life and character are determined by the thoughts in which he habitually dwells.
October Twelfth.

WHILE, at first, the time spent in actual meditation is short—perhaps only half an hour in the early morning—the knowledge gained in that half-hour of vivid aspiration and concentrated thought is embodied in practice during the whole day. In meditation, therefore, the entire life of a man is involved; and as he advances in its practice he becomes more and more fitted to perform the duties of life in the circumstances in which he may be placed, for he becomes stronger, holier, calmer, and wiser.

The principle of meditation is twofold, namely:

1. Purification of the heart by repetitive thought on pure things. 2. Attainment of divine knowledge by embodying such purity in practical life.

By practice, association, and habit, thoughts tend to repeat themselves.
October Thirteenth.

BY daily dwelling upon pure thoughts, the man of meditation forms the habit of pure and enlightened thinking which leads to pure and enlightened actions and well-performed duties. By the ceaseless repetition of pure thoughts, he at last becomes one with those thoughts, and is a purified being, manifesting his attainment in pure actions, in a serene and wise life.

The majority of men live in a series of conflicting desires, passions, emotions, and speculations, and there are restlessness, uncertainty, and sorrow; but when a man begins to train his mind in meditation, he gradually gains control over this inward conflict by bringing his thoughts to a focus upon a central principle.

It is easy to mistake reverie for meditation.

Selfishness, the root of the tree of evil and of all suffering, derives its nourishment from the dark soil of ignorance.

October Fourteenth.

THE rich and the poor alike suffer for their own selfishness; and none escape. The rich have their particular sufferings as well as the poor. Moreover, the rich are continually losing their riches; the poor are continually acquiring them. The poor man of to-day is the rich man of to-morrow, and vice versa. Fear, also, follows men like a great shadow, for the man who obtains and holds by selfish force will always be haunted by a feeling of insecurity, and will continually fear its loss; whilst the poor man, who is selfishly seeking or coveting material riches, will be harassed by the fear of destitution. And one and all who live in this under-world of strife are overshadowed by one great fear—the fear of death.

Each individual suffers by virtue of his own selfishness.

The spirit is strengthened and renewed by meditation upon spiritual things.

October Fifteenth.

A MAN must pass through three Gateways of Surrender. The first is the Surrender of Desire; the second is the Surrender of Opinion; the third is the Surrender of Self. Entering into meditation, he will commence to examine his desires, tracing them out in his mind, and following up their effects in his life and upon his character; and he will quickly perceive that, without the renunciation of desire, a man remains a slave both to himself and to his surroundings and circumstances. Having discovered this, the first Gate, that of the Surrender of Desire, is entered. Passing through this Gate, he adopts a process of self-discipline which is the first step in the purification of the soul.

The lamp of faith must be continually fed and assiduously trimmed.

The loss of to-day will add to the gain of to-morrow for him whose mind is set on the conquest of self.

October Sixteenth.

LET a man, therefore, press on courageously, heeding neither the revilings of his friends without, nor the clamourings of his enemies within; aspiring, searching, striving; looking ever towards his Ideal with eyes of holy love; day by day ridding his mind of selfish motive, his heart of impure desire; stumbling sometimes, sometimes falling, but ever travelling onward and rising higher; and recording each night in the silence of his own heart the journey of the day, let him not despair if but each day, in spite of all its failures and falls, records some holy battle fought, though lost, some silent victory attempted, though unachieved.

Learn to distinguish between the real and the unreal, the shadow and the substance.

Acquire the priceless possession of spiritual discernment.

October Seventeenth.

CLOTHING his soul with the colourless Garment of Humility, a man bends all his energies to the uprooting of those opinions which he has hitherto loved and cherished. He now learns to distinguish between Truth, which is one and unchangeable, and his own and others' opinions about Truth, which are many and changeable. He sees that his opinions about Goodness, Purity, Compassion, and Love, are very distinct from those qualities themselves, and that he must stand upon those divine Principles, and not on his own opinions. Hitherto he has regarded his own opinions as of great value, but now he ceases so to elevate his own opinions, and to defend them against those of others, and comes to regard them as utterly worthless.

Stand upon the divine Principles of Purity, Wisdom, Compassion, and Love.

Find the Divine Centre within.

October Eighteenth.

HE who resolves that he will not rest satisfied with appearances, shadows, illusions shall, by the piercing light of that resolve, disperse every fleeting phantasy, and shall enter into the substance and reality of life. He shall learn how to live, and he shall live. He shall be the slave of no passion, the servant of no opinion, the votary of no fond error. Finding the Divine Centre within his own heart, he shall be pure and calm and strong and wise, and will ceaselessly radiate the Heavenly Life in which he lives—which is himself.

Not to know that within you that is changeless, and defiant of time and death, is not to know anything, but is to play vainly with unsubstantial reflections in the Mirror of Time.

Having betaken himself to the Divine Refuge within, and remaining there, a man is free from sin. No doubt shall shake his trust, no uncertainty shall rob him of repose.

October Nineteenth.

MEN love their desires, for gratification seems sweet to them, hut its end is pain and vacuity; they love the argumentations of the intellect, for egotism seems most desirable to them, but the fruits thereof are humiliation and sorrow. When the soul has reached the end of gratification and reaped the bitter fruits of egotism, it is ready to receive the Divine Wisdom and to enter into the Divine Life. Only the crucified can be transfigured; only by the death of self can the Lord of the heart rise again into the Immortal Life, and stand radiant upon the Olivet of Wisdom.

Where self is not, there is the Garden of the Heavenly Life.

Life is more than motion, it is Music; more than rest, it is Peace; more than work, it is Duty; more than labour, it is Love.

October Twentieth.

LET the impure turn to Purity, and they shall be pure; let the weak resort to Strength, and they shall be strong; let the ignorant fly to Knowledge, and they shall be wise. All things are man's, and he chooses that which he will have. To-day he chooses in ignorance, to-morrow he shall choose in wisdom. He shall "work out his own salvation," whether he believe it or not, for he cannot escape himself, nor transfer to another the eternal responsibility of his own soul. By no theological subterfuge shall he trick the Law of his being, which shall shatter all his selfish makeshifts and excuses for right thinking and right doing. Nor shall God do for him that which it is destined his soul shall accomplish for itself.

Life is more than enjoyment, it is Blessedness.

He who would find Blessedness, let him find himself.

October Twenty-First.

MEN fly from creed to creed, and find unrest; they travel in many lands, and discover—disappointment; they build themselves beautiful mansions, and plant pleasant gardens, and reap—ennui and discomfort. Not until a man falls back upon the Truth within himself does he find rest and satisfaction; not until he builds the inward Mansion of Faultless Conduct does he find the endless and incorruptible Joy, and, having obtained that, he will infuse it into all his doings and possessions.

When a man can no longer carry the weight of his many sins, let him fly to the Christ, whose throne is the centre of his own heart, and he shall become light-hearted, entering the glad company of the Immortals.

The spiritual Heart of man is the Heart of the universe.

All power, all possibility, all action is now.
October Twenty-Second.

WHILST a man is dwelling upon the past or future he is missing the present; he is forgetting to live now. All things are possible now, and only now. Without wisdom to guide him, and mistaking the unreal for the real, a man says, "If I had done so-and-so last week, last month, or last year, it would have been better with me to-day"; or," I know what is best to be done, and I will do it to-morrow." The selfish cannot comprehend the vast importance and value of the present, and fail to see it as the substantial reality of which past and future are the empty reflections. It may truly be said that past and future do not exist except as negative shadows, and to live in them—that is, in the regretful and selfish contemplation of them —is to miss the reality in life.

To put away regret, to anchor anticipation, to do and work now, this is wisdom.

Virtue consists in fighting sin day after day,
October Twenty-Third.

CEASE to tread every byway of dependence, every winding side way that tempts thy soul into the shadowland of the past and the future, and manifest thy native and divine strength now. Come out into "the open road."

That which you would be, and hope to be, you may be now. Non-accomplishment resides in your perpetual postponement, and, having the power to postpone, you also have the power to accomplish—to perpetually accomplish; realise this truth, and you shall be to-day, and every day, the ideal man of whom you dreamed.

Act now, and lo! all things are done; live now, and behold! thou art in the midst of Plenty; be now, and know that thou art perfect.

Holiness consists in leaving sin, unnoticed and ignored, to die by the wayside.

Say not unto thy soul, "Thou shalt be purer tomorrow"; but rather say, "Thou shalt be pure now."

October Twenty-Fourth.

TO-MORROW is too late for anything, and he who sees help and salvation in to-morrow shall continually fail and fall to-day. Thou didst fall yesterday! Didst sin grievously! Having realised this, leave it instantly and forever, and watch that thou sinnest not now. The while thou art bewailing the past every gate of thy soul remains unguarded against the entrance of sin now.

The foolish man, loving the boggy side of procrastination rather than the firm highway of Present Effort, says, "I will rise early tomorrow; I will get out of debt to-morrow; I will carry out my intentions to-morrow," But the wise man, realising the momentous import of the Eternal Now, rises early to-day; keeps out of debt to-day; carries out his intentions to-day; and so never departs from strength and peace and ripe accomplishment.

Thou shalt not rise by grieving over the irremediable past, but by remedying the present.

Looking back to happy beginnings, and forward to mournful endings, a man's eyes are blinded so that he beholds not his own immortality.

October Twenty-Fifth.

IT is wisdom to leave that which has not arrived, and to attend to that which is; and to attend to it with such a consecration of soul and concentration of effort as shall leave no loophole for regret to creep in.

A man's spiritual comprehension being clouded by the illusions of self, he says, "I was born on such a day, so many years ago, and shall die at my allotted time." But he was not born, neither will he die, for how can that which is immortal, which eternally is, be subject to birth and death? Let a man throw off his illusions, and then he will see that the birth and death of the body are the mere incidents of a journey, and not its beginning and end.

The universe, with all that it contains, is now.

Let a man put away egotism, and he will see the universe in all the beauty of its pristine simplicity.

October Twenty-Sixth.

LET life cease to be lived as a fragmentary thing, and let it be lived as a perfect Whole; the simplicity of the Perfect will then be revealed. How shall the fragment comprehend the Whole? Yet how simple that the Whole should comprehend the fragment. How shall sin perceive Holiness? Yet how plain that Holiness should understand sin. He who would become the Greater let him abandon the lesser. In no form is the circle contained, but in the circle all forms are contained. In no colour is the radiant light imprisoned, but in the radiant light all colours are embodied. Let a man destroy all the forms of self, and he shall apprehend the Circle of Perfection.

When a man succeeds in entirely forgetting (annihilating) his personal self, he becomes a mirror in which the universal Reality is faultlessly reflected.

In the perfect chord of music the single note, though forgotten, is indispensably contained, and the drop of water becomes of supreme usefulness by losing itself in the ocean.

October Twenty-Seventh.

SINK thyself compassionately in the heart of humanity, and thou shalt reproduce the harmonies of Heaven; lose thyself in unlimited love toward all, and thou shalt work enduring works and shalt become one with the eternal Ocean of Bliss.

Man evolves outward to the periphery of complexity, and then involves backward to the Central Simplicity. When a man discovers that it is mathematically impossible for him to know the universe before knowing himself, he then starts upon the Way which leads to Original Simplicity. He begins to unfold from within, and as he unfolds himself, he enfolds the universe.

Cease to speculate about God, and find the all-embracing Good within thee.

The pure man knows himself as pure being.

October Twenty-Eighth.

HE who will not give up his secret lust, his covetousness, his anger, his opinion about this or that, can see nor know nothing; he will remain a dullard in the school of Wisdom, though he be accounted learned in the colleges.

If a man would find the key of Knowledge, let him find himself. Thy sins are not thyself; they are not any part of thyself; they are diseases which thou hast come to love. Cease to cling to them, and they will no longer cling to thee. Let them fall away, and thyself shall stand revealed. Thou shalt know thyself as Comprehensive Vision, Invincible Principle, Immortal Life, and Eternal Good.

Purity is extremely simple, and needs no argument to support it.

Truth lives itself.

October Twenty-Ninth.

MEEKNESS, Patience, Love, Compassion, and Wisdom—these are the dominant qualities of Original Simplicity; therefore the imperfect cannot understand it. Wisdom only can apprehend Wisdom, therefore the fool says, "No man is wise." The imperfect man says, "No man can be perfect," and he therefore remains where he is. Though he live with a perfect man all his life, he shall not behold his perfection. Meekness he will call cowardice; Patience, Love, Compassion he will see as weakness; and Wisdom will appear to him as folly. Faultless discrimination belongs to the Perfect Whole, and resides not in any part, therefore men are exhorted to refrain from judgment until they have themselves manifested the Perfect Life.

A blameless life is the only witness of Truth.

He who has found the indwelling Reality of his own being has found the original and universal Reality.

October Thirtieth.

KNOWING the Divine Heart within, all hearts are known, and the thoughts of all men become his who has become master of his own thoughts; therefore the good man does not defend himself, but moulds the minds of others to his own likeness.

As the problematical transcends crudity, so Pure Goodness transcends the problematical. All problems vanish when Pure Goodness is reached; therefore the Good man is called "The Slayer of illusions." What problem can vex where sin is not? O thou who strivest loudly and resteth not! retire into the holy silence of thine own being, and live therefrom. So shalt thou, finding Pure Goodness, rend in twain the Veil of the Temple of Illusion, and shalt enter into the Patience, Peace, and transcendent Glory of the Perfect, for Pure Goodness and Original Simplicity are one.

So extremely simple is Original Simplicity that a man must let go his hold of everything before he can perceive it.

Great will be his pain and unrest who seeks to stand upon the approbation of others.

October Thirty-First.

TO detach oneself from every outward thing, and to rest securely upon the inward virtue, this is the Unfailing Wisdom. Having this Wisdom, a man will be the same whether in riches or poverty. The one cannot add to his strength, nor the other rob him of his serenity. Neither can riches defile him who has washed away all the inward defilement, nor the lack of them degrade him who has ceased to degrade the temple of his soul.

To refuse to be enslaved by any outward thing or happening, regarding all such things and happenings as for your use, for your education, this is Wisdom. To the wise all occurrences are good, and, having no eye for evil, they grow wiser every day. They utilise all things, and thus put all things under their feet. They see all their mistakes as soon as made, and accept them as lessons of intrinsic value, knowing that there are no mistakes in the Divine Order.

To love where one is not loved; herein lies the strength which shall never fail a man.

The wise man is always anxious to learn, but never anxious to teach.
November First.

ALL strength and wisdom and power and knowledge a man will find within himself, but he will not find it in egotism; he will only find it in obedience, submission, and willingness to learn. He must obey the higher and not glorify himself in the lower. He who stands upon egotism, rejecting reproof, instruction, and the lessons of experience, will surely fall; yea, he is already fallen. Said a great teacher to his disciples, "Those who shall be a lamp unto themselves, relying upon themselves only, and not relying upon any external help, but holding fast to the Truth as their lamp, and, seeking their salvation in the Truth alone, shall not look for assistance to any beside themselves, it is they among my disciples who shall reach the very topmost height! But they must be witling to learn." The true Teacher is in the heart of every man.

Dispersion is weakness; concentration is power.
November Second.

THINGS are useful and thoughts are powerful in the measure that their parts are strongly and intelligently concentrated. Purpose is highly concentrated thought. All the mental energies are directed to the attainment of an object, and obstacles which intervene between the thinker and the object are, one after another, broken down and overcome. Purpose is the keystone in the temple of achievement. It binds and holds together in a complete whole that which would otherwise lie scattered and useless. Empty whims, ephemeral fancies, vague desires, and half-hearted resolutions have no place in purpose. In the sustained determination to accomplish there is an invincible power which swallows up all inferior considerations and marches direct to victory.

All successful men are men of purpose.

Know this—thou makest and unmakest thyself.

November Third.

DOUBT, anxiety, and worry are unsubstantial shades in the underworld of self, and shall no more trouble him who will climb the serene altitudes of his soul. Grief, also, will be for ever dispelled by him who will comprehend the Law of his being. He who so comprehends shall find the Supreme Law of Life, and he shall find that it is Love, that it is imperishable Love. He shall become one with Love, and loving all, with mind freed from all hatred and folly, he shall receive the invincible protection which Love affords. Claiming nothing, he shall suffer no loss; seeking no pleasure, he shall find no grief; and employing all his powers as instruments of service, he shall evermore live in the highest state of blessedness and bliss.

Thou art a slave if thou preferrest to be; thou art a master if thou wilt make thyself one.

He who has found Meekness has found divinity.

November Fourth.

THE mountain bends not to the fiercest storm, but it shields the fledgling and the lamb; and though all men tread upon it, yet it protects them, and bears them up upon its deathless bosom. Even so is it with the meek man who, though shaken and disturbed by none, yet compassionately bends to shield the lowliest creature, and, though he may be despised, lifts up all men, and lovingly protects them.

As glorious as the mountain in its silent might is the divine man in his silent Meekness; like its form, his loving compassion is expansive and sublime. Truly his body, like the mountain's base, is fixed in the valleys and the mists; but the summit of his being is eternally bathed in cloudless glory, and lives with the Silence.

The meek man has realised the divine consciousness and knows himself as divine.

He who lives in Meekness is without fear, knowing the Highest, and having the lowest under his feet.

November Fifth.

THE meek man shines in darkness, and flourishes in obscurity. Meekness cannot boast, nor advertise itself, nor thrive on popularity. It is practised, and is seen and not seen; being a spiritual quality it is perceived only by the eye of the spirit. Those who are not spiritually awakened see it not, nor do they love it, being enamoured of, and blinded by, worldly shows and appearances. Nor does history take note of the meek man. Its glory is that of strife and self-aggrandisement; his is the glory of peace and gentleness. History chronicles the earthly, not the heavenly acts. Yet though he lives in obscurity, he cannot be hidden (how can light be hid?); he continues to shine after he has withdrawn himself from the world, and is worshipped by the world which knew him not.

The meek man is found in the time of trial; when other men fall he stands.

The meek man resists none, and thereby conquers all.

November Sixth.

HE who imagines he can be injured by others, and who seeks to justify and defend himself against them, does not understand Meekness, does not comprehend the essence and meaning of life. "He abused me, he beat me, he defeated me, he robbed me. In those who harbour such thoughts hatred will never cease ... for hatred ceases not by hatred at any time; hatred ceases by love." What sayest thou? Thy neighbour has spoken thee falsely? Well, what of that? Can a falsity hurt thee? That which is false is false, and there is an end of it. It is without life, and without power to hurt any but him who seeks to be hurt by it. It is nothing to thee that thy neighbour should speak falsely of thee, but it is much to thee that thou shouldst resist him, and seek to justify thyself, for, by so doing, thou givest life and vitality to thy neighbour's falseness, so that thou art injured and distressed.

Take all evil out of thine own heart, then shalt thou see the folly of resisting it in another.

Great is the power of purpose.

November Seventh.

PURPOSE goes with intelligence.

There are lesser and greater purposes, according with degrees of intelligence.

A great mind will always be great of purpose. A weak intelligence will be without purpose. A drifting mind argues a measure of undevelopment.

The men who have moulded the destinies of humanity have been men mighty of purpose. Like the Roman laying his road, they have followed along a well-defined path, and have refused to swerve aside even when torture and death confronted them. The Great Leaders of the race are the mental road-makers, and mankind follows in the intellectual and spiritual paths which they have carved out and beaten.

Inert matter yields to a living force, and circumstance succumbs to the power of purpose.

All things at last yield to the silent, irresistible all-conquering energy of purpose.
November Eighth.

THE weak man, who grieves because he is misunderstood, will not greatly achieve; the vain man, who steps aside from his resolve in order to please others and gain their approbation, will not highly achieve; the double-minded man, who thinks to compromise his purpose, will fail. The man of fixed purpose who, whether misunderstandings and foul accusations, or flatteries and fair promises, rain upon him, does not yield a fraction of his resolve is the man of excellence and achievement; of success, greatness, and power.

Hindrances stimulate a man of purpose; difficulties nerve him to renewed exertion; mistakes, losses, pains, do not subdue him; and failures are steps in the ladder of success, for he is ever conscious of the certainty of final achievement.

The intensity of the purpose increases with the growing magnitude of the obstacles encountered.

Joy is always the accompaniment of a task successfully accomplished.
November Ninth.

OF all miserable men, the shirker is the most miserable. Thinking to find ease and happiness in avoiding difficult tasks, which require the expenditure of labour and exertion, his mind is always uneasy and disturbed, he becomes burdened with an inward sense of shame, and forfeits manliness and self-respect. "He who will not work according to his faculty, let him perish according to his necessity," says Carlyle; and it is a moral law that the man who avoids duty, and does not work to the full extent of his capacity, does actually perish, first in his character, and last in his body and circumstances. Life and action are synonymous, and immediately a man tries to escape exertion, either physical or mental, he has commenced to decay.

An undertaking completed, or a piece of work done, always brings rest and satisfaction.

The price of life is effort.
November Tenth.

EVERY successful accomplishment, even in worldly things, is repaid with its own measure of joy; and in spiritual things the joy which supervenes upon the perfection of purpose is sure, deep, and abiding. Great is the heartfelt joy (albeit ineffable) when, after innumerable and apparently unsuccessful attempts, some ingrained fault of character is at last cast out, to trouble its erstwhile victim and the world no more. The striver after virtue—he who is engaged in the holy task of building up a noble character—tastes, at every step of conquest over self, a joy which does not leave him again, but which becomes an integral part of his spiritual nature.

The reward of accomplishment is joy.

Everything that happens is just.
November Eleventh.

AS you think, you travel; as you love, you attract. You are to-day where your thoughts have brought you; you will be to-morrow where your thoughts take you. You cannot escape the results of your thoughts, but you can endure and learn, can accept and be glad.

You will always come to the place where your love (your most abiding and intense thought) can receive its measure of gratification. If your love be base, you will come to a base place; if it be beautiful, you will come to a beautiful place.

You can alter your thoughts, and so alter your condition. You are powerful, not powerless.

Nothing is fated, everything is formed.

The man whose thoughts, words, and acts are sincere is surrounded by sincere friends; the insincere man is surrounded by insincere friends.
November Twelfth.

EVERY fact and process in Nature contains a moral lesson for the wise man. There is no law in the world which is not to be found operating with the same mathematical certainty in the mind of man and in human life. All the parables of Jesus are illustrative of this truth, and are drawn from the simple facts of Nature. There is a process of seed-sowing in the mind and life, a spiritual sowing which leads to a harvest according to the kind of seed sown. Thoughts, words, and acts are seeds sown, and, by the inviolable law of things, they produce after their kind.

The man who thinks hateful thoughts brings hatred upon himself. The man who thinks loving thoughts is loved.

When you know yourself you will perceive that every event in your life is weighed in the faultless balance of equity.

He who would be blessed, let him scatter blessings.

November Thirteenth.

THE farmer must scatter all his seed upon the land, and then leave it to the elements. Were he to covetously hoard his seed, he would lose both it and his produce, for his seed would perish. It perishes when he sows it, but in perishing it brings forth a greater abundance. So in life, we get by giving; we grow rich by scattering. The man who says he is in possession of knowledge which he cannot give out because the world is incapable of receiving it either does not possess such knowledge, or, if he does, will soon be deprived of it—if he is not already deprived of it. To hoard is to lose; to exclusively retain is to be dispossessed.

He who would be happy, let him consider the happiness of others.

Men reap that which they sow.

November Fourteenth.

IF a man is troubled, perplexed, sorrowful, or unhappy, let him ask:

"What mental seeds have I been sowing?" "What seeds am I sowing?" "What is my attitude towards others?" "What seeds of trouble and sorrow and unhappiness have I sown that I should thus reap these bitter weeds?"

Let him seek within and find, and having found, let him abandon all the seeds of self, and sow, henceforth, only the seeds of Truth.

Let him learn of the farmer the simple truths of wisdom, and sow broadcast the seeds of kindness, gentleness, and love.

The way to obtain peace and blessedness is to scatter peaceful and blessed thoughts, words, and deeds.

Destroying the idols of self, we draw nearer to the great, silent Heart of Love.

November Fifteenth.

WE have reached one of those epochs in the world's progress which witnesses the passing of the false gods; the gods of human selfishness and human illusion. The new-old revelation of one universal impersonal Truth has again dawned upon the world, and its searching light has carried consternation to the perishable gods who take shelter under the shadow of self.

Men have lost faith in a god who can be cajoled, who rules arbitrarily and capriciously, subverting the whole order of things to gratify the wishes of his worshippers, and are turning, with a new light in their hearts, to the God of Law. And to Him they turn, not for personal happiness and gratification, but for knowledge, for understanding, for wisdom, for liberation from the bondage of self.

Enter the Path of obedience to the Law.

Perfection, which is knowledge of the Perfect Law, is ready for all who earnestly seek it.

November Sixteenth.

ENTERING that Path—the Path of the Supreme Law—men no longer accuse, no longer doubt, no longer fret and despond, for they know now that God is right, the universal laws are right, the cosmos is right, and that they themselves are wrong, if wrong there is, and that their salvation depends upon themselves, upon their own efforts, upon their personal acceptance of that which is good, and deliberate rejection of that which is evil. No longer merely hearers, they become doers of the Word, and they acquire knowledge, they receive understanding, they grow in wisdom, and they enter into the glorious life of liberation from the bondage of self.

Adopt the life of self-obliteration.

God does not alter for man, for this would mean that the perfect must become imperfect; man must alter for God.

November Seventeenth.

THE Children of Truth are in the world to-day; they are thinking, writing, speaking, acting; yea, even prophets are amongst us, and their influence is pervading the whole earth. An undercurrent of holy joy is gathering force in the world, so that men and women are moved with new aspirations and hopes, and even those who neither see nor hear, feel within them strange yearnings after a better and fuller life.

The Law reigns, and it reigns in men's hearts and lives; they have come to understand the reign of Law who have sought out the Tabernacle of the true God by the fair pathway of unselfishness.

The Law cannot be broken for man, otherwise confusion would ensue; this is in accordance with harmony, order, justice.

There is no more painful bondage than to be at the mercy of one's inclinations.

November Eighteenth.

THE Law is that the heart shall be purified, the mind regenerated, and the whole being brought in subjection to Love, till self be dead and Love is all in all, for the reign of Law is the reign of Love. And Love waits for all, rejecting none. Love may be claimed and entered into now, for it is the heritage of all.

Ah, beautiful Truth! To know that now man may accept his divine heritage, and enter the Kingdom of Heaven!

Oh, pitiful error! To know that man rejects it because of love of self!

Obedience to one's selfish inclinations means the drawing about one's soul clouds of pain and sorrow which darken the light of Truth; the shutting out of oneself from all real blessedness; for "whatsoever a man sows that shall he also reap."

There is no greater liberty than utmost obedience to the Law of Being.

The moral universe is sustained and protected by the perfect balance of its equivalents.

November Nineteenth.

IS there, then, no injustice in the universe? There is injustice, and there is not. It depends upon the kind of life and the state of consciousness from which a man looks out upon the world and judges. The man who lives in his passions sees injustice everywhere; the man who has overcome his passions, sees the operations of Justice in every department of human life.

Injustice is the confused feverish dream of passion, real enough to those who are dreaming it; Justice is the permanent reality in life, gloriously visible to those who have wakened out of the painful nightmare of self.

As in the physical world Nature abhors a vacuum, so in the spiritual world disharmony is annulled.

The Divine Order cannot be perceived until passion and self are transcended.

November Twentieth.

THE man who thinks, "I have been slighted, I have been injured, I have been insulted, I have been treated unjustly," cannot know what justice is; blinded by self, he cannot perceive the pure Principles of Truth, and, brooding upon his wrongs, he lives in continual misery.

In the region of passion there is a ceaseless conflict of forces causing suffering to all who are involved in them. There is action and reaction, deed and consequence, cause and effect; and within and above all is the divine Justice regulating the play of forces with the utmost mathematical accuracy, balancing cause and effect with the finest precision.

Justice is not perceived—cannot be perceived—by those who are engaged in conflict.

Having no knowledge of cause and effect in the moral sphere, men do not see the exacting process which is momentarily proceeding.

November Twenty-First.

MEN blindly inflict suffering upon themselves, living in passion and resentment, and not finding the true way of life. Hatred is met with hatred, passion with passion, strife with strife. The man who kills is himself killed; the thief who lives by depriving others, is himself deprived; the beast that preys on others is hunted and killed; the accuser is accused, the condemner is condemned, the denouncer is persecuted. "By this the slayer's knife doth stab himself, The unjust judge has lost his own defender, The false tongue dooms its lie, the creeping thief And spoiler rob to render.

"Such is the Law."

Ignorance keeps alive hatred and strife.

Cause and effect cannot be avoided; consequence cannot be escaped.

November Twenty-Second.

THE good man, having put away all resentment, retaliation, self-seeking, and egotism, has arrived at a state of equilibrium, and has thereby become identified with the Eternal and Universal Equilibrium. Having lifted himself above the blind forces of passion, he understands those forces, contemplates them with a calm penetrating insight, like the solitary dweller on a mountain who looks down upon the conflict of the storms beneath his feet. For him, injustice has ceased, and he sees ignorance and suffering on the one hand, and enlightenment and bliss on the other. He sees that not only do the fool and the slave need his sympathy, but that the fraud and the oppressor are equally in need of it, and so his compassion is extended towards all.

Unerring Justice presides over all.

They who refuse to trim their lamps of reason will never perceive the Light of Truth.

November Twenty-Third.

HE who will use the light of reason as a torch to search for Truth, will not be left at last in comfortless darkness.

"Come now, and let us reason together, saith the Lord; though your sins be as scarlet, they shall be as white as snow."

Many men and women pass through untold sufferings, and at last die in their sins, because they refuse to reason; because they cling to those dark delusions which even a faint glimmer of the light of reason would dispel; and all must use their reason freely, fully, and faithfully, who would exchange the scarlet robe of sin and suffering for the white garment of blessedness and peace.

They who despise the light of reason, despise the Light of Truth.

A man does not live until he begins to discipline himself; he merely exists.
November Twenty-Fourth.

BEFORE a man can accomplish anything of an enduring nature in the world he must first of all acquire some measure of success in the management of his own mind. This is as mathematical a truism as that two and two are four, for "out of the heart are the issues of life." If a man cannot govern the forces within himself, he cannot long hold a firm hand upon the outer activities which form the visible life. On the other hand, as a man succeeds in governing himself he rises to higher and higher levels of power and usefulness and success in the world. Hitherto his life has been without purpose or meaning, but now he begins to consciously mould his own destiny; he is "clothed and in his right mind."

With the practice of self-discipline a man begins to live.

In the process of self-discipline there are three stages— control, purification, and relinquishment.
November Twenty-Fifth.

A MAN begins to discipline himself by controlling those passions which have hitherto controlled him; he resists temptation, and guards himself against all those tendencies to selfish gratifications which are so easy and natural, and which have formerly dominated him. He brings his appetite into subjection, and begins to eat as a reasonable and responsible being, practising moderation and thoughtfulness in the selection of his food, with the object of making his body a pure instrument through which he may live and act as becomes a man, and no longer degrading that body by pandering to gustatory pleasure. He puts a check upon his tongue, his temper, and, in fact, his every animal desire and tendency.

There is in the heart of every man and woman a selfless centre.

The Rock of Ages, the Christ within, the divine and immortal in all men!
November Twenty-Sixth.

AS a man practises self-control he approximates more and more to the inward reality, and is less and less
swayed by passion and grief, pleasure
and pain, and lives a steadfast and virtuous life, manifesting manly strength and fortitude. The restraining of the passions, however, is merely the initial stage in self-discipline, and is immediately followed by the process of Purification. By this a man so purifies himself as to take passion out of the heart and mind altogether; not merely restraining it when it rises within him, but preventing it from rising altogether. By merely restraining his passions a man can never arrive at peace, can never actualise his ideal; he must purify these passions.

It is in the purification of his lower nature that a man becomes strong and godlike.

Purification is effected by thoughtful care, earnest meditation, and holy aspiration.

November Twenty-Seventh.

TRUE strength and power and usefulness are born of self-purification, for the lower animal forces are not lost, but are transmuted into intellectual and spiritual energy. The pure life (pure in thought and deed) is a life of conservation of energy; the impure life (even should the impurity not extend beyond thought) is a life of dissipation of energy. The pure man is more capable, and therefore more fit to succeed in his plans and to accomplish his purposes than the impure. Where the impure man fails, the pure man will step in and be victorious, because he directs his energies with a calmer mind and a greater definiteness and strength of purpose.

With the growth in purity, all the elements which constitute a strong and virtuous manhood are developed.

By self-discipline a man rises higher and higher, approximating more and more nearly to the divine.

November Twenty-Eighth.

AS a man grows purer, he perceives that all evil is powerless, unless it receives his encouragement, and so he ignores it, and lets it pass out of his life. It is by pursuing this aspect of self-discipline that a man enters into and realises the divine life, and manifests those qualities which are distinctly divine, such as wisdom, patience, non-resistance, compassion, and love. It is here, also, where a man becomes consciously immortal, rising above all the fluctuations and uncertainties of life, and living in an intelligent and unchangeable peace.

By self-discipline a man attains to every degree of virtue and holiness, and finally becomes a purified son of God, realising his oneness with the central heart of all things.

A life without resolution is a life without aims, and a life without aims is a drifting and unstable thing.

November Twenty-Ninth.

WHEN a man makes a resolution, it means that he is dissatisfied with his condition, and is commencing to take himself in hand, with a view to producing a better piece of workmanship out of the mental materials of which his character and life are composed, and in so far as he is true to his resolution he will succeed in accomplishing his purpose.

The vows of the saintly ones are holy resolutions directed toward some victory over self, and the beautiful achievements of holy men and the glorious conquests of the Divine Teachers were rendered possible and actual by unswerving resolution.

Resolution—the companion of noble aims and lofty ideals.

True resolution is the crisis of long thought,

November Thirtieth.

HALF-HEARTED and premature resolution is no resolution at all, and is shattered at the first difficulty.

A man should be slow to form a resolution. He should searchingly examine his position and take into consideration every circumstance and difficulty with his decision, and should be fully prepared to meet them. He should be sure that he completely understands the nature of his resolution, that his mind is finally made up, and that he is without doubt in the matter. With the mind thus prepared, the resolution that is formed will not be departed from, and by the aid of it a man will, in due time, accomplish his strong purpose.

Hasty resolutions are futile.

Indolence is the twin sister of indifference, hat ready action is the friend of contentment.

December First.

CONTENTMENT is a virtue which becomes lofty and spiritual, as the mind is trained to perceive and the heart to receive the guidance, in all things, of a merciful law.

To be contented does not mean to forgo effort; it means to free effort from anxiety; it does not mean to be satisfied with sin ' and ignorance and folly, but to rest happily in duty done, and work accomplished.

A man may be said to be content to lead a grovelling life, to remain in sin and in debt, but such a man's true state is one of indifference to his duty, his obligations, and the just claims of his fellow-men. He cannot truly be said to possess the virtue of contentment; he does not experience the pure and abiding joy which is the accompaniment of active achievement.

True contentment is the outcome of honest effort and true living.

The truly contented man works energetically and faithfully, and accepts all results with an untroubled spirit.

December Second.

THERE are three things with which a man should be content: With whatever happens; with his friendships and possessions; and with his pure thoughts. Contented with whatever happens, he will escape grief; with his friendships and possessions, he will avoid anxiety and wretchedness; and with his pure thoughts, he will never go back to suffer and grovel in impurities.

There are three with which a man should not be content: With his opinions; with his character; and with his spiritual condition. Not content with his opinions, he will continually increase in intelligence; not content with his character, he will ceaselessly grow in strength and virtue; and not content with his spiritual condition, he will, every day, enter into a larger wisdom and a fuller blessedness.

Results exactly correspond with efforts.

Universal Brotherhood is the supreme Ideal of Humanity, and towards that Ideal the world is slowly but surely moving.

December Third.

BROTHERHOOD as a human organisation cannot exist so long as any degree of self-seeking reigns in the hearts of men and women who band themselves together for any purpose, as such self-seeking must eventually rend the Seamless Coat of loving unity. But although organised Brotherhood has so largely failed, any man may realise Brotherhood in its perfection, and know it in all its beauty and completion, if he will make himself a wise, pure, loving spirit, removing from his mind every element of strife, and learning to practise those divine qualities without which Brotherhood is but a mere theory, opinion, or illusive dream.

In whatsoever heart discord rules, Brotherhood is not realised.

Brotherhood is at first spiritual, and its outer manifestation in the world must follow as a natural result.
December Fourth.

FROM the spirit of Humility proceed meekness and peacefulness; from Self-surrender come patience, wisdom, and true judgment; from Love spring kindness, joy, harmony; and from Compassion proceed gentleness and forgiveness.

He who has brought himself into harmony with these four qualities is divinely enlightened; he sees whence the actions of men proceed and whither they tend, and therefore can no longer live in the exercise of the dark tendencies. He has realised Brotherhood in its completion, as freedom from malice, from envy, from bitterness, from contention, from condemnation. All men are his brothers, those who live in the dark tendencies as well as those who live in the enlightening qualities. He has but one attitude of mind towards all, that of goodwill.

Where pride, self-love, hatred, and condemnation are, there can be no Brotherhood.

Brotherhood consists, first of all, in the abandonment of self by the individual.
December Fifth.

THEORIES and schemes for propagating Brotherhood are many, but Brotherhood itself is one and unchangeable, and consists in the complete cessation from egotism and strife, and in practising goodwill and peace; for Brotherhood is a practice and not a theory. Self-surrender and Goodwill are its guardian angels, and peace is its habitation.

Where two are determined to maintain an opposing opinion, the clinging of self and ill-will are there, and Brotherhood is absent.

Where two are prepared to sympathise with each other, to see no evil in each other, to serve and not to attack each other, the love of Truth and Good-will are there and Brotherhood is present.

Brotherhood is only practised and known by him whose heart is at peace with all the world.

Prejudice and cruelty are inseparable.
December Sixth.

SYMPATHY is not required towards those who are purer and more enlightened than one's self, as the purer one lives above the necessity for it. In such a case reverence should be exercised, with a striving to lift one's self up to the purer level, and so enter possession of the larger life. Nor can a man fully understand one who is wiser than himself, and before condemning, he should earnestly ask himself whether he is, after all, better than the man whom he has singled out as the object of his bitterness. If he is, let him bestow sympathy. If he is not, let him exercise reverence.

When a man is prone to harshly judge and condemn others, he should inquire how far he falls short himself

Dislike, resentment, and condemnation are all forms of hatred, and evil cannot cease until these are taken out of the heart.

December Seventh.

THE obliterating of injuries from the mind is merely one of the beginnings in wisdom. There is a still higher and better way. And that way is to purify the heart and enlighten the mind that, far from having to forget injuries, there will be none to remember. For it is only pride and self that can be injured and wounded by the actions and attitudes of others; and he who takes pride and self out of his heart can never think the thought, "I have been injured by another," or, "I have been wronged by another."

From a purified heart proceeds the right comprehension of things; and from the right comprehension of things proceeds the life that is peaceful, freed from bitterness and suffering, calm and wise.

He who is troubled and disturbed about the sins of others is far from the Truth.

He who is troubled and disturbed about his own sins is very near to the Gate of Wisdom.

December Eighth.

HE in whose heart the flames of resentment burn, cannot know peace nor understand Truth; he who will banish resentment from his heart, will know and understand.

He who has taken evil out of his own heart, cannot resent or resist it in others, for he is enlightened as to its origin and nature, and knows it as a manifestation of the mistakes of ignorance. With the increase of enlightenment, sin becomes impossible. He who sins, does not understand; he who understands, does not sin. The pure man maintains his tenderness of heart toward those who ignorantly imagine that they can do him harm. The wrong attitude of others toward him does not trouble him; his heart is at rest in Compassion and Love.

Let those who aim at the right life, calmly and wisely understand.

A pure heart and a righteous life are the great and all-important things.
December Ninth.

THE deeds and thoughts that lead to suffering are those that spring from self-interest and self-seeking; the thoughts and deeds that produce blessedness are those that spring from Truth. The process by which the mind is thus changed and transmuted is two-fold; it consists of meditation and practice. By silent meditation, the ground and reason of right conduct is sought, and by practice, right-doing is accomplished in daily life.

For Truth is not a matter of book learning, or subtle reasoning, or disputation, or controversial skill; it consists in right-doing.

Truth is not something that can be gleaned from a book; it can be learned and known by practice only.

He only has Truth who has found it by practice.
December Tenth.

HE who wishes to acquire Truth must practise it. He must begin at the very first lesson in self-control, thoroughly master it, and then pass on to the next and the next, until he attains to the moral perfection at which he aims. It is common with men to imagine that Truth consists in holding certain ideas or opinions. They read a number of treatises, and then form an opinion which they call "Truth," and then they go about disputing with their fellow-men in order to try to prove that their opinion is the Truth. In worldly matters men are wise, for they do things in order to achieve their ends, but in spiritual things they are foolish, for they merely read, and do not do things, and then imagine they have acquired Truth.

He only has Truth whose life shows it forth in pure and blameless conduct.

Love, all inclusive.
December Eleventh.

BY its very nature, Love can never be the exclusive possession of any religion, sect, school, or brotherhood. The common claim, therefore, of such sections of the community to the exclusive possession of Truth in their particular religious doctrine is a denial of Love. Truth is a spirit and a life, and though it may manifest through manifold doctrines, it can never be confined to any one particular form of doctrine. Love is a winged angel that refuses to be chained to any letter doctrine whatsoever. Love is above and beyond, outside and greater than all the opinions, doctrines, and philosophies of men; yet Love includes all—the righteous and the unrighteous, the fair and foul, the clean and the unclean. He whose Love is so deep and wide as to envelop all men of all creeds is he who has most of religion, and most of wisdom, and also most of insight, for he knows and sees men as they are.

Hatred is absence of Love, and therefore absence of all that is included in Love.

Love broadens and expands the mind of a man until it embraces in its kindly folds all mankind without distinction.

December Twelfth.

THE way of Love is the way of Life— Immortal Life—and the beginning of that way consists in getting rid of our carpings, quarrellings, fault-findings, and suspicions. If these petty vices possess us, let us not deceive ourselves, but let us confess that we have not Love. To be thus honest with ourselves is to be prepared to find Love; but to be self-deceived is to be shut out from Love. If we are to grow in Love, we must begin at the beginning, and remove from our minds all mean and suspicious thoughts about our fellow-workers and fellow-men. We must learn to treat them with large-hearted freedom, and to perceive the right reason for their actions, to excuse them on grounds of personal right and personal freedom when their opinions, methods, or actions are contrary to us; thus shall we come at last to love them with that Love of which St. Paul speaks, a Love that is a permanent principle.

He who has Love—of whatsoever creed or none— is enlightened with the Light of Truth.

The Life of Truth is that in which wrong-thinking and wrong-doing are abandoned, and right-thinking and right-doing are embraced.

December Thirteenth.

IT is the wrong deeds of men which bring all the unhappiness into the world. It will be right deeds which will transform all its misery into happiness. By wrong deeds we come to sorrow; by right deeds we come to bliss.

But a man must not think the thought: "It is the wrong deeds of others which have made me unhappy," for such a thought produces bitterness towards others and increases hatred. He must understand that his unhappiness is from something wrong within himself; he must regard it as a sign that he is yet imperfect, that there is some weak spot within which must be strengthened. He must never accuse others for his lapses of conduct, or for his troubles, but must gain more steadfastness of heart, must establish himself more firmly in the Truth.

Walk with lowly footsteps the holy way of Truth.

The principles of Truth are fixed and eternal, and cannot be made or unmade by anyone.

December Fourteenth.

THE principles of Truth were discovered by searching and practice, and are so stated and arranged as to make the path plainer for other feet to tread; and it is the path along which every being has travelled who has passed from sin to sinlessness, from error to Truth. It is the ancient Way along which every saint, every Buddha, every Christ has walked to divine perfection, and along which every imperfect being in the future will pass to reach this glorious goal. It matters not what religion a man professes, if he is daily striving with his own sins, and purifying his heart, he is walking this path; for while opinions, theologies, and religions differ, sin does not differ, the overcoming of sin does not differ, and Truth does not differ.

Religions change from age to age, but the principles of divine virtue are eternally the same.

Truth is one, though it has a variety of aspects, and is adaptable to men in various stages of growth.

December Fifteenth.

WE have sat at the feet of all the Great Teachers, and have learned of them. Unspeakable has been our rejoicing to have found, in the lives and precepts of gentle Indian and Chinese Teachers, the same divine qualities and the same preceptive truths which adorn the character of Jesus Christ. To us they are all wonderful and adorable, and so great and good and wise that we can but reverence and learn of them. They have also had the same marvellous influence for good over the various races among which they have appeared, and have all equally called forth the undying worship of millions of human beings.

Great Teachers are perfected flowers of humanity, types of what all men will one day be.

Perfect purity of heart is a condition of emancipation from all the cravings and indulgences of self.

December Sixteenth.

THERE is a distinction between a worldly life and a religious life. He who is daily following his impure inclinations, with no wish to give them up, is irreligious; while he who is daily controlling and purging away his impure inclinations is religious.

The religious man should curb his passions and the indulgence of his desires, for that is what constitutes religion. He must learn to see men and things as they are, and must perceive that they are living in accordance with their nature, and their right of choosing their path as intelligent human beings. He must never intrude his rules of life upon them; and never presume to be, or even think of himself as being, on a "higher plane" than they are. He must learn to put himself in their place, and to see from their standpoint.

A lover of Truth must be a lover of all men. He must let his love go out without restraint or stint.

The ground of certainty on which we can securely rest amid all the incidents of life, is the mathematical exactitude of the moral law.

December Seventeenth.

THE unceasing change, the insecurity and the mystery of life make it necessary to find some basis of certainty on which to rest if happiness and peace of mind are to be maintained. This basic principle, a knowledge of which the whole race will ultimately acquire, is best represented by the term Divine Justice. Human justice differs with every man according to his own light or darkness, but there can be no variation in that Divine Justice by which the universe is eternally sustained. Divine Justice is spiritual mathematics. As with figures and objects, so with the thoughts and deeds of men, two and two equally make four.

Given the same cause, there will always be the same effect.

All the spiritual laws with which men are acquainted have, and must have, the same infallibility in their operations.

December Eighteenth.

GIVEN the same thought or deed in a like circumstance, the result will always be the same. Without this fundamental ethical justice there could be no human society, for it is the just reactions of the deeds of individuals which prevents society from tottering to its fall.

It thus follows that the inequalities of life, as regards the distribution of happiness and suffering, are the outworking of moral forces operating along lines of flawless accuracy. This flawless accuracy, this perfect law, is the one great fundamental certainty in life, the finding of which insures a man's perfection, makes him wise and enlightened, and fills him with rejoicing and peace.

The moral order of the universe is not, cannot be disproportionate, for if it were, the universe would fall.

Nothing can transcend right.
December Nineteenth.

TAKE away a belief in this certainty from a man's consciousness, and he is adrift on a self-created ocean of chance, without rudder, chart, or compass. He has no ground on which to build a character or life, no incentive for noble deeds, no centre for moral action; he has no island of peace and no harbour of refuge. Even the crudest idea of God as of a great man whose mind is perfect, who cannot err, and who has "no variableness nor shadow of turning," is a popular expression of a belief in this basic principle of Divine Justice.

According to this principle there is neither favour nor chance, but unerring and unchangeable right. Thus all the sufferings of men are right as effects, their causes being the mistakes of ignorance; but as effects they will pass away.

Man cannot suffer for something which he has never done, or never left undone, for this would be an effect without a cause.

Talent, genius, goodness, greatness, are not launched upon the world ready-made. They are the result of a long train of causes and effects.
December Twentieth.

THE process of growth is seen in the flower, but though not seen in the mental growth, it is nevertheless there.

I said the process of mental growth was not seen; but this is only true in a general sense. The true thinker and sage does see, with his spiritual eye, the process of spiritual growth. Just as the natural scientist has made himself acquainted with natural causes and effects— as, indeed, the ordinary observer is so acquainted—so he has made himself familiar with spiritual causes and effects. He sees the process by which characters, like plants, come into being; and when he sees the flowers of genius and virtue appear, he knows from what mental seeds they sprang, and how they gradually came to perfection through long periods of silent growth.

Nothing appears ready-made. There is always a changing, a growing, a becoming.

An awakened vision calls us to a nobler life.
December Twenty-First.

AS a man cannot live in two countries at the same time, but must leave the one before he can settle in the other, so a man cannot inhabit two spiritual countries at the same time, but must leave behind the land of sin before he can live at peace in the land of truth. When one leaves his native land, that he may begin anew in an adopted country, he leaves behind all beloved associations, sweet companionships, dear friends and relatives, yea, all upon which his heart has been ever set must be parted with and left behind. So when one resolves to live in the new world of Truth, the old world of error, with its loved pleasures, cherished sins, and vain associations, must be renounced. By such renunciation the individual gains, humanity gains, and the universe becomes a brighter and more beautiful habitation.

We must shake the mud of the valley from our feet if we are to commune with the mountain silence.

Right thoughts spring from a right mental attitude, and lead to right actions.
December Twenty-Second.

THAT is the right mental attitude which seeks the good in all the occurrences of life, and extracts strength, knowledge, and wisdom from them. Right thoughts are thoughts of cheer, of joy, of hope, of confidence, of courage, of constant love, of large generosity, of abounding faith and trust. These are the affirmations that make strong characters and useful and noble lives, and that build up those personal successes which make the progress of the world. Such thoughts are inevitably followed by right action, by the putting forth of energy and effort in work, in the accomplishment of some legitimate object; and as the climber at last reaches the hill-top, so the earnest, cheerful, and untiring worker at last accomplishes his end.

All the successful people, through all time, have reached their particular success by labouring for it.

Suffering is a purifying and perfecting process. "We become obedient by the things which we suffer."
December Twenty-Third.

TO inflict suffering upon others is to become more deeply involved in ignorance; but to suffer ourselves is to come nearer to enlightenment. Pain teaches men how to be kind and compassionate. It at last makes them tender-hearted and thoughtful for the sufferings of others. When a man does a cruel deed, he thinks, in his ignorance, that that is the end of it, but it is only the beginning. Attached to the deed is a train of consequences which will plunge him in a tormenting hell of pain. For every wrong thought we think, or unkind deed we do, we must suffer some form of mental or bodily pain; and the kind of pain will be in accordance with the initiative thought or act.

By acquainting man with suffering, it enables him to feel for the sufferings of others.

Every resource is already with you and within you.

December Twenty-Fourth.

JUST as the strong doing of small tasks leads to greater strength, so the doing of those tasks weakly leads to greater weakness. What a man is in his fractional duties that he is in the aggregate of his character. Weakness is as great a source of suffering as sin, and there can be no true blessedness until some measure of strength of character is evolved. The weak man becomes strong by attaching value to little things and doing them accordingly. The strong man becomes weak by falling into looseness and neglect concerning small things, thereby forfeiting his simple wisdom and squandering his energy.

There is no way to strength and wisdom but by acting strongly and wisely in the present moment.

The year is passing, and blessed are they who can let its mistakes, its injuries, and wrongs pass away for ever, and be remembered no more.

December Twenty-Fifth.

THE past is dead and unalterable; let it sink into oblivion, but extract and retain its divine lessons; let those lessons be strength to you now, and make them the starting-points of a nobler, purer, more perfect life in the coming years. Let all thoughts of hatred, resentment, strife, and ill-will die with the dying years; erase from the tablet of your heart all malicious memories, all unholy grudges. Let the cry, "Peace on earth and good-will to men!" which at this season re-echoes through the world from myriads of lips, be to you something more than an oft-reiterated platitude. Let its truth be practised by you; let it dwell in your heart; and do not mar its harmony and peace by thoughts of ill-will.

Blessed is he who has no wrongs to remember, no injuries to forget; in whose pure heart no hateful thought about another can take root and flourish.

No man can be confronted with a difficulty which he has not the strength to meet and subdue.

December Twenty-Sixth.

DO not regard your difficulties and perplexities as portentous of ill; by so doing you will make them ill; but regard them as prophetic of good, which, indeed, they are. Do not persuade yourself that you can evade them: you cannot. Do not try to run away from them; this is impossible, for wherever you go they will still be there with you—but meet them calmly and bravely; confront them with all the dispassion and dignity which you can command; weigh up their proportions; measure their strength; understand them; attack them, and finally vanquish them. Thus will you develop strength and intelligence; thus will you enter one of those byways of blessedness which are hidden from the superficial gaze.

There is no peace in sin, no rest in error, no final refuge but in Wisdom.

Go to your task with love in your heart and you will go to it light-hearted and cheerful.

December Twenty-Seventh.

WHAT heavy burden is a man weighted with which is not made heavier and more unendurable by weak thoughts or selfish desires? If your circumstances are "trying" it is because you need them, and can evolve the strength to meet them. They are trying because there is some weak spot in you, and they will continue to be trying until that spot is eradicated. Be glad that you have the opportunity of becoming stronger and wiser. No circumstances can be trying to wisdom; nothing can weary love. Stop brooding over your own trying circumstances and contemplate the lives of some of those about you.

The duty which you shirk is your reproving angel; the pleasure which you race after is your flattering enemy.

Animal indulgence is alien to the perception of Truth.

December Twenty-Eighth.

THERE are little selfish indulgences, some of which appear harmless, and are commonly fostered; but no selfish indulgence can be harmless, and men and women do not know what they lose by repeatedly and habitually succumbing to effeminate and selfish gratifications. If the God in man is to rise strong and triumphant, the beast in man must perish. The pandering to the animal nature, even when it appears innocent and seems sweet, leads away from truth and blessedness. Each time you give way to the animal within you, and feed and gratify him, he waxes stronger and more rebellious, and takes firmer possession of your mind, which should be in the keeping of Truth.

Live superior to the craving for sense-excitement, and you will live neither vainly nor uncertainly.

Sacrifice all hatred, slay it upon the altar of devotion— devotion to others.
December Twenty-Ninth.

WHATEVER others may say of you, whatever they may do to you, never take offence. Do not return hatred with hatred. If another hates you perhaps you have, consciously or unconsciously, failed somewhere in your conduct, or there may be some misunderstanding which the exercise of a little gentleness and reason may remove; but under all circumstances "Father, forgive them" is infinitely better than "I will have nothing more to do with them." Hatred is so small and poor, so blind and wretched. Love is so great and rich, so far-seeing and blissful.

Open the floodgates of your heart for the inpouring of that sweet, great, beautiful love which embraces all.

Inside the gateway of unselfishness lies the elysium of Abiding Joy.
December Thirtieth.

KNOWING this—that selfishness leads to misery, and unselfishness to joy, not merely for one's self alone—for if this were all how unworthy would be our endeavours!—but for the whole world, and because all with whom we live and come in contact will be the happier and the truer for unselfishness; because Humanity is one, and the joy of one is the joy of all—knowing this, let us scatter flowers and not thorns in the common ways of life—yea, even in the highway of our enemies let us scatter the blossoms of unselfish love—so shall the pressure of their footprints fill the air with the perfume of holiness and gladden the world with the aroma of joy.

Seek the highest Good, and you will taste the deepest, sweetest joy.

The universe has no favorites; it is supremely just, and gives to every man his rightful earnings.

December Thirty-First.

HAPPY in the Eternal Happiness is he who has come to that Life from which the thought of self is abolished. Already, even now and in this life, he has entered the Kingdom of Heaven. He is at rest on the bosom of the Infinite.

Sweet is the rest and deep the bliss of him who has freed his heart from its lusts and hatreds and dark desires; and he who, without any shadow of bitterness or selfishness, can breathe, in his heart, the blessing:

Peace unto all living things,

making no exceptions or distinctions—such a man has reached that happy ending which can never be taken away, the fulness of peace, the consummation of Perfect Blessedness.

Man can find the right way in life, and, having found it, can rejoice and be glad.

Lightning Source UK Ltd.
Milton Keynes UK

177599UK00001B/189/P